Truth and Paradox

Truth and Paradox

Solving the Riddles

TIM MAUDLIN

CLARENDON PRESS · OXFORD

OXFORD
UNIVERSITY PRESS

Great Clarendon Street, Oxford OX2 6DP

Oxford University Press is a department of the University of Oxford.
It furthers the University's objective of excellence in research, scholarship,
and education by publishing worldwide in

Oxford New York

Auckland Bangkok Buenos Aires Cape Town Chennai
Dar es Salaam Delhi Hong Kong Istanbul Karachi Kolkata
Kuala Lumpur Madrid Melbourne Mexico City Mumbai Nairobi
São Paulo Shanghai Taipei Tokyo Toronto

Oxford is a registered trade mark of Oxford University Press
in the UK and in certain other countries

Published in the United States
by Oxford University Press Inc., New York

British Library Cataloguing in Publication Data

Data available

Library of Congress Cataloging in Publication Data

Data available

ISBN 0-19-924729-3

1 3 5 7 9 10 8 6 4 2

Typeset in 10.5 on 12pt Ehrhardt by
Kolam Information Services, Pvt. Ltd., Pondicherry, India
Printed in Great Britain
on acid-free paper by
Biddles Ltd., King's Lynn, Norfolk

To my parents:

Who, if this sentence is true, put up with all this nonsense.

Preface

I trust that I am not absolutely the last human being on the face of the Earth who might be expected to write a book on truth and the Liar paradox, but my name would not be among the first dozen, or first score, or first hundred to come to mind as a likely candidate for such an undertaking. I am not trained as a logician, or a specialist in semantics. Some explanation is in order.

I did not set out to write a book on the Liar paradox. Indeed, I did not set out to write a book at all, and the non-book I did set out to write was not about the Liar paradox. So what you have before you is the end product of a very long and difficult struggle in which one problem led to another and yet another, with the problem of truth ultimately emerging as the center of attention. The original project was concerned instead with attempts by John Lucas and, more recently, Roger Penrose to draw consequences about the structure of the human mind from Gödel's incompleteness proof. The basic line of argument is well known: suppose that human reasoning capacity can be reduced to some sort of algorithmic procedure, such that the sentences about, say, arithmetic that one takes to be provably true with certainty can be characterized as a recursively enumerable set of sentences. Gödel's procedure then shows how to identify a sentence which, if the system is consistent, is certain to be both true and not identified by the system as a truth. The idea is now this: *We* can recognize the Gödel sentence of the system as true even though the system itself cannot. Therefore *our* insight into what is certainly true outruns that of the system. But the system has not been characterized in any way except to say that it is consistent and, in some sense, algorithmic. Therefore our insight is, in principle, more extensive than that of any consistent algorithmic system. Therefore, our insight cannot be the result of any consistent algorithmic system. Therefore, the power of our minds cannot be captured by any algorithm. Therefore we are not like computers. Yet further, according to Penrose, it follows that the physics that governs our brains cannot even be computable, otherwise our insights would, in the relevant sense, be the output of an algorithm (viz. the algorithm which specifies the dynamics of the physics of the brain).

There are obviously lots of lacunae in this argument, and the foregoing sketch is only the barest skeleton of the complete defense of the conclusion. But even without going into the details, there is something extremely odd about the conclusion. It seems to rely on the idea that our insight into the truth of the Gödel sentence of a (consistent) system is evidence of some almost mystical intellectual power, a power that cannot even be mimicked by a computer. But when one looks at the reasoning that leads to the conclusion that the Gödel sentence is true, one finds nothing remarkable or difficult or unformalizable. What one finds instead is a simple *reductio ad absurdum*. One constructs a sentence that says, in effect, that it is not a theorem, or recognized as an unassailable truth, by the algorithmic system in question. Then one asks whether the sentence in question is in fact recognized by the system as an unassailable truth. If it is, then the system in question judges as an unassailable truth a sentence which is, in fact, quite obviously false. So the system is not consistent, or at least makes obvious mistakes in what it recognizes as certainly true. Such a system cannot represent our reasoning power, since we would not make such an obvious mistake. So any consistent system cannot judge the sentence in question to be obviously true. But then, as *we* can see, the sentence *is* obviously true. So, providing the system is consistent, we can grasp more truths than it can.

Let us try to formulate the *reductio* in a rigorous way. We need a predicate $P(x)$ which will stand for "x is recognized as certainly true by the system" (if the system can be reduced to an algorithm, $P(x)$ will ultimately specify the algorithm, but this will do for now). Then we can characterize the Gödel sentence of the system, which we will call γ, as $\sim P(\gamma)$. The sentence γ says of itself that it is not provable by the system. Now suppose that we accept that the system in question is absolutely reliable: everything it recognizes as certainly true is, in fact, true. Then we will endorse the inference from the fact that a sentence is provable by the system, or recognized as true by the system, to that sentence itself. That is, we will typically accept as valid the inference from $P(n)$ to the sentence denoted by n (I am being cavalier about the use/mention distinction here, but in an obvious way). Let us call that inference rule *Trust*, reflecting the fact that we ourselves trust every sentence the system can prove. (If we don't trust the system, e.g. if we think the system might be inconsistent or might allow us to prove falsehoods, then the whole argument breaks down.) To employ the inference rule, we need an algorithm which can determine what sentence is denoted by an individual term like γ, but in this case it is easy to specify this: γ denotes the sentence $\sim P(\gamma)$.

Now we can reproduce the *reductio* we use to establish the truth of the Gödel sentence by a simple four-line proof in a natural deduction system:

$$
\begin{array}{lll}
& P(\gamma) & \text{Hypothesis} \\
& P(\gamma) & \text{Reiteration} \\
& \sim P(\gamma) & \text{Trust} \\
\sim P(\gamma) & & \sim \text{Introduction}
\end{array}
$$

Since $\sim P(\gamma)$ is the sentence denoted by γ, we have managed to prove $\sim P(\gamma)$ and simultaneously to prove that the system cannot prove $\sim P(\gamma)$, since that is just what the sentence derived says. So we can prove more than the system.

There is nothing mystical or non-algorithmic about the reasoning just reproduced: it requires nothing more than the syntactically specifiable inference rules Trust and $\sim$ Introduction. (We count Trust as syntactically specifiable since we are allowing information about the denotation of γ into the inference rules themselves.) And similar reasoning can be produced for any predicate for which we accept the analog to the rule Trust, that is, for any predicate such that we accept that every sentence that satisfies the predicate is true. If we believe that, then we believe that the rule Trust is valid. In other words, the proof above seems to give us a general recipe: find any property of sentences such that every sentence which has that property is true, then we can construct a sentence which *does not* have that property but which we can recognize (by an analog of the proof above) as true. The *reductio* seems to have a magical power to reveal the truth of a sentence that does *not* have whatever truth-guaranteeing property we can specify: namely the sentence which says of itself that it does not have the truth-guaranteeing property.

Now this is just too good to be true. The argument is too general, and too simple, to really have the power ascribed to it. It occurs to one, in the first place, that we might as well let $P(x)$ stand for "sentence which *I* can recognize, by whatever means, as unassailably true". Now the little argument seems to prove, beyond any doubt, that $\sim P(\gamma)$ is true and (hence) that I cannot recognize $\sim P(\gamma)$ as unassailably true. For I must surely endorse the principle Trust in this case: it says that if I recognize a sentence as unassailably true then it is true. If I do not endorse Trust, then I recognize that there are sentences which I regard as certainly true but which I suspect may not be true: a clear contradiction. So the little proof above would seem to prove, to my own satisfaction, the truth of $\sim P(\gamma)$. Hence, I can apparently prove (to my own satisfaction) a sentence that, if true, I cannot prove to my own satisfaction. But things get worse.

We have said that the little proof goes through for any predicate that denotes a property of a sentence which guarantees truth, and that we must regard the proof as going through for any such predicate which we regard as denoting such a property (so we accept the rule Trust). But the most obvious and undeniable such predicate is "true". If we accept the argument above, letting $P(x)$ stand for "true", then we seem to be able to prove the truth of a sentence to which that predicate does not apply, i.e. we seem to be able to prove a sentence which (if our proofs are to be trusted) *is not true*. Further, if we let $P(x)$ stand for "true", then γ is a sentence which says *that it is not true*, i.e. it is a classical Liar sentence. Our original concern with Gödel's argument has led us back to the Liar.

This route to the Liar is rather different from the usual approaches. One typically begins by considering the Liar sentence, and arguing that one cannot consistently hold it to be true (since that leads to a contradiction) and cannot consistently hold it not to be true (since that leads to a contradiction as well). That is, indeed, a puzzle. But what is even more puzzling, and more upsetting, is that we apparently can *prove* both the Liar and its negation, so if we really trust the standard system of inferences, we are forced to accept both the Liar and its negation. This is what will be called the *Inferential Version* of the Liar paradox. What the Inferential Version really shows, of course, is that we cannot consistently accept the validity of all of the inferences that we intuitively take to be valid. We must somehow amend or restrict logic to keep ourselves from falling into contradiction.

My original suspicion was that the very modifications to our inference schemes needed to save us from the inferential paradox might also undercut the arguments that we use to convince ourselves of the truth of the Gödel sentence of a formal system. The informal Gödel reasoning is so close to our reasoning about the Liar that it seemed likely that whatever error infects the latter also infects the former. My plan was to fix up logic to escape from the Liar problem, and then see how the necessary modifications affect arguments that depend on Gödel's results. The project did not proceed smoothly.

My first attempt to solve the inferential problem still resides on my hard disk, in a file entitled "Truth". It comes to an abrupt end after 78 pages. The original scheme, of which nothing now remains, never exactly died, but it became progressively more cumbersome and baroque. Every solution to one problem engendered another difficulty, which could in turn be addressed. Conditions piled on conditions and clauses on clauses, with no end in sight. Eventually, the attempt was simply abandoned. I salvaged what I could, and started a second file, entitled "New Truth".

"New Truth" puttered along for 124 pages before finally giving out. I had hit on the solution to the inferential problem, but was only slowly coming to realize that defending the solution required one to tackle the problem of truth directly, by producing a semantics for the language. The problem is fairly simple: in defending a set of inference rules, one would like to show that they are truth-preserving. But without an explicit theory of truth, this cannot be done. So "New Truth" had to be retooled.

The next file was entitled "Final Truth". It soldiered on for 164 pages before being abandoned. "Final Truth" contains the key to the semantic theory that ultimately survived: the idea of the graph of a language, and the analogy between the problem of semantics and boundary value problems as they appear in mathematics and mathematical physics. But the means for avoiding the Liar paradox were still clumsy and complicated, and the restrictions imposed on the language felt *ad hoc*. "Final Truth", I decided, was too much of a contraption to be the final truth.

Running out of both patience and superlatives, I opened a file called "Ultimate Truth". That file contains the text before you. The theory in "Ultimate Truth" is vastly more compact and elegant than any of its forebears, and I had hoped that the end result would be a more compact paper. But new ideas and applications kept crowding in, new paradoxes came forward and were resolved, the scope of the paper enlarged. In the end, Gödel's theorem, the original object of inquiry, takes up a scant few pages. But having gone through so many different ideas, and abandoned so many different approaches, I feel secure that there is some value to what survives.

Composing a book by fits and starts, wandering into cul-de-sacs and then starting over again, is not an intrinsically pleasant enterprise. Still, writing this book has been as enjoyable as such a tortuous journey could be. The bulk of the text was written in the first half of 1997, while on sabbatical in Cambridge, Massachusetts. Following a tradition set the previous semester when I had been visiting at Harvard, Ned Hall, Jim Pryor, Jennifer Noonan, and Justin Broakes would join my wife Vishnya, my daughter Clio, and me weekly for a banquet of gourmet food (Vishnya's masterpieces) and conversation. Any mild disaster becomes comic in the telling. In such delightful company, the seemingly endless series of failures, reversals and dead-ends on my path to this theory was transformed from a chronic frustration to a serialized shaggy dog story. Ned especially was taxed with every gory detail, and his boundless acuity and cheer made the whole process not merely bearable, but fun. His insights were always sharp and to the point. Vann McGee provided very valuable comments on the penultimate draft, and pushed me to face the Permissibility Paradox directly, rather than trying to finesse it. It was also a great help to be able to present some preliminary results at the London School of Economics. And without the generous support of Rutgers University during the sabbatical, this work would never have been done.

The final draft has benefited greatly from the generous comments of Hartry Field, and the joint comments of a reading group at MIT and Harvard. I am also very grateful to the Department of Philosophy at the University of Massachusetts, Amherst, and the Language and Mind Seminar at New York University for allowing me to present an overview of the final theory, and vigorously challenging the approach. The topic of the NYU seminar was non-factual discourse, and without the invitation to participate, much of Chapter 9 would not have been written. Jim Pryor made a lovely observation about the analogy with continued fractions discussed in Appendix B; I wish I could have found a more elegant way to include it than in a footnote. Two anonymous referees at Oxford University Press provided extremely helpful suggestions, and I hope they find the final result a bit more palatable. And Ned Hall once again provided unstinting support by reviewing the final draft and offering good advice and pertinent questions.

My greatest, unrepayable debt is to Vishnya, who lived through every modification, retraction, and short-lived enthusiasm, day after day, for months. I would be fortunate beyond measure if only for her constant affection, but to have in addition a partner in life with whom a project like this can be shared is more than anyone could deserve.

Contents

1. Two Versions of the Liar Paradox   1

2. On the Origin of Truth Values   26

3. What is Truth, and What is a Theory of Truth?   68

4. A Language That Can Express Its Own Truth Theory   79

5. The Norms of Assertion and Denial   95

6. Solving the Inferential Liar Antinomy   105

7. Reasoning about Permissible Sentences   141

8. The Permissibility Paradox   168

9. The Metaphysics of Truth   178

References   204

Index   207

1 Two Versions of the Liar Paradox

The Liar paradox is the most widely known of all philosophical conundrums. Its reputation stems from the simplicity with which it can be presented. In its most accessible form, the Liar appears as a kind of parlor game. One imagines a multiple-choice questionnaire, with the following curious entry:

* This sentence is false.
The starred sentence is
(a) True
(b) False
(c) All of the above
(d) None of the above.

There follows a bit of informal reasoning. If (a) is the right answer, then the sentence is true. Since it says it is false, if it is true it must really be false. Contradiction. Ergo, (a) is not the right answer. If (b) is the right answer, then the sentence is false. But it says it is false, so then it would be true. Contradiction. Ergo, (b) is not the right answer. If both (a) and (b) are wrong, surely (c) is. That leaves (d). The starred sentence is neither true nor false.

The conclusion of this little argument is somewhat surprising, if one has taken it for granted that every grammatical declarative sentence is either true or false. But the reasoning looks solid, and the sentence is a bit peculiar anyhow, so the best advice would seem to be to accept the conclusion: some sentences are neither true nor false. This conclusion will have consequences when one tries to formulate an explicit theory of truth, or an explicit semantics for a language. But it is not so hard after all to cook up a semantics with truth-value gaps, or with more than the two classical truth values, in which sentences like the starred sentence fail to be either true or false. From this point of view, there is nothing deeper in the puzzle than a pathological sentence for which provision must be made.

In more sophisticated parlors, the questionnaire is a bit different:

* This sentence is not true.
The starred sentence is
(a) True
(b) False
(c) All of the above
(d) None of the above.

By a similar piece of reasoning we are left with (d) again, but our conscience is uneasy. If the answer is "none of the above", then (a) is not right, but if (a) is not right, then the sentence is not true, but that is just what the starred sentence says, so the starred sentence is true and (a) is right after all. But if (a) is right, then the sentence is true, but it says it isn't true, so . . .

Problems become yet more acute with a third questionnaire:

* This sentence is not true.

The starred sentence is
(a) True
(b) Not True
(c) All of the above
(d) None of the above.

Both the first and second answers lead straight to contradictions, and so can be ruled out by *reductio*. This leaves (d) again, but the *intrinsic* tenability of (d) is suspect. Maintaining that a sentence is neither true nor false appears to be a coherent option: one might, for example, assert that nonsense sentences, or ungrammatical strings, or commands, are neither. Falsity is, as it were, a positive characteristic, to which only appropriately constructed sentences can aspire (prefixing "It is not the case that . . . " to a false sentence should yield a true sentence). But "Not True" takes in even ungrammatical strings: it is merely the complement class of "True". Surely every sentence, ungrammatical or not, either falls within the extension of "True" or outside it, so how could (d) even be an option? The only available alternative is that the extension of "True" is somehow not well defined, that "True" is a vague predicate with an indeterminate boundary, and that the starred sentence falls in the region of contention. But this does not explain how there could be apparently flawless arguments *demonstrating* that the sentence cannot consistently be held to be true or not true. For other vague predicates, the opposite obtains: a borderline bald person can consistently be regarded either as bald or not.

What conclusion is one to draw from these three puzzles? Perhaps nothing more than that these sentences are peculiar, and that, if we trust the first argument, we should make room in our semantics for sentences which are neither true nor false. Let the final semantics determine their ultimate fate: since we have no coherent strong intuition about what to do with them, it is a clear case of spoils to the victor. In many semantic schemes, the Liar sentence, in both its forms, falls into a truth-value gap. Perhaps there is no more to be said of it.

This rather benign assessment of the Liar is belied as soon as one turns to the *locus classicus* of serious semantics. At the end of the first section of "The Concept of Truth in Formalized Languages", Alfred Tarski arrives at a stark and entirely negative assessment of the problem of defining truth in a language which contains its own truth predicate. The allegedly insuperable difficulties are motivated by the antinomy of the Liar, leading Tarski to this conclusion:

If we analyse this antinomy in the above formulation we reach the conviction that no consistent language can exist for which the usual laws of logic hold and which at the same time satisfies the following conditions: (I) for any sentence which occurs in the language a definite name of this sentence also belongs to the language; (II) every sentence formed from (2) [i.e. *"x is a true sentence if and only if p"*] by replacing the symbol *"p"* by any sentence of the language and the symbol *"x"* by a name of this sentence is to be regarded as a true sentence of this language; (III) in the language in question an empirically established premise having the same meaning as (α) [i.e. the sentence which asserts that the denoting term which occurs in the Liar sentence refers to the sentence itself] can be formulated and accepted as a true sentence.   (Tarski 1956: 165)

Tarski assumed that all natural ("colloquial") languages satisfy conditions (I) and (III), and also that any acceptable account of a truth predicate must entail (II), at least in the metalanguage. Consequently, no natural language that serves as its own metalanguage can consistently formulate its own account of truth. If one adds to this the claim that every user of a natural language must regard the T-sentences formulable in that language as true (whether there exists any explicit "theory of truth" or not), one arrives at the striking conclusion that every user of a natural language who accepts all the classical logical inferences must perforce be inconsistent.

This last conclusion has not met with universal approbation. Robert Martin, for example, remarks:

> In at least three places Tarski argues essentially as follows:
>
> > Every language meeting certain conditions (he speaks earlier of *universality*, later of *semantic closure*), and in which the normal laws of logic hold, is inconsistent.
>
> Although Tarski acknowledges difficulties in making precise sense in saying so, it is fairly clear that he thinks that colloquial English meets the conditions in question, and is in fact inconsistent. This argument has made many philosophers, including, perhaps, Tarski himself, quite uncomfortable. It is not clear even what it means to say that a natural language is inconsistent; nor is one quite comfortable arguing in the natural language to such a conclusion about natural language.   (Martin 1984: 4)

Martin goes on to suggest that Tarski ought to have drawn a different conclusion, viz. that the concept of truth is not expressible in any natural language (ibid. 5), and hence, presumably, that speakers of only natural languages either have no concept of truth, or else are unable to express it. This is surely as odd a conclusion as Tarski's. If one has no such concept available before constructing a formalized language, what constraints are to guide the construction? It is rather like saying that although there is no concept expressed by "Blag" in English, one can set about constructing a theory of Blag in a formalized language, which theory can somehow be judged intuitively as either right or wrong. On the other hand, if speakers of natural language do have a concept of truth, why can't they express it simply by introducing a term for it (e.g. "truth")? Expressing a concept does not require offering an analysis of it in other terms.

Pace Martin, Tarski's claim can be made quite precise, and anyone attempting to construct a theory of truth for natural languages must be prepared to answer it. There is, indeed, a swarm of theories of truth designed to apply to languages which contain their own truth predicate, including, for example, Bas van Fraassen's supervaluation approach (1968, 1970), Saul Kripke's fixed-point theory (1975), and Anil Gupta's revision theory (1982). At first glance, it even seems obvious how these theories will block Tarski's conclusion. But on second glance, matters become rather more complicated, and it is not so clear after all how Tarski's objections are to be met. Fully responding to Tarski's concerns will lead us to a slightly different theory of truth than the aforementioned, one more adequate to our actual practice of reasoning about truth. Our first task, then, is to make Tarski's argument explicit, and take the first and second glances.

The Liar in Language L

Consider the simplest possible language in which the Liar paradox can be framed, which language we will call L. The language is a simple propositional language without quantification that contains terms for atomic propositions (P, Q, R, P_1, etc.), the classical connectives, and, in addition, singular terms (α, β, γ, etc.) and a single monadic predicate $T(x)$. For simplicity's sake, and unlike any normal language, the singular terms of L *can only denote sentences of L*. We could, in principle, expand L to allow for singular terms which denote things other than sentences, but this would only create complications with no addition of insight. The wffs of L are (i) the atomic propositions, (ii) any proposition of the form $T(x)$ where the x is replaced by a singular term, and (iii) all the usual molecular sentences constructable from (i) and (ii) and the classical connectives. The metalanguage for L also comes with an interpretation function $\mathscr{F}(x)$ which maps the singular terms to the sentences they denote. We require that the function be completely well defined, either by an explicit listing of the values of the singular terms (using lists like δ: P or $\mathscr{F}(\delta) = P$) or by some algorithm (e.g. if quotation names are added to the language, the algorithm could specify that the quotation name denotes the sentence one obtains by stripping the quotation marks off the name). *Any such function $\mathscr{F}(x)$ is allowed so long as it is well-defined and computable, so any sentence can, in principle, be designated by any singular term.* It is now easy to specify a schema for the T-sentences of L: they are all instances of the sentence form $T(n) \equiv \mathscr{F}(n)$, i.e. the sentences which result from replacing n with a singular term and $\mathscr{F}(n)$ with the image of that singular term under the function $\mathscr{F}(x)$.

We can now produce the Liar paradox in L.[1] First, we specify the designation of the singular term λ explicitly as follows:

$\lambda: \sim T(\lambda)$

or alternatively

$\mathcal{F}(\lambda) = \sim T(\lambda)$

The T-sentence for λ is therefore

T-Lambda: $T(\lambda) \equiv \sim T(\lambda)$.

According to one understanding of the paradox, we have already produced the antinomy of the Liar. That understanding, which we may call the *semantic* understanding, goes as follows: on the one hand, it is required of any acceptable concept of truth that the T-sentences containing that truth predicate, such as T-Lambda, all be considered true (cf. Tarski's (II) above). On the other hand, according to *the classical two-valued compositional semantics for* $\sim$ *and* $\equiv$, the sentence T-Lambda must come out false. That is, no matter whether $T(\lambda)$ be assigned the value true or the value false, T-Lambda will come out false since T-Lambda is a classical contradiction.

On this reading of the antinomy, when Tarski uses the phrase "for which the usual laws of logic hold" he means "for which the usual two-valued compositional semantics for logical connectives hold". If every sentence in such a

---

[1] The Liar sentence we will consider is constructed by simply stipulating that the denotation of the singular term λ shall be the sentence $\sim T(\lambda)$. This reflects the simplicity with which the original Liar paradox was produced, similar to the little puzzles with which we began. In modern mathematical logic, the Liar sentence is constructed in a more roundabout way: sentences are designated by Gödel numbers according to a coding scheme, and then a computable diagonalization function is used to achieve the self-reference needed for the Liar. This technique has the advantage of showing that there is nothing illegitimate about the self-reference: it can be achieved by standard mathematical means. But having been so assured, there is really no cogent objection to the simpler expedient of simple stipulation. As Kripke remarks: "A simpler, and more direct, form of self-reference uses demonstratives and proper names: Let 'Jack' be a name of the sentence 'Jack is short', and we have a sentence that says of itself that it is short. I can see nothing wrong with 'direct' self-reference of this type. If 'Jack' is not already a name in the language, why can we not introduce it as a name of any entity we please? In particular, why can it not be a name of the (uninterpreted) finite sequence of marks 'Jack is short'? (Would it be permissible to call the sequence of marks 'Harry' but not 'Jack'? Surely prohibitions on naming are arbitrary here.) There is no vicious circle in our procedure, since we need not interpret the sequence of marks 'Jack is short' before we name it. Yet if we name it 'Jack', it at once becomes meaningful and true" (Kripke 1975, in Martin 1984: 56) An advantage of Gödel numbering is that one can compute the denotation of a name from the name, as one can do with quotation-mark names, and so various sorts of inferences can be automated. But so too can they be automated if the function we are calling $\mathcal{F}(x)$ is computable, which it certainly is if the function is specified by a finite list. Having been told that $\mathcal{F}(\lambda) = \sim T(\lambda)$, or $\mathcal{F}(\text{Jack}) =$ Jack is short, we can easily automate the inferences. Of course, the information about what $\mathcal{F}(x)$ is must be given, but then so must, e.g., the coding for the Gödel numbers.

language is to get a classical truth value, then T-Lambda will come out false, contrary to the requirement that all T-sentences come out true. End of story.

If this is all that Tarski has in mind, then the response of theorists such as van Fraassen, Kripke, and Gupta is clear: each rejects both the classical two-valued compositional semantics *and* the requirement that all of the T-sentences come out true. On Kripke's approach, for example, T-Lambda turns out to have no truth value since the truth value of $\sim T(\lambda)$ is undefined. On a super-valuation approach, T-Lambda comes out false, exactly because it is a classical contradiction, while $\sim T(\lambda)$ is again undefined.

Tarski could try to hold his ground by insisting that the acceptability of the T-sentences is somehow *analytic* of the notion of truth, so that any purported truth predicate not all of whose T-sentences are true is *ipso facto* not an acceptable candidate for *truth*. But given the problematic status of the ana-lytic/synthetic distinction, this looks like a losing cause.

It seems, then, at first glance that Tarski's pessimistic evaluation of the prospects for defining truth in a natural language can be easily surmounted by relaxing the requirement that the T-sentences all be true. Of course, T-sentences for grounded[2] sentences, i.e. for most of everyday discourse, will come out true, and so Tarski's intuition holds for the most part, and only breaks down where we have independent reasons to suspect trouble.

There is, however, another way of understanding the antinomy of the Liar, and on this second approach the problem is somewhat more tenacious. The second approach arises from the following dissatisfaction with the semantic approach. According to the semantic approach, when Tarski writes of "the laws of logic" he must be referring to the classical bivalent compositional semantics. But this is not the usual understanding of "the laws of logic": rather one typically uses that phrase to refer to certain *inference rules*, such as Modus Ponens and the disjunctive syllogism. There is, further, a use of "inconsistent" which applies to a set of inference rules: the rules are inconsistent if some sentence and its negation are both theorems, or if every sentence in the language is a theorem. Thus there is also available an alternative understanding of what Tarski could mean when he says that there is no consistent language for which the laws of logic and the three conditions listed above hold.

Postulating the validity of the classical inference rules is not the same thing as postulating the classical bivalent compositional semantics. This is proven by the existence of, e.g., many-valued compositional semantics in which all of the classical inferences are valid (i.e. truth-preserving).[3] Or one can stick with bivalence and abandon compositionality (i.e. that the connectives are truth-

---

[2] I am using the term "grounded" in Kripke's sense; cf. Kripke (1975, in Martin 1984: 71). The grounded sentences are the sentences which have a truth value in the smallest fixed point.

[3] Take any Boolean lattice and interpret the nodes as truth values. Let the supremum be classical truth, the infimum classical falsehood, and the other nodes (if any) various non-classical truth values. Let the truth value of the negation of a sentence be the orthocomplement of the

functional). If one demands a bivalent semantics and postulates that the inference rules for conjunction are valid, one can derive the truth table for conjunction: the semantics for "and" is uniquely determined and is compositional. But the same does not go for negation: the validity of the classical inferences does not entail that the semantics for "not" be compositional.[4]

The upshot of all this is that accepting the validity of the classical inferences does not entail accepting the classical bivalent compositional semantics. And this raises the question: is there an *inferential* version of the Liar paradox, i.e. a version that shows that there is going to be trouble with the classical *inferences* in our little language L?

Indeed there is. Let us begin by allowing all of the classical logical inferences in L. We will use a standard natural deduction system. (Details of this system are provided in Appendix A.) Let us further take all of the T-sentences for L as *axioms*. The resulting inferential structure is inconsistent, as can be shown by the following derivation:

$T(\lambda)$	Hypothesis
$T(\lambda)$	Reiteration
$T(\lambda) \equiv \sim T(\lambda)$	Axiom
$\sim T(\lambda)$	$\equiv$ Elimination
$\sim T(\lambda)$	$\sim$ Introduction
$T(\lambda) \equiv \sim T(\lambda)$	Axiom
$T(\lambda)$	$\equiv$ Elimination

The classical rules of inference, together with the T-sentences for L, allow one to derive both the Liar and its negation.

Prima facie, it appears that the solution to the inferential version of the paradox is exactly the same as the solution of the semantic version. Just as the semantic version can be resolved by denying that all of the T-sentences are true, so the inferential version is solved by disallowing at least some of the T-sentences as axioms. Without the axiom T-Lambda, the derivation above cannot be formulated.

But on further reflection, a puzzle arises. For consider the *use* to which the T-sentences are put in the derivation above. The T-sentences are used, together with the rule of $\equiv$ Elimination, to secure inferences from one side

truth value of the sentence, and the truth value of a conjunction be the meet of the truth values of the conjuncts. All classical inferences come out valid. The classical compositional semantics is given by the simplest such lattice, the one with only two nodes.

[4] Of the Boolean lattices mentioned in the previous footnote, take one that has more than two nodes, and interpret the supremum as truth and all the rest of the nodes as falsehood. The resulting semantics is bivalent, but non-compositional: in it some sentences and their negations both turn out to be false, even though their disjunction is true. Yet in such a bivalent non-compositional semantics, all of the classical inferences are valid.

of the T-sentence to the other. The T-sentences allow one to infer from any sentence of the form $T(n)$ to $\mathscr{F}(n)$, i.e. from the sentence which claims that the sentence named by n is true to the sentence named by n, and vice versa. Let us call any such inference a *T-Inference*. More precisely, let us call an inference from $\mathscr{F}(n)$ to $T(n)$ an *Upward T-Inference*, and an inference from $T(n)$ to $\mathscr{F}(n)$ a *Downward T-Inference*, reflecting the idea that the notion of truth can be used for semantic ascent, for converting talk about things into talk about sentences.[5]

Just as we can augment a logical system by adding new *axioms*, like adding all of the instances of the T-Schema, so too can we augment it by adding new *inference rules*. In order for it to count as a formal system, we need to specify the inference rules in such a way that one can check by an algorithmic procedure whether the rules are being followed. What we are now proposing is the addition of two new rules, whose specification depends upon a computable specification of the function $\mathscr{F}(x)$. That is, one must specify $\mathscr{F}(x)$ in such a way that a computer could check, for a given singular term and a given wff, whether the value of $\mathscr{F}(x)$ for that singular term is that wff. For the purposes of our proof, we need only specify the value of $\mathscr{F}(\lambda)$, which we have done: $\mathscr{F}(\lambda) = {\sim}T(\lambda)$. So in this case, the Upward T-Inference allows us to infer $T(\lambda)$ from ${\sim}T(\lambda)$ (i.e. allows us to infer a sentence which says that ${\sim}T(\lambda)$ is true from ${\sim}T(\lambda)$) and the Downward T-Inference allows us to infer ${\sim}T(\lambda)$ from $T(\lambda)$ (i.e. allows us to infer ${\sim}T(\lambda)$ from a sentence which says that ${\sim}T(\lambda)$ is true).

Given use of the Upward and Downward T-Inferences, the little proof above can be simplified, in a form we will call *Proof Lambda*:

$T(\lambda)$	Hypothesis
$T(\lambda)$	Reiteration
${\sim}T(\lambda)$	Downward T-Inference
${\sim}T(\lambda)$	$\sim$ Introduction
$T(\lambda)$	Upward T-Inference

Adding the T-Inferences to the classical inferences again makes L inconsistent. So it appears to be not so much the T-sentences themselves but rather the T-Inferences that they support, which are getting us into trouble.

Now our new puzzle can be stated. Let us take Kripke's theory of truth as a clinical example. Kripke specifies an ascending hierarchy of interpretations of the monadic predicate $T(x)$ which he adds to his simple language L. According

---

[5] The terminology "Upward" and "Downward" T-Inference is idiosyncratic: these inferences are commonly called T-Intro and T-Elim. These latter terms, however, can be misleading, since T-Elim may not, for example, result in the elimination of the T-predicate. If $\mathscr{F}(\beta) = T(\beta)$, then applying either T-Elim or T-Intro to $T(\beta)$ yields $T(\beta)$ itself, and nothing has been either introduced or eliminated. The inferences are rather from $\mathscr{F}(n)$ to $T(n)$ ("upward") or from $T(n)$ to $\mathscr{F}(n)$ ("downward"). In the case of $T(\beta)$, traveling in either direction leads back to $T(\beta)$.

to him, "if $T(x)$ is to be interpreted as truth for the very language L containing $T(x)$ itself", then the extension of $T(x)$ must be a *fixed point* in this hierarchy of interpretations, that is, a sentence lies in the extension of $T(x)$ if and only if that sentence comes out true using the usual semantics with that same extension for $T(x)$ (Kripke 1975: 67, in Martin 1984). For Kripke, being a fixed point under this mapping is *constitutive* of being the extension of a truth predicate: "*Being a fixed point, L_σ is a language that contains its own truth predicate*" (ibid. 69, emphasis in the original).

But if the extension of the truth predicate is a fixed point in Kripke's construction, then both the Upward and Downward T-Inferences are valid. For suppose a sentence of the form $T(n)$ is true, where n denotes some sentence. Then the sentence denoted by n is in the extension of $T(x)$. But all sentences in the extension of $T(x)$ are sentences which have been assigned the value "true" by the semantics. So the Downward T-Inference is valid. And suppose some sentence denoted by the term n is true. Then at the next round of the iterative hierarchy, that sentence will be included in the extension of $T(x)$. But when it is a fixed point, the extension of $T(x)$ does not change on the next iteration: that is the definition of a fixed point. So at a fixed point, the sentence named by n is in the extension of $T(x)$. So $T(n)$ is true, and the Upward T-Inference is valid.

If it is analytic (as it were) of any truth predicate that its extension be a fixed point in Kripke's hierarchy, then it is analytic that the T-Inferences be valid for any acceptable truth predicate. But now we are right back in the soup. Proof Lambda above uses only the T-Inferences and inferences of standard classical logic. So it seems after all that Tarski was right: if the validity of the T-Inferences is guaranteed by the very notion of truth itself, then no consistent language can both contain an acceptable truth predicate and employ classical logic.

Indeed, it is very hard to see how to sensibly deny the validity of the T-Inferences on even the weakest conceptions of truth. The so-called "deflationary" concept of truth is sometimes characterized as the claim that the notion of truth is *exhausted* by the T-sentences. This is already too strong a notion to be consistent with classical logic if it is interpreted as accepting the T-sentences as all true. An even weaker notion is this: the sentence $T(n)$ is just a *notational variant* for the sentence denoted by the term n, i.e. for $\mathscr{F}(n)$; $T(n)$ makes exactly the same claim as $\mathscr{F}(n)$ does. It is an unavoidable step from here to the conclusion that the truth value of $T(n)$ is identical to that of $\mathscr{F}(n)$: after all, they are just two ways of saying the same thing. If so, then the T-Inferences are certainly valid: they are just inferences from one sentence to a notational variant, rather like changing from regular to italic fonts. Note that again this notion of truth does *not* entail the truth of the T-sentences, since it only requires that the sentences on either side of the biconditional have the same truth value, not that they both be true or false. If only the usual two truth values are available, then the T-sentences must all be true, but if a biconditional flanked by sentences with undefined truth value is itself undefined, then the T-sentence for an undefined sentence will not be true.

Kripke discusses this sort of approach in his paper:

> The approach adopted here has presupposed the following version of Tarski's "Convention T", adapted to the three-valued approach: If "k" abbreviates the name of the sentence A, $T(k)$ is to be true, or false, respectively if A is true, or false. This captures the intuition that $T(k)$ is to have the same truth conditions as A itself; it follows that $T(k)$ suffers a truth-gap if A does.   (ibid. 80 in Martin 1984)

Since the validity of the T-Inferences entails the invalidity of some of the classical logic, *from the point of view of classical logic, even the most deflationary conceptions of truth are overcommitted.*[6]

If the foregoing arguments are correct, then the admission of any "acceptable" theory of truth for a language like L must entail either inconsistency or a modification or restriction of classical logic, just as Tarski claimed. But it is as yet obscure what modifications will do the job, and how much of classical logic can remain without rendering the language inconsistent. It is also unclear whether the classical inferences really must be the ones to go: perhaps the most rational response to the dilemma is to restrict the T-Inferences in some way, even though the arguments in favor of their necessary validity seem quite strong. These questions are entirely untouched on by most of the standard approaches to the Liar, which focus exclusively on the semantic reading of the paradox.

A Remark on Logical Systems

In the foregoing section, I have presented two variants of the Inferential Version of the Liar paradox, one of which supplements a classical logical system with a set of *axioms* (viz. the T-sentences formulable in L) and the other of which supplements the system with a pair of *inference rules* (viz. the Upward and Downward T-Inferences). I also argued that these two variants are importantly different, and in particular that the variant which uses the inference rules is the more difficult of the two to solve. This claim will likely appear implausible at first sight, since the differences between the two versions only appear when one begins to question the fundamental assumptions that underpin classical logic. Furthermore, the same observations apply to logical systems in general, so it will be worthwhile to pause to reflect on this point in a bit more detail.

Classical logical systems can be built in different, but equivalent, ways. In particular, one can construct a system that economizes on its inference rules by expanding its set of axioms, or one can economize on the axioms by expanding

---

[6] By "classical logic", we here mean the natural deduction system being used, which is an acceptable way of formulating classical first-order predicate calculus. Other ways of formulating "classical logic" may react differently to the introduction of the T-Inferences. See Appendix A.

the set of inference rules. Which approach one takes is (in the classical context) purely a matter of taste, since the resulting systems can have exactly the same set of theorems.

Suppose, for example, one has a logical system that includes negation, disjunction, conditional and biconditional, but does not yet have a symbol for conjunction. One can introduce the conjunction symbol into the language in either of two ways. On the one hand, one can introduce a set of *axiom schemata* such as

(A ⊃ (B ⊃ (A & B)))
(A & B) ⊃ A
(A & B) ⊃ B,

so that any sentence one gets by replacing A and B by wffs is an axiom. The inference rules need not be changed: Modus Ponens can be used together with the axioms to introduce and eliminate sentences that include the conjunction sign.

On the other hand, one can avoid the use of axiom schemata by introducing new inference rules, viz. & Introduction and & Elimination. & Introduction states: if one has already derived a sentence on one line of a proof and another sentence on another line, then one is allowed to write the conjunction of the two sentences. & Elimination states: if one has already derived a conjunction, then one is allowed to write either conjunct.

Given the supporting environment of the classical inference rules, the axiom schemata and the inference rules have identical effects on the proof structure. That is: given the inference rules one can derive any instance of the axiom schemata as a theorem, and given the axiom schemata, one can mimic, via some intermediary steps, the action of the inference rules. A simple example will make this clear.

Let's take the case of & Introduction. If I add the rule & Introduction to a system, then I can derive any instance of the corresponding axiom schema as follows:

A	Hypothesis
B	Hypothesis
A	Reiteration
B	Reiteration
A & B	& Introduction
B ⊃ (A & B)	⊃ Introduction
A ⊃ (B ⊃ (A & B))	⊃ Introduction

In the other direction, the effect of any application of the rule & Introduction can be achieved by use of the axiom schema and repeated use of ⊃ Elimination (Modus Ponens):

> A
> B
> A ⊃ (B ⊃ (A & B))   Axiom
> B ⊃ (A & B)   ⊃ Elimination
> A & B   ⊃ Elimination

So given the supporting environment, viz. the rules ⊃ Elimination and ⊃ Introduction, it appears to be purely a matter of personal preference whether one adds to the axioms or to the inference rules to introduce conjunction.

But further reflection shows that this cannot be all there is to the story. For consider how one goes about *justifying* the addition of either the new axiom schema or the new inference rule. The aim of a system of logical inference is to be *valid*, i.e. *truth-preserving*. One aspires to a system of inferences that will never allow an untrue conclusion to be derived from true premises. So consider how one would argue, in each of the cases considered above, that the new rules will be truth-preserving.

The argument will have to advert to the semantic properties of conjunction. In the case of the rule for & Introduction, all one needs to show is that whenever the premises of the inference (the conjuncts) are both true, so is the conclusion (the conjunction). And in order to show *that*, one need merely check *a single line on the truth table for conjunction, viz. the line on which both conjuncts are true*. Since on that line the conjunction is also true, the rule of & Introduction can be justified. Notice that for the purposes of the justification, it does not matter whether there are any truth values other than true and false, and it certainly does not matter what the semantics of the horseshoe happen to be.

One the other hand, justifying the corresponding axiom schema is a much more convoluted business. If we add the axiom schema, then we want to be assured that every instance of the schema, every well-formed sentence that has the structure (A ⊃ (B ⊃ (A & B)), is true. And to prove *this*, one needs to know quite a bit more than the truth value of A & B on a single line of a truth table. One has, in the first place, to know about the semantics of the horseshoe. Furthermore, one has to know about the semantic value of material implication and conjunction for *all* possible semantic values of their constituents. So moving from a bivalent to a multivalent semantics will have a significant impact on the justification of the axiom schema, and no impact at all on the justification of inference rule & Introduction. And since one of the apparent upshots of the Liar paradox is the need to move beyond a bivalent semantics, this difference in justification is likely to loom large in our investigation.

When constructing a formal system of inferences, there are two competing forms of parsimony that can be pursued. One can seek to minimize the number of inference rules in a system, employing axiom schemata in their stead, or one can minimize the axioms by increasing the inference rules. If one pursues the first strategy, the minimal number of inference rules required is one: Modus Ponens. Everything else can be taken care of by axiom schemata in the manner we have just seen. If one pursues the other strategy, then the minimal number of axiom schemata one can achieve is zero: the system can consist entirely of inference rules with no axioms at all. Such a system is a *Natural Deduction* system, which is the system that will be employed in this book. The details of the system, and some more technical remarks, are presented in Appendix A. In a standard classical setting, the choice between an axiomatic system and a natural deduction system is purely one of preference: the power of the systems can be shown to be identical. *But as soon as one contemplates moving beyond a classical (bivalent) setting, the differences between the systems become substantive.* As we have seen, the projects of justifying corresponding elements of the two systems become very different. There is no problem at all in justifying the rule of & Introduction even if there are more than the usual two truth values, whereas justifying the axiom schema (A ⊃ (B ⊃ (A & B)) will be more diffi-cult, and perhaps impossible.

So the observations made above concerning the two variants of the Inferen-tial Version generalize to a wider application. Just as & Introduction is easier to justify than the corresponding axiom schema, so too are the Upward and Downward T-Inference rules easier to justify than the axiom schema for the T-sentences. And this make the problem posed by Proof Lambda much more *difficult* to solve than the variant which uses the T-sentences as axioms. For it is plausible that the T-sentence for the Liar (T-Lambda) ought not to be an axiom since it is not true. But it is very implausible that any objection can be lodged against the T-Inferences: it at least appears simple to show that they are always valid. The first version of the argument, which uses only classical logic and the T-sentences, can be defused by a plausible observation, while Proof Lambda, which uses only classical logic and the T-Inferences, cannot be. Indeed, if no objection can be found to the T-Inferences, then the only way to respond to Proof Lambda is *by modifying classical logic*. This is what we will eventually be forced to do.

The Virtues of the Inferential Version of the Paradox

The inferential version of the Liar antinomy is not a trivial variant of the semantic version. This has been illustrated by Kripke's approach, since there the solution to the semantic version is clear but the solution to the inferential version still obscure. If the Liar sentence has no truth value, and if one uses the Strong Kleene rules for the biconditional, T-Lambda also has no truth value, so we can see how the demand that all T-sentences be true fails. But still, if one then asks how the inferential problem is solved, how either the T-Inferences or the rules of classical logic are to be amended, no answer immediately presents itself. Perhaps the only suggestion is to abandon the project of standardizing inferences altogether, in favor of reasoning directly *with the semantics*, i.e. instead of reasoning from premises to conclusion by some syntactically specifiable rules, use the semantics to try to figure out if a given sentence is true, given that others are either true or false. Of course, in Kripke's case such reasoning is highly non-trivial, involving as it does transfinite inductions, the existence of multiple fixed points, etc. Further, Kripke's proof of the existence of any fixed point is non-constructive, so it is unclear what general methods can be used to determine the truth values of arbitrary sentences.

Attacking the inferential problem directly means attempting to discover syntactically specifiable inference rules for L which are not inconsistent and which save as much of classical logic and the T-Inferences as possible. But one also wants the inferential structure to be valid, i.e. truth-preserving, and that is a property which depends on the semantics for the language. So questions of the semantics of L, i.e. of how the truth values of the sentences of L are determined, cannot be left behind. Indeed, the best counsel is to investigate the semantics and the inferential structure for L jointly. At times, the semantics may suggest how to proceed with the inferences; at times the inferences may suggest how to proceed with the semantics. Our aim is to produce a semantics and a set of inference rules which mesh so as to ensure that the inferences will be valid. By this sort of triangulation on the problem of truth, we will ultimately be able to use the solution to the inference problem to provide essential support for the treatment of the semantics of the language. We will eventually see that the most counterintuitive properties of the semantics are exactly what one would expect given the natural solution to the inference problem.

Before entertaining any semantic considerations, though, let us canvass some of the options available for defusing the unacceptable Proof Lambda.

If one declares the T-Inferences to be sacrosanct, then there is not much wiggle room to defeat Proof Lambda. The rule of Reiteration is beyond reproach, so that leaves only Hypothesis and $\sim$ Introduction. The rule of Hypothesis also seems safe, since it never, on its own, results in the *assertion* of any claim, but rather marks the beginning of a subderivation. Hypothesis allows one to begin a subderivation with any wff, and one would suspect that if some unacceptable result eventually appears *outside* the subderivation (as in Proof Lambda), then the problem lies with the rule which *dismisses* the subderivation. This leaves $\sim$ Introduction as the only questionable inference in Proof Lambda, which is perhaps an intuitively appealing result. *Reductio* has always been a somewhat suspect means of proof: so perhaps our focus should center on the rule of $\sim$ Introduction.

Another suggestive aspect of Proof Lambda is that the contradiction derived consists of a *paradoxical* sentence and its negation. This might not seem so bad a result as the derivation of a *grounded* sentence and its negation, which would really be intolerable. Of course, in a standard classical scheme, if any sentence and its negation are theorems, then so are all well-formed sentences, but this feature of classical logic has also been found intuitively objectionable. So perhaps the lesson of Proof Lambda is that we should adopt some Relevance Logic or some Paraconsistent Logic in place of classical logic.

However, further examples of the inconsistency of the classical inferences together with the T-Inferences undercut both of these lines of reasoning. One can demonstrate the inconsistency of these inferences without the use of $\sim$ Introduction, and one can also derive any sentence one likes without first deriving a paradoxical sentence and its negation and then arguing that anything follows from a contradiction. The manner of proof, sometimes called *Löb's Paradox*, is well known, though it tends to get less attention than the Liar. Let X stand for an arbitrary wff in L. Then stipulate the denotation of the sentence name γ as follows

$\gamma: T(\gamma) \supset X.$

We can prove X by means of the T-Inferences, $\supset$ Introduction, $\supset$ Elimination, Hypothesis and Reiteration. Let us call this *Proof Gamma*:

	$T(\gamma)$	Hypothesis
	$T(\gamma)$	Reiteration
	$T(\gamma) \supset X$	Downward T-Inference
	X	$\supset$ Elimination
$T(\gamma) \supset X$		$\supset$ Introduction
$T(\gamma)$		Upward T-Inference
X		$\supset$ Elimination

Proof Gamma is much more deadly than Proof Lambda, since it shows directly that the system allows for any sentence to be proven, and by seemingly innocuous inferences. $\supset$ Elimination is just Modus Ponens, and $\supset$ Introduction is grounded in the seeming truism that if Y can be derived via valid inferences from X, then one is entitled to assert: If X, then Y. It is not clear how Intuitionist Logic or Relevance Logic or Paraconsistent Logic could block any of these inferences. So perhaps the problem is really with the T-Inferences after all, although every acceptable account of truth seems to imply that they must be valid, and although, even including paradoxical and other ungrounded sentences, there is no clear example of such an inference being *invalid*, that is, leading from a true premise to a conclusion which is other than true.

The inconsistency of the T-Inferences with the classical inferences even apart from $\sim$ Introduction is also shown by the fact that the T-Inferences together with the other classical inferences allow one to derive the T-sentences as theorems. So even though the claim that the T-Inferences are valid is logically weaker than the claim that all the T-sentences are true (as we have seen), the former together with classical inferences (and without $\sim$ Introduction) imply the T-sentences. If some of the T-*sentences* must go, then either we must deny the T-*Inferences* or deny some of classical logic besides ~ Introduction.

One added incentive to look carefully at the inferential paradox is provided by the observation that, although Löb's paradox is recognized, the invalidity of arguments using classical logic and the T-Inferences is widely overlooked. Remarkably, it is not uncommon for popular puzzles to *teach* or *encourage* invalid inferences as a test of reasoning skill! I refer to certain "logic puzzles" which make reference to truth and falsity, or truth-telling and lying. The genre is long-lived and well known, so familiar that it takes some effort to recognize how startling the uncritical acceptance of such puzzles should be.

Consider an example of such a puzzle from a recent computer game.[7] One is confronted with three switches, labeled "#1", "#2" and "#3", each of which may be set either to a position marked "true" or one marked "false". The following instructions are provided:

Key:
Set switch to false if any statement associated with it is false.
Set switch to true if any statement associated with it is true.
Password statements for today:
Statement for switch #1 = All switches are false.
Statement for switch # 3 = One and only one switch is true.

The task is to set all three switches. The statement for #1 cannot be true on pain of contradiction, so #1 is false and hence at least one switch must be set to "true". If the statement for switch #3 is false, #2 must be true (since at least one is true), which would make the statement for #3 true after all. So #3 is true and #2 false. Mission accomplished, go on to the next phase of the game.

"Logical" puzzles such as that just given hardly raise an eyebrow: one is rewarded for "deducing" the "right" answer. But the "right" answer apparently involves "proving" that the statement associated with switch #2 is false completely *a priori, and without even knowing what the statement is.* If the statement associated with switch #2 happens to be "The Earth is round", have we just undone two millennia of scientific progress by the use of pure logic? The puzzle requires the use of something like Löb's paradox to get the "right" answer. But at least Löb's paradox is regarded as a *paradox*: these puzzles are instead presented as *good training in logic*!

Less blatant but also disturbing are examples like the following:

Sam says "Sue is lying". Sue says "Joe is lying". Joe says "Both Sam and Sue are lying". Who is telling the truth?

---

[7] *Connections*, Discovery Channel Multimedia, 1995.

Using standard hypothetical reasoning and the analog of the T-Inferences which is appropriate for falsehood, one can derive that only Sue is telling the truth, as the only "consistent" allocation of truth and falsity to the three claims. But the result that Sue is telling the truth and the other two lying is at some level bizarre. After all, their little conversation has no content at all beyond referring to one another: what could be the grounds that make any of their claims true or false?

The upshot of the inferential understanding of the Liar antinomy is a rather confused and puzzling situation. Purely semantic approaches, such as Kripke's, seem to do some justice to the way we reason about the *semantic evaluation* of the Liar, but the resulting theory also endorses the validity of the T-Inferences. This seems to require that some part of classical logic be rejected (which?), and, just as Tarski had originally claimed, it appears that any language containing its own truth predicate, names for any arbitrary wff, and employing classical logic must be inconsistent. As Martin noted, since natural languages seem to satisfy these requirements, they all are *prima facie* inconsistent.

Since Tarski's claim has been the source of much puzzlement it behooves us to be somewhat more exact about how it should be understood. Recall Tarski's claim: any language is inconsistent if it satisfies four conditions:

(I) For any sentence which occurs in the language a definite name of this sentence also belongs to the language.

(II) Every sentence formed from (2) [i.e. "*x is a true sentence if and only if p*"] by replacing the symbol "*p*" by any sentence of the language and the symbol "*x*" by a name of this sentence is to be regarded as a true sentence of this language.

(III) In the language in question an empirically established premise having the same meaning as (α) [i.e. the sentence which asserts that the denoting term which occurs in the Liar sentence refers to the sentence itself] can be formulated and accepted as a true sentence.

(IV) "The usual laws of logic hold."

The puzzle is, of course, that a natural language such as English appears to satisfy all of the constraints, and so would have to be inconsistent. But what could it even mean to say that English is inconsistent, and how could it be that English, and every other natural language, is?

In *Understanding Truth*, Scott Soames reports a suggestion of Nathan Salmon on this question of interpretation: "Salmon's suggestion is that Tarski's notion of an inconsistent language is to be understood as one in which some sentence and its negation are jointly true in the language and hence as a language in which at least one contradiction is true" (Soames 1999: 54). Soames goes on to opine that Tarski himself actually accepted this conclusion, and therefore "rejected [natural] languages themselves as inadequate for the construction of serious theories of truth and proposed that they be replaced, for these purposes, by formalized languages for which restricted truth predicates could be defined in a way that made the construction of Liar-paradoxical sentences impossible" (ibid. 55). Soames himself finds the conclusion unacceptable: even in English, no contradiction is true, so there must be something wrong with Tarski's argument.

In light of our discussion of the Liar, we are now in a position to provide an alternative reading of Tarski's claim, a reading which does not require the conclusion that any contradiction in English is true. Instead of focusing on *semantic values*, we will consider instead the properties of an inferential system. Conditions (I) and (III) above are used by Tarski to guarantee that a Liar-like sentence can be constructed in the language. So let us combine them more simply into the following condition:

(I*) sentences like $\sim T(\lambda)$ and $T(\gamma) \supset X$ (as defined above) can be constructed in the language.

English, and any other natural language, clearly satisfies this criterion: the singular terms λ and γ need only be replaced by either proper names or definite descriptions that denote the relevant sentence.

Tarski's condition (II) requires that each T-sentence of the language "be regarded as a true sentence" (NB Tarski does not say that they *are* true but that they are *regarded* as true). Tarski's concern here is not with what is true but rather what is *accepted* by speakers of the language: speakers of English will tend to accept the T-sentences for English. And because they regard these sentences as true, they are willing to *use* the sentences when constructing arguments. As we have seen, the T-sentences can be used in constructing a variant of Proof Lambda that uses axiom schemata, and similarly T-sentences as axioms could be used to construct an axiomatic variant of Proof Gamma. But if this is the *purpose* for which the T-sentences are being used, then it is simpler and more direct to require only that the T-Inferences be regarded as valid rather than have the T-sentences be regarded as true. So let us construct a second condition:

(II*) The Upward and Downward T-Inferences are *accepted* (regarded as valid) by speakers of the language.

Finally, we can give a similar construal for condition (IV). Tarski writes of a language in which "the usual laws of logic hold", but he does not further explicate what he means by "holding". It *could* mean that the usual laws of logic are *valid* (i.e. truth-preserving), but then it would be difficult for Tarski to maintain that the laws hold *for English* since he thinks that there is no acceptable theory of truth for English. It makes more sense to construe "holding" on a par with "be regarded as a true sentence", i.e. as a *psychological* claim. The laws of logic "hold" in English (for a community) insofar as speakers of English in that community are inclined to *accept* certain logical inferences, or regard them as valid. So we then have a third condition:

(III*) The usual laws of logic are *accepted* (regarded as valid) by speakers of the language.

Let us assume that (I*), (II*), and (III*) all obtain for some language and some community of speakers. Then the language will be *inconsistent for those speakers* in the following sense: it will be possible to construct arguments that are accepted by the speakers as valid yet which have contradictory conclusions. Indeed, as Proof Gamma shows, it will be possible to construct proofs that are accepted by the speakers to any conclusion at all.

It no doubt seems unlovely to import psychological notions like "accepted as valid" into Tarski's argument. But since the psychological notion "regarded as true" is explicitly in the argument, it seems a minor step to just extend the psychological aspect to the logical requirement. In any case, whether this is a defensible interpretation of Tarski or not, it is a clearly stated argument with interest in its own right. For *prima facie* it appears that English, as used by the general population (and perhaps most obviously by philosophers) satisfies all three conditions. It satisfies condition I* since sentences like the Liar can be constructed. And at least the community of philosophers satisfies III*: philosophers are inclined to accept the standard logical inferences, to regard them as valid. And furthermore, philosophers (and even the common folk) are inclined to accept the T-Inferences as valid: no one *objects* when a speaker infers " 'Snow is white' is true" from "Snow is white". Even common folk enjoy and "solve" logic puzzles such as those cited above. So it appears that for most speakers English is an inconsistent language as defined above: given the language together with inference rules that the speakers accept, one can construct a proof of any arbitrary sentence.

Of course, this is not exactly right. It is true that typical English speakers *tend to accept* both the standard logical inferences and the T-Inferences, but that acceptance is not absolute. As a psychological experiment, it is instructive to try to *convince* someone of something by the use of Proof Gamma. (Indeed, it is instructive to try this experiment on oneself.) The steps of the argument can be laid out and reviewed—each step appears to be unobjectionable—but the whole procedure produces no conviction. When I tried out Proof Gamma on a friend (not a philosopher), he followed it in detail, saw the apparent justification for each inference, and then simply rejected the conclusion. When pressed on exactly *where* the chain of argument went wrong, he said that it was "like dividing by zero": *something* illegitimate had happened, even though he could not say exactly what. And outside a very select group of people, this reaction is typical: no one will actually accept the argument, but few will even venture an opinion about exactly what is wrong with it. Each step appears to be valid, even though the end result is clearly unacceptable.

So normal human beings (quite sensibly) have rules that allow them to *overrule* arguments, even when every step of the argument appears *prima facie* to be valid. In the case of Proof Gamma, one observes that if it is to be accepted in one case, then it must be accepted in all cases, and so anything can be proven. This is reason enough to reject the argument *without any diagnosis of where it went wrong*. And of course Proof Gamma does go wrong—although it is by no means obvious where. But the existence of an undiagnosed flaw in Proof Gamma ought to give us pause: who is to say that there are not other arguments which make the same mistake but which are not *obviously* invalid in the way that Proof Gamma is? The rules that allow us to overrule arguments are crude: they will not catch every fallacious piece of reasoning. What is urgently needed is a diagnosis of Proof Gamma and Proof Lambda.

The following conclusion is therefore defensible: the grammatical structure of English allows for the construction of arguments which appear *prima facie* to be valid to most English speakers (there is no individual step in the argument that would be rejected), but which are inconsistent in the straightforward sense that they allow any claim to be proven. These arguments employ as logical apparatus only classical logical inferences and the T-Inferences (or alternatively the T-sentences as axioms "regarded to be true"). English speakers are not inclined to *accept* these arguments when they see that they are inconsistent, but they are also typically not able to identify any step in the argument that is objectionable. It is therefore an open problem to exactly identify where these arguments go wrong. Unfortunately, most discussions of the Liar paradox and related paradoxes in the philosophical literature do not address these questions. It ought to be a test of the adequacy of any account of the Liar paradox that it be able to explain where Proof Lambda and Proof Gamma go wrong, even when they are presented in colloquial English. We will use this question as a touchstone for our account as we proceed.

Having gone to some lengths to attract attention to the Inferential Version of the Liar paradox, I must now beg the reader's indulgence: the Inferential Version will disappear from consideration for quite a while. We have three distinct tasks before us. The first is to provide an account of how sentences get truth values, particularly in languages that contain a truth predicate. This will directly address the semantic status of the Liar sentence. Let us call this the *technical* problem. The second is to consider exactly what a theory of truth, i.e. an explication of the nature of truth, can be. We must also provide a clear account of what truth is. Let us call this the *metaphysical* problem. And the third is solving the Inferential Version of the Liar. Aside from its intrinsic interest, our examination of inferential structures will reinforce the results of the purely semantic issues with which we will begin. This last is the *inference* problem.

The relationship between these three problems is a matter of some delicacy. As we have already noted, if we want our inferences to be truth-preserving, we must have some account of how truth values are determined (the technical problem) before we can provide a satisfactory solution to the inference problem. But in approaching the technical problem, we need to have some notions about what results the semantics ought to give. For example, the little puzzles we began this chapter with suggest that the Liar sentence ought not to turn out to be either true or false. But as we can now see, the way we reason through those puzzles uses collections of inference principles that are jointly inconsistent. So until we have solved the inference problem, we really will not know exactly which of our arguments about truth values we ought to trust. So we have to proceed with caution, trying to make progress along each of our three fronts, then pausing to consider how that progress comports with investigations of the other questions. Bearing all this in mind, we will begin with the technical problem.

Appendix A: The Natural Deduction System

We will be using a standard natural deduction, based on that presented in LeBlanc and Wisdom (1976), supplemented with some axioms for identity and the T-Inferences. We will omit the reference to line numbers in the application of the rules since our proofs are typically short. The standard rules are as follows:

Reiteration: One may reiterate any sentence above the hypothesis bar of the derivation one is in, or of any derivation of which it is a subderivation.

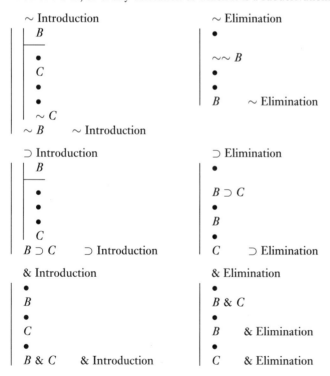

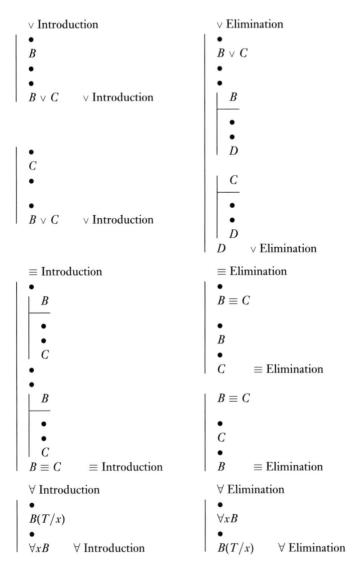

Restriction: In ∀ Introduction, the term T must be foreign to all hypotheses and premises of the derivation and of any derivation of which the line is a subderivation, and must be foreign to B.

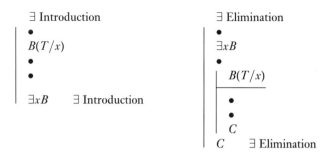

Restriction: In ∃ Elimination, the term T must be foreign to all hypotheses and premises of the derivation and of any derivation of which the line is a subderivation, and must be foreign to $\exists x B$ and to C.

These rules are sufficient to derive all classical theorems of the first-order predicate calculus, and so deserve the name *classical logic*. They also reflect closely the sort of informal reasoning that is commonly used.

As it turns out, mathematical logicians seldom use such systems, which accounts for some discrepancies between the results we obtain and results reported in the literature. Friedman and Sheard (1987), for example, examine exactly the question of how a standard system of Peano Arithmetic can be supplemented with either axioms or inference rules for a truth-like predicate (called "T") without becoming inconsistent. All of the T-sentences cannot be added as axioms, so various other weaker axioms and inference rules are considered. In particular, Friedman and Sheard consider both the pair of axiom schemata

$$A \rightarrow T(\text{ins}(\#A, \ x_n)) \qquad\qquad T\text{-In}$$
$$T(\text{ins}(\#A, \ x_n)) \rightarrow A \qquad\qquad T\text{-Out}$$

and the pair of inference rules

From A derive $T(\text{ins}(\#A, \ x_n))$ T-Intro
From $T(\text{ins}(\#A, \ x_n))$ derive A T-Elim

(Friedman and Sheard 1987: 5)

They show that while there are no consistent extensions of their system that add both T-In and T-Out, there are consistent extensions that add both T-Intro and T-Elim. This result is also reported in, for example, Ketland (1999) and Tennant (2002).

The system that Friedman and Sheard begin with is an axiomatic system quite different from the natural deduction system we are using. To take an obvious example, their system simply stipulates as axioms "All tautologies of $L(T)$", i.e. all of these tautologies are simply *stipulated*, not *derived* by any rules of inference. So it is perhaps not surprising that the interaction of the T-Inferences with the rest of the system might be different. The main point of difference must certainly be the absence of conditional proofs in their system, for if one has the usual natural deduction rule for ⊃ Introduction, then adding the rules T-Intro and T-Elim is tantamount to adding the axiom schemata T-In and T-Out: every instance of the schemata will be a theorem. Since no consistent extension of Friedman and Sheard's system includes both T-In and T-Out, no consistent extension of a version with ⊃ Introduction can include T-Intro and T-Elim.

All of this focuses attention, quite appropriately, on $\supset$ Introduction. As we will see, it is a rule that must be amended to make our system consistent with the T-Inferences. One advantage here of using the natural deduction system is that $\supset$ Introduction mimics well the informal reasoning one uses when confronted with the Liar sentence: "Well, if the sentence is true, then (since it says it is not true) it is not true…"

The ability of the natural deduction system to represent intuitive reasoning about truth can also be illustrated by formalizing a somewhat more complicated case, related to the one used by Tarski. In this case, we do not use a stipulation like $\mathscr{F}(\lambda) = {\sim}T(\lambda)$ but rather an *empirical premise* to achieve the self-reference. Consider the sentence

* $\forall x(S(x) \supset {\sim}T(x))$

Let $S(x)$ represent "x is a starred sentence in Appendix A of *Truth and Paradox*". We can then translate the sentence above as

Every starred sentence in Appendix A of *Truth and Paradox* is not true.

The sentence above is not *per se* paradoxical, but does play a role in deriving contradictory sentences from the evidently true (contingent) premise

$$\forall x(S(x) \equiv (x = \ulcorner\forall x(S(x) \supset {\sim}T(x))\urcorner)),$$

where the corner quotes are used to form a quotation name (or a Gödel number, if one wishes) for the sentence within the quotes. This last sentence says that the only starred sentence in Appendix A of *Truth and Paradox* is the sentence $\forall x(S(x) \supset {\sim}T(x))$. The important thing here is that one can determine, simply from the form of the term itself, that $\ulcorner\forall x(S(x) \supset {\sim}T(x))\urcorner$ denotes $\forall x(S(x) \supset {\sim}T(x))$, and one can then use that to apply the T-Inferences.

To get our problematic proof, all we need are the rules of standard deduction, the T-Inferences, the axiom

$\forall x(x = x)$

and a rule that says if we have derived $n = m$ and some sentence B, then we are allowed to write $B[n/m]$, i.e. the sentence one gets by replacing n everywhere it occurs in B with m. Let's call this last rule "= Replace". The problematic proof then runs:

$\forall x(S(x) \equiv (x = \ulcorner\forall x(S(x) \supset {\sim}T(x))\urcorner))$	Premise
$\forall x(S(x) \supset {\sim}T(x))$	Hypothesis
$\forall x(S(x) \equiv (x = \ulcorner\forall x(S(x) \supset {\sim}T(x))\urcorner))$	Reiteration
$S(\ulcorner\forall x(S(x) \supset {\sim}T(x))\urcorner) \equiv$ $\;(\ulcorner\forall x(S(x) \supset {\sim}T(x))\urcorner = \ulcorner\forall x(S(x) \supset {\sim}T(x))\urcorner)$	$\forall$ Elimination
$\forall x(x = x)$	Axiom
$\ulcorner\forall x(S(x) \supset {\sim}T(x))\urcorner = \ulcorner\forall x(S(x) \supset {\sim}T(x))\urcorner$	$\forall$ Elimination
$S(\ulcorner\forall x(S(x) \supset {\sim}T(x))\urcorner)$	$\equiv$ Elimination
$\forall x(S(x) \supset {\sim}T(x))$	Reiteration
$T(\ulcorner\forall x(S(x) \supset {\sim}T(x))\urcorner)$	Upward T-Inference
$S(\ulcorner\forall x(S(x) \supset {\sim}T(x))\urcorner) \supset$ $\quad {\sim}T(\ulcorner\forall x(S(x) \supset {\sim}T(x))\urcorner)$	$\forall$ Elimination
${\sim}T(\ulcorner\forall x(S(x) \supset {\sim}T(x))\urcorner)$	$\supset$ Elimination
${\sim}\forall x(S(x) \supset {\sim}T(x))$	$\sim$ Introduction

$S(\alpha)$	Hypothesis
$T(\alpha)$	Hypothesis
$\forall x(S(x) \equiv (x = \ulcorner \forall x(S(x) \supset \sim T(x))\urcorner))$	Reiteration
$S(\alpha) \equiv (\alpha = \ulcorner \forall x(S(x) \supset \sim T(x))\urcorner)$	$\forall$ Elimination
$S(\alpha)$	Reiteration
$\alpha = \ulcorner \forall x(S(x) \supset \sim T(x))\urcorner$	$\equiv$ Elimination
$T(\alpha)$	Reiteration
$T(\ulcorner \forall x(S(x) \supset \sim T(x))\urcorner)$	$=$ Replace
$\forall x(S(x) \supset \sim T(x))$	Downward T-Inference
$S(\alpha) \supset \sim T(\alpha)$	$\forall$ Elimination
$\sim T(\alpha)$	$\supset$ Elimination
$\sim T(\alpha)$	$\sim$ Introduction
$S(\alpha) \supset \sim T(\alpha)$	$\supset$ Introduction
$\forall x(S(x) \supset \sim T(x))$	$\forall$ Introduction

So one can derive the contradictory conclusions $\forall x(S(x) \supset \sim T(x))$ and $\sim \forall x(S(x) \supset \sim T(x))$ from the premise $\forall x(S(x) \equiv (x = \ulcorner \forall x(S(x) \supset \sim T(x))\urcorner))$, which is an embarrassment since the premise happens to be true.

Of course, the derivation would be an embarrassment even if the premise were not true since the premise might have been true. The pathology here is not so ostentatious as in Proof Lambda, which demonstrates that the inferential system is inconsistent, but it is at root just as damning. In Proof Lambda, we show that a sentence and its negation are both theorems. Given the usual set of inferences, that means that every sentence is a theorem (as is shown directly by Proof Gamma), but that is not the nub of the problem. The problem is rather that Proof Lambda shows that not every theorem of the system is true, since the two contradictory conclusions cannot both be true. The result is just as bad if a system of inferences has a theorem that just happens, contingently, to be false, for that is enough to show that the system cannot be trusted.

The proof above does not establish any theorems, but it can be easily adapted to the purpose. If we treat the entire proof as a subderivation, with $\forall x(S(x) \equiv (x = \ulcorner \forall x(S(x) \supset \sim T(x))\urcorner))$ as a *hypothesis* rather than a *premise*, then we could conclude with $\sim \forall x(S(x) \equiv (x = \ulcorner \forall x(S(x) \supset \sim T(x))\urcorner))$ as a *theorem* by means of $\sim$ Introduction. And what this shows is that adding the T-Inferences to the natural deduction system yields a non-conservative extension: with the addition one can derive more sentences *which do not contain the truth predicate* than one could before. (The truth predicate does not occur in $\sim \forall x(S(x) \equiv (x = \ulcorner \forall x(S(x) \supset \sim T(x))\urcorner))$, as is obvious if the corner quotes are used to indicate the Gödel number of the quoted sentence.) And according to the semantics, the new theorem is not a tautology, and so could be false. Hence the extended system cannot be trusted.

It is perhaps worthwhile to go through the proof above in order to be assured that the troubles with Proof Lambda and Proof Gamma do not arise from the stipulation of the denotation of the terms λ and γ. But having so convinced ourselves, it is much to our advantage to attend to simpler proofs like Lambda and Gamma. Since they are shorter, they provide fewer targets for criticism and emendation: by reflection on them we will be led more quickly and surely to a resolution of the problems they illustrate.

2 On the Origin of Truth Values

The first task before us now is the construction of a complete semantic theory for a language with its own truth predicate. To make the task more significant, we will add to our language L (the minimal language in which the Liar can be constructed) quantifiers which range over sentences, and also whatever non-semantic predicates of sentences one likes (e.g. $S(x)$ for "Sam uttered x"). Since all of the predicates in the language are predicates of sentences, and since the language only contains denumerably many sentences, we can stipulate that at least one name exists for each sentence, viz. its quotation name. We shall use corner quotes for quotation names in our language, so that $\lceil \sim T(\lambda) \rceil$ is a singular term which denotes the Liar sentence $\sim T(\lambda)$. (Of course, the letter λ is another singular term that denotes the same sentence.) Quantification can therefore be treated substitutionally. These assumptions are merely for convenience. In a more realistic language, the quantifiers would range over things other than sentences, and there would be singular terms denoting things other than sentences, but the extra complications involved in adding these luxuries will not advance our purposes here.

Any proposal for a semantic theory enters a crowded marketplace. Treatments of the Liar paradox and theories of truth are numerous and variform, and a complete defense of a new proposal would demand explicit comparisons with all other competitors. This will not be attempted. The plausibility of the proposal will rest almost entirely on the plausibility, indeed near inescapability, of the foundational picture of language and consequent analysis of the Liar. But it will nonetheless be useful to have some touchstones by which the adequacy of the theory can be assessed.

We will consider two benchmark theories: Tarski's theory of the hierarchy of languages and metalanguages and Kripke's fixed-point theory of truth. Each of these theories is, in its own way, designed to respond to the Liar paradox, but the results could hardly be more dissimilar. Tarski deals with the paradox by confining his account of truth to formalized languages in which the paradoxical sentence, as informally understood, cannot be constructed at all. This is achieved by denying that there is any single univocal truth predicate for the language: a truth predicate must always be part of a metalanguage that is distinct from the language to which the predicate applies. No truth predicate is satisfied by a sentence which contains that very predicate, although every sentence may fall in the extension of a truth predicate from a higher metalanguage. The informal Liar cannot be constructed because it purports to contain a single, univocal truth predicate that can be satisfied by sentences that contain it: in Tarski's scheme, no such predicate exists. As is well known, there results an infinite hierarchy of languages and truth predicates.

Kripke's approach is diametrically opposed. Kripke insists (at least initially) on a language with a single univocal truth predicate, predicable of every sentence in the language. Further, the language allows arbitrary proper names for sentences, as L does, so the Liar sentence can be constructed. The extension of the truth predicate is postulated to be a fixed point in Kripke's iterative procedure for calculating the extension and anti-extension of the truth predicate. The Liar sentence ends up neither in the extension nor in the anti-extension, and so is neither true nor false. No metalanguage is employed.

Kripke's theory seems to stand as a rebuke to Tarski's claims about the impossibility of a consistent language which contains its own truth predicate and which contains a Liar sentence. But Tarski is not without his own grounds for criticizing Kripke's theory in turn. First, Tarski claimed that there can be no consistent language with a Liar sentence *in which all of the T-sentences are regarded as true*. The T-sentence for the Liar, which we called T-lambda, is $T(\lambda) \equiv \sim T(\lambda)$. In the Kripke scheme using the Strong Kleene connectives, this sentence does not come out true: it falls in a truth-value gap. (If one uses van Fraassen's supervaluation techniques, this sentence comes out false.) Since Tarski regards the T-sentences as truisms concerning truth, he would reject Kripke's approach as providing a proper theory of truth.

Furthermore, using fixed points and the Strong Kleene rules, the Liar is not true. But if one tries to *say* this in the language, using, e.g. $\sim T(\lceil \sim T(\lambda) \rceil)$, this sentence also falls in the gap. So although one can *comment* in giving the theory that the Liar is not true, one cannot say so truly in the language itself.

Kripke notices this problem at the end of his paper, and suggests a solution. The relevant passage is worth quoting in full.

It is not difficult to modify the present approach so as to accommodate such an alternate intuition. Take any fixed point $L'(S_1, S_2)$. Modify the interpretation of $T(x)$ so as to make it false of any sentence outside S_1. [We call this "closing off" $T(x)$.] A modified version of Tarski's Convention T holds in the sense of the conditional $(T(k) \vee T(neg(k))). \supset .A \equiv T(k)$. In particular, if A is a paradoxical sentence, we can now assert $\sim T(k)$. Equivalently, if A had a truth value before $T(x)$ was closed off, then $A \equiv T(k)$ is true.

Since the object language obtained by closing off $T(x)$ is a classical language with every predicate totally defined, it is possible to define a truth predicate for that language in the usual Tarskian manner. This predicate will *not* coincide in extension with the predicate $T(x)$ of the object language, and it is certainly reasonable to suppose that it is really the metalanguage predicate which expresses the "genuine" concept of truth for the closed-off object language; the $T(x)$ of the closed-off language defines truth for the fixed point *before* it was closed off. So we still cannot avoid the need for a meta-language.   (Kripke 1975: 80–1 in Martin 1984)

It is remarkable to see the main points in favor of a theory abandoned so completely and in such an off-hand manner. In order to make it come out *true* that the Liar is not true, we must admit a metalanguage after all, so the language/metalanguage dichotomy is not avoided. There seem to be two truth predicates, but the predicate in the object language is not "genuine". But since the Liar sentence is framed using the *object language* predicate, it is not really a Liar sentence after all, merely a sentence which denies that some predicate symbolized using a T applies to itself. By jumping to the metalanguage predicate, we have undercut the relevance of the very sentence we were concerned about.

Kripke's attempt to secure the truth of "The Liar is not true" must therefore be rejected. We want to construct a semantics for a language with a single univocal truth predicate. Kripke's fixed-point theory manages this quite nicely, and shows the way to the right account of semantics. Indeed, the theory we will develop employs Kripke's technique for proving a fixed-point theorem, and the results, with respect to truth and falsity, are exactly those one gets in the minimal fixed point using the Kleene treatment of connectives. But our understanding of the significance of the fixed point will differ somewhat from Kripke's and our understanding of sentences which are neither true nor false will be the polar opposite of his. More importantly, if the *only* demand one puts on the extension of the truth predicate is that it be a fixed point in Kripke's construction, one's theory of truth will be underdetermined: as Kripke points out, the fixed-point technique can be wedded to either Kleene's treatment of connectives or to a supervaluational treatment, and even the choice of one of these is consistent with many fixed points. If *all* that one demands of the extension of the truth predicate is that it constitute a fixed point, then there are many equally adequate candidates: the minimal fixed point, the maximal intrinsic fixed point, any of the various maximal fixed points, etc. Our theory will have a *unique* account of truth, secured by our understanding of sentences that are neither true nor false. And we will come to see the *significance* of Kripke's results in a rather different way than he does.

A Picture of Language and Semantics

Consider any formal language with rules for well-formedness, with the usual logical connectives, as well, perhaps, as a truth predicate and a quantifier which ranges over sentences. If the language contains a truth predicate, it also contains a name for each sentence (e.g. a quotation name). If the language has individual terms that denote sentences, we assume the function $\mathscr{F}(n)$ which maps those terms to the sentences they denote is given.

The truth values of various sentences in such a language are related to one another. Indeed, the truth values of some of the sentences are *derived from* the truth values of others, in fairly obvious ways. The truth value of a conjunction, for example, is derived from the truth values of the conjuncts, and the truth value of a negation is derived from the truth value of the sentence negated. "Derived from", in this context, means more than merely "can be inferred from". The truth value of a negation can be inferred from the truth value of the negated sentence, but so too can the truth value of the negated sentence be inferred from the truth value of the negation. The basic picture of semantics we are constructing insists on more: the truth value of a negation is *defined in terms of* the truth value of the negated sentence, but not vice versa. To understand semantics, we need a vivid means to present these relations of *semantic dependence* among the various sentences in a language.

Consider every well-formed formula of the language as a point in an abstract space. We construct a *directed graph* connecting these points by the following rule: an arrow is to be drawn from every immediate semantic constituent of a sentence to that sentence. For the usual logical connectives, the immediate semantic constituents are obvious. The immediate semantic constituent of a negation is the sentence negated (and similarly for any unary connective). The immediate semantic constituents of a conjunction are the conjuncts, of a disjunction the disjuncts, and similarly for other binary connectives, and higher-order connectives if any. But in our language, we want to treat the truth predicate as a truth-functional logical particle, even though it does not have any sentences as parts. Rather, the truth value of a sentence of the form $T(n)$ is a function of the truth value of the sentence which is denoted by n. That is, the immediate semantic constituent of $T(n)$ is $\mathscr{F}(n)$, and similarly for any other *semantic* predicates there may be (e.g. a falsity predicate).[1] The immediate semantic constituents of a quantified sentence are all of the instances generated by replacing the variable by an individual term (again, we assume that every item in the domain of the quantifier has a name).

The basic intuition of any compositional semantics is that *the truth value of any sentence which has immediate semantic constituents is a given function of the truth values of those constituents*. The relevant function is determined by the logical form of the sentence and the meanings of the logical particles.

Notice that the treatment of the truth predicate in our language is modeled on the treatment of the *truth-functional logical connectives* in standard logic rather than on the treatment of other *predicates*. The semantics (and hence the meaning) of a truth-functional connective like & or $\sim$ is specified completely by the truth function associated with the connective. One understands what

---

[1] The general notion of a semantic predicate is that of a predicate whose satisfaction conditions are defined at least in part in terms of the truth value of its argument. "John knows" is a semantic predicate given that a sentence must be true to be known.

$\sim$ is in standard (bivalent) logic when one understands that $\sim$ applied to a true sentence yields a false sentence and vice versa. Similarly, we could, if we wish, introduce a standard unary truth-functional connective T'' (pronounced "It is true that . . . ") associated with the following truth function: T'' applied to a true sentence yields a true sentence, and T'' applied to a false sentence yields a false sentence (or more generally, T'' applied to any sentence yields a sentence with the same truth value). Notice that T'' is not a *predicate* and so does not have an *extension*, any more than $\sim$ does. Clearly, A would be an immediate semantic constituent of T'' A, just as it is of $\sim A$.

We could just as easily decide to write this new connective as T'' . . . ", with an additional quotation mark at the end, so "It is true that A" is rendered as T'' A''. And now our unary connective starts to look suspiciously like a predicate. But still, T'' . . . " is understood as a truth functional connective, not a predicate. And the jump from here to the truth predicate proper is easy to make: just as T'' . . . " is a truth function which takes the truth value of the sentence it is applied to as input, so $T(n)$ is a truth function which takes the truth value of $\mathscr{F}(n)$ as input (supposing $\mathscr{F}(n)$ is a sentence). It is a truth function of the *denotation of its argument* rather than a truth function of its *argument*, but still it is semantically akin to negation rather than to a predicate like " . . . is a mouse". " . . . is a mouse" is not a truth function at all, whether of its argument or the denotation of its argument (if the argument happens to denote anything). This observation gives one way of understanding the claim that truth is not a *property* of sentences.

It is because the truth predicate is a truth function that it deserves to be treated as a *logical* particle, and inferences involving it (the T-Inferences) ought to be treated by logic. It is the truth-functionality that guarantees that the T-Inferences (both Upward and Downward) are valid. This is exactly because $\mathscr{F}(n)$ is an immediate semantic constituent of $T(n)$ in the sense we have described (when $\mathscr{F}(n)$ is a sentence). So we are entitled to put arrows from $\mathscr{F}(n)$ to $T(n)$ in the semantic graph of our language.[2]

The existence of such a directed graph representing a given language (*cum* $\mathscr{F}(x)$) is uncontroversial. The graph itself has a perfectly determinate form independently of any attribution of truth values to sentences. Among the features of the graph are the following.

The graph will typically have a *boundary*, i.e. a set of nodes that have no immediate semantic constituents, nodes that have no arrows leading *into* them (every node has arrows leading out). The truth values of sentences on the boundary are not assigned in virtue of, or as a consequence of, the truth values

---

[2] Again, we simplify the case by making the domain of $\mathscr{F}(n)$ sentences. If the individual terms in the language can denote non-sentences, or the quantifier can range over non-sentences, then not every sentence of the form $T(n)$ will have an immediate semantic constituent. If n denotes a non-sentence, then $T(n)$ will be a false boundary sentence, and will so appear in the graph of the language.

of any other sentences. Again, this is not to say that the truth values of boundary sentences cannot be *inferred* from the truth values of other sentences: they can. For example, the truth value of any sentence can be inferred from the truth value of that sentence conjoined with itself. But in the order of being (as it were) the conjunction has its truth value in virtue of the truth value of the conjuncts, and not vice versa. The "order of being", i.e. the order of semantic dependence, is indicated by the arrows in the graph.

The truth values of the boundary points of the graph are determined not by the truth values of other bits of language but by *the world*. We will assume that the boundary sentences (the non-semantic atomic sentences in L, i.e. the atomic sentences which do not contain the truth or falsity predicates) all have classical truth values, but that is not a necessary part of the picture. If the terms used in the boundary sentences are vague or ambiguous, as in "France is hexagonal", then it may be appropriate to regard the truth value of the boundary sentence as something other than true or false. Even so, it is the world which makes this so: France could have been a perfect geometrical hexagon, or a square. For the sake of simplicity we will regard the boundary sentences as either true or false, but that idealization can be abandoned if other considerations require it. As we will see, the problems posed by the Liar have nothing to do with vagueness or ambiguity: they have rather to do with the mathematical features of the directed graph and the truth functions represented in it.

Once we have the representation of the language as a directed graph with a boundary, all of the riddles of paradox can be seen as species of the general *boundary value problem*. Boundary value problems are a staple in mathematical physics, where one is interested in finding solutions to certain dynamical equations over a space-time manifold. Typically, one is given a space-time manifold, a set of equations (such as Maxwell's equations or Newton's equations of motion and gravity) and the physical state of a system along a boundary of the manifold. The boundary is usually an instant in time (together, perhaps, with a characterization of the system at spatial infinity). What we typically ask is whether, given the state of a system at some moment and the laws of physics, there is a *single unique* solution of those laws everywhere on the manifold that is consistent with the state on the boundary. In the ideal case, a boundary value problem is well-posed: for every set of boundary conditions there exists a unique global solution. Much of mathematical physics is concerned with proofs of existence and uniqueness of solutions.

A simple example, indeed the simplest possible example, can illustrate the nature of a boundary value problem in physics. Consider the physics of perfectly elastic, equally massive Newtonian particles that move in one dimension. Only two things can happen to such particles. Either they move freely, in which case they maintain a constant velocity, or else they collide, in which case they exchange momenta like perfectly elastic billiard balls: each particle moves off with the velocity that the other one had before the collision.[3] If we draw the trajectories of these particles in a two-dimensional space-time, then the dynamics implies that the trajectories of particles are either straight lines (when they don't collide) or form x's (when they do). So given trajectories of a set of particles like this in a two dimensional space-time, we can tell whether we have a global solution to the dynamical equations quite easily by checking that the trajectories are straight when there is no collision and form an x when there is.

The instantaneous state of such a system specifies how many particles there are, where each particle is, and what its velocity is. An example of a boundary condition is given in Figure 2.1: there are three particles, two traveling to the right and one to the left. We will call the moment of time at which the boundary condition is given S.

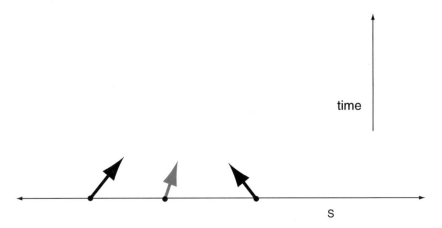

FIG. 2.1. Initial State with Three Particles.

We want to find out what will happen to these particles according to the dynamical laws. Since the laws are so simple, it is quite easy in this case to specify how to find a global solution: simply continue the three trajectories of the three particles by drawing straight lines in the appropriate directions: collisions will take care of themselves. The solution is given in Figure 2.2.

The center particle is first hit from the right and sent left, then collides with the left-most particle, and then collides for a second time with the particle on the right.

One might well think that such boundary-value problems are always well posed for this system: specify how many particles there are and how they are moving at any moment, and there will be a *unique* global solution from those boundary conditions that everywhere satisfies the equations of motion. That unique solution would be generated by the procedure just explained.

[3] It is possible for more than two particles to collide at once, but the solution in this case is forced by continuity considerations.

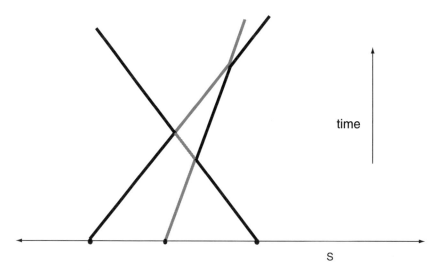

FIG. 2.2. Complete Solution from the Boundary Conditions.

But in fact the situation is a bit more complicated than one might imagine. For whether or not a boundary condition specifies a unique solution depends not just on the equations of motion but also on the topology of the space-time manifold. We have been assuming up to now that the space-time on which the solution is defined has the topology of two-dimensional Euclidean space. But other topologies are possible, and they radically change the nature of our problem.

Suppose, for example, that we put a *loop* into our space-time structure, so the space-time is no longer topologically simple. We do this by hand, by a cut-and-paste procedure. First, cut our original manifold along two lines, L+ and L−. The lines themselves belong to the regions below them. Now paste the manifold back together in this way: L+ gets joined to the open region above L− and L− gets joined to the open region above L+ (see Figure 2.3).

Particles "going in" to L+ from below "emerge" from L−, and particles "going in" to L− from below "emerge" from L+. It may help to think of the loop we have just formed as a time machine: particles that enter the machine at L+ are transported back in time to L−, and particles that enter at L− are transported forward in time to L+.

How does this loop in the space-time manifold affect the boundary value problem? Before we put in the loop, arbitrary data on S could be continued to a unique global solution. But with the loop in place, the uniqueness of the solution disappears. There will always be not just one solution consistent with the boundary values, but many.

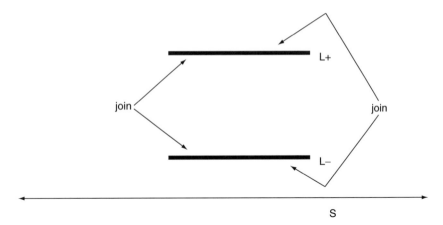

FIG. 2.3. Changing the Topology by Cut-and-Paste.

The easy way to see that there always is a solution is to construct the *minimal* solution in the following way. Start drawing straight lines from S as required by the initial data. If a line hits L− from the bottom, just continue it coming out of the top of L+ in the appropriate place, and if a line hits L+ from the bottom, continue it emerging from L− at the appropriate place. Figure 2.4 represents the minimal solution for a single particle that enters the time-travel region from the left:

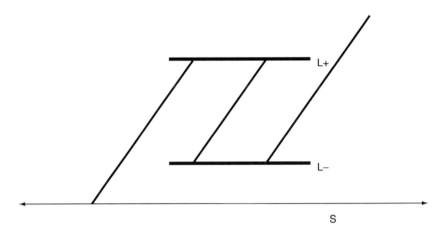

FIG. 2.4. The Minimal Solution.

The particle "travels back in time" twice. It is obvious that this minimal solution is a global solution, since the particle always travels inertially.

But the same initial state on S is also consistent with other global solutions. The new requirement imposed by the topology is just that the data going into L+ from the bottom match the data coming out of L− from the top, and the data going into L− from the bottom match the data coming out of L+ from the top. So we can add any number of vertical lines connecting L− and L+ to a solution and still have a solution. For example, adding a few such lines to the minimal solution yields:

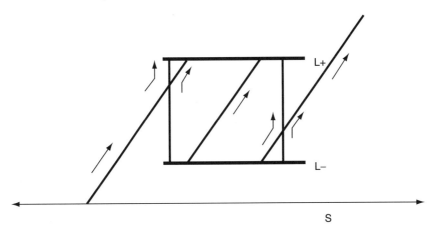

FIG. 2.5. A Non-Minimal Solution.

The particle now collides with itself twice: first before it reaches L+ for the first time, and again shortly before it exits the time-travel region. From the particle's point of view, it is traveling to the right at a constant speed until it hits an older version of itself and comes to rest. It remains at rest until it is hit from the right by a younger version of itself, and then continues moving off, and the same process repeats later. It is clear that this is a global model of the dynamics, and that any number of distinct models could be generated by varying the number and placement of vertical lines.

So in the case of physics, we set a problem by specifying data along a boundary in space-time, and then we have laws, equations of motion, which constrain how the values of the physical magnitudes in space-time are related to each other. We can then ask whether there is a unique solution of those equations consistent with the values on the boundary. The answer to this question will depend on the topology of the space: if the topology is simple, in this case, then there is a unique solution, but if the topology is not, then many solutions can exist.

Given the graph of a language, as defined above, we have an exactly analogous situation. The boundary of the graph, where truth values must be provided from the outside, is the set of non-semantic atomic sentences. The analogs to the equations of motion are the truth functions that specify how the truth value of a non-boundary sentence depends on the truth values of its immediate semantic constituents. What we would like to know is whether these truth functions serve to fix a unique truth value for all the sentences, given the truth values at the boundary. Not surprisingly, the answer to this question depends on the topology of the language, and in particular on whether the directed graph of the language contains loops.

In the standard propositional calculus, the graph of the language is *acyclic*: tracing back successively from a sentence to its immediate semantic constituents will never lead in a circle. This is obvious because in the standard propositional calculus the immediate semantic constituents of a sentence are strictly *shorter* than the sentence of which they are constituents: each constituent contains fewer symbols than the sentence of which it is a constituent. Further, since every sentence is of finite length, every *backward path* from a sentence (i.e. every path which begins at a sentence and continues backwards along arrows) must terminate at the boundary, i.e. at the atomic sentences, after a finite number of steps. Every sentence can be assigned a *rank*, which is the maximal length of a backward path from it to the boundary. Atomic sentences have rank zero; the rank of A $\vee$ ($\sim\sim$B & C) is 4, as there are three backward paths from it to the boundary, of lengths 1, 2, and 4. In a natural way, one can regard the truth values of all sentences in the language as "flowing" in a step-by-step process from the boundary. First the truth values of the boundary sentences are fixed. At the first step, the truth values of all rank 1 sentences are determined from the values on the boundary. (Higher-ranked sentences may also be determined: e.g. if A happens to be true, then the fourth rank sentence above is rendered true at the first step.) Every sentence of rank n is guaranteed to have been assigned a truth value by the nth step, and every sentence eventually gets a truth value.

The unproblematic determinacy of the semantics of the standard propositional calculus, then, derives from the fact that *every sentence in the language has a finite rank*. Given any sentence, after a finite number of "steps" of semantic evaluation, truth values will have migrated up *every* backward path from the sentence to the boundary. The truth value of every immediate semantic constituent will have been settled, and so the truth value of the sentence itself will be fixed.

This determinacy is not shaken if not every boundary sentence is either true or false. We can imagine the possibility of more truth values, and even the possibility that some boundary sentences have no truth value at all. Furthermore, the language can contain logical connectives that are defined by *any* function from the truth values of immediate constituents to the truth value of the sentence whose constituents they are. For example, in a three-valued semantics, the language can contain both the Kleene negation, and what we may call Strong negation, whose truth table is given below.

A	~A
T	F
F	T
U	U

A	¬A
T	F
F	T
U	T

Kleene Negation   Strong Negation

Or again, the language can contain the following three conditionals, among others, the Weak and Strong Kleene conditionals, and a third we will represent as "⇒":

⇒	T	F	U
T	T	F	U
F	T	T	T
U	T	T	T

⊃	T	F	U
T	T	F	U
F	T	T	T
U	T	U	U

⊃w	T	F	U
T	T	F	U
F	T	T	U
U	U	U	U

Strong Kleene   Weak Kleene

It is evident that the addition of many truth values and many truth-functional connectives to the propositional calculus causes no semantic indeterminacy or paradox. For every possible boundary condition there exists a unique global solution which everywhere respects the truth-functional connection between a sentence and its immediate constituents. So there is nothing *inherently* incoherent about connectives like ⇒ and ¬ in a language with more than two truth values.

This may seem a long way round to an obvious conclusion: the unproblematic semantics of standard propositional calculus. But more interesting results can easily be proven.

First, consider adding a truth predicate to the language *and only allowing quotation names of sentences*. $\mathscr{F}(n)$ is the immediate semantic constituent of $T(n)$, and the truth function associated with the truth predicate is the identity function: $T(n)$ has the same truth value as $\mathscr{F}(n)$. This language, which contains a truth predicate and names for every sentence, still has an acyclic graph in which every sentence has a finite rank. The proof follows from the observation that *every immediate semantic constituent of every sentence contains strictly fewer typographical symbols than the sentence of which it is a constituent.* A *typographical symbol* is a letter or other symbol used in writing the language, including each individual letter in the quotation name of a sentence. Thus $\sim T(^{\lceil}\sim B^{\rceil})$ contains eight typographical symbols, even though from the point of view of grammatical structure it is just a tilde, a predicate denoted by tau, and an individual term. It is obvious that the immediate semantic constituents of negations, conjunctions, etc. all contain fewer typographical symbols than the sentences whose constituents they are, and, in this language, so do the immediate semantic constituents of atomic sentences which contain the truth predicate. Since the immediate semantic constituents always contain fewer typographical symbols, and since every well-formed formula contains a finite number of typographical symbols, every well-formed formula has a finite rank. This language can contain many truth values as well as the truth predicate, and a name for every sentence, without any semantic difficulties. Truth functions like $\Rightarrow$ and $\neg$ can coexist with the truth predicate without paradox.

Suppose, in the language just described, one assigns a non-classical truth value to a boundary sentence. Suppose, for example, the sentence "France is hexagonal", symbolized by F, is regarded as neither true nor false, and assigned the truth value *Undetermined*. There is no problem in this language for there to be the two sorts of negation, Kleene negation and Strong negation, with different symbols, $\sim$ and $\neg$ respectively. Then $\sim$ F receives the truth value Undetermined while $\neg$ F is true. This language has the resources to say that F is not true by means of a true sentence, with no paradoxes. Of course, no direct or indirect self-reference is possible in this language since the only means of referring to a sentence is by its quotation name. Reflection on languages like this one suggest the conclusion that any language with multiple truth values *ought to be able to contain* a connective like the Strong negation, which renders a true sentence whenever its immediate semantic constituent is anything other than true, and a false sentence if its immediate semantic constituent is true. But as we will see, the existence of such a connective allows for the construction of a new and deadlier Liar, which cannot be digested by the many-valued semantics.

We have raised this point about the different sorts of negation available in a theory with multiple truth values because in the languages just described the possibility of such different connectives is manifest. A standard propositional calculus can be supplemented by a truth predicate, multiple truth values, and multiple connectives ($\neg$ and $\Rightarrow$ as well as $\sim$ and $\supset$) without paradox or inconsistency if only quotation names are allowed. Of course, if only quotation names are allowed, using the truth predicate looks like a pointlessly roundabout way of asserting the sentence said to be true.

The propositional language can also be expanded in another way without harm. We can replace it with a predicate calculus with quantifiers *so long as no semantic predicates are admitted*. One may employ other predicates which apply to sentences, and refer to sentences by proper names other than quotation names, and have quantifiers which range over sentences (and other objects as well), so long as no semantic predicates exist. Semantic predicates are distinguished by this characteristic: the truth value of an atomic sentence containing a semantic predicate depends (at least sometimes) on the *truth value* of the sentences of which it is predicated. For example, "Maxwell uttered" is not a semantic predicate, while "Maxwell truly uttered" is.

The graph of such a language is acyclic, and every sentence has a finite rank. The proof is similar to the proof given above, with one crucial change. It is no longer true that every immediate semantic constituent of a sentence must contain fewer *typographical* symbols than the sentence of which it is a constituent. For example, let "Maxwell uttered every sentence Clio uttered" be symbolized as $\forall x((M(x) \,\&\, Sen(x)) \supset C(x))$, and suppose quotation names are allowed. Then one of the (infinite number of) immediate semantic constituents of that sentence is

$$(M(^\ulcorner\forall x((M(x) \,\&\, Sen(x)) \supset C(x))^\urcorner) \,\&\, Sen(^\ulcorner\forall x((M(x) \,\&\, Sen(x))$$
$$\supset C(x))^\urcorner)) \supset C(^\ulcorner\forall x((M(x) \,\&\, Sen(x)) \supset C(x))^\urcorner),$$

which obviously contains many more *typographical* symbols than the former. But it still contains few *grammatical* symbols, where we regard an individual term like $^\ulcorner\forall x((M(x) \,\&\, Sen(x)) \supset C(x))^\urcorner$ as a *single* symbol despite its typographical length. Every instance of a quantified sentence is grammatically shorter than the sentence itself, just as a conjunct is grammatically shorter than the conjunction of which it is a part, etc. So in this language immediate semantic constituents always are grammatically shorter than the sentences of which they are constituents, and every sentence contains only finitely many grammatical parts. It follows again that every sentence has a finite rank and that every backward path from a sentence terminates at the boundary. Multiple truth values and multiple truth-functional connectives can therefore be introduced into this language without harm.

In a quantified language, a sentence can have an infinite number of immediate semantic constituents. For simplicity, we have supposed that the quantifiers range only over denumerable domains, and that every element of the domain has a standard name. These are useful simplifications, but not strictly necessary. If a domain is non-denumerable, then the natural thing to do is to postulate that the language has non-denumerably many names, and each object has a name. We may even adopt David Lewis's suggestion of a Lagadonean language, in which every object is its own name.[4] Such a language may be hard to *use*, but that is neither here nor there: it has the advantage that the truth value of every sentence is a determinate function of the truth values of its immediate semantic constituents. The techniques needed to deal with languages whose domains of quantification are larger than the stock of individual terms are really of no interest for the problem at hand.

Since every sentence in this quantified language is of finite rank, each sentence will receive a truth value after a finite number of iterations of the evaluative procedure (starting from the truth values on the boundary), and the truth values so calculated are guaranteed to satisfy the functional relations between the sentence and its constituents encoded in the logical connective. If

---

[4] Lewis (1986: 145).

some sentences fail to have classical truth values then one can say *truly* of them that they are not true by using the Strong negation. No paradoxes or inconsistencies arise. The boundary value problem for such a language is always well posed.

By now the drift of this analysis should become clear. Although semantic predicates can be admitted into a language without harm (if only quotation names, or other names typographically longer than the sentences they denote are allowed), and although quantifiers and arbitrary proper names can be admitted into a language without harm (if no semantic predicates are allowed) and although each of these expansions of the language can also be accompanied by the admission of multiple truth values and arbitrary truth-functional connectives, *both semantic predicates and quantifiers (or arbitrary proper names) cannot be allowed into a language without harm.* For the admission of *both* of these innovations allows the language to have a graph that is not acyclic, to have sentences of no finite rank, sentences whose truth value may not be uncontroversially settled by calculation from the truth values on the boundary. In such a language the boundary-value problem may not be well posed: there may be no global solution which respects all of the necessary functional constraints between sentences and their immediate semantic constituents, or there may be many. The uniqueness and universality of the semantics is at risk.

The existence of cycles in the directed graph of such a language is obviously illustrated by the Liar. The immediate semantic constituent of $\sim T(\lambda)$ is $T(\lambda)$, and the immediate semantic constituent of this is $\mathscr{F}(\lambda)$, i.e. $\sim T(\lambda)$. An even simpler cycle is produced by the Truthteller: let β denote the sentence $T(\beta)$. The immediate semantic constituent of $T(\beta)$ is $\mathscr{F}(\beta)$, i.e. $T(\beta)$ itself. The graphs of these parts of the language obviously contain cycles:

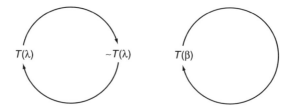

Backwards paths from these sentences never reach the boundary, so the sentences are of no finite (or infinite!) rank. Obviously, the truth values at the boundary cannot "flow up" to these sentences: if they have truth values at all, it is not because of the way the world is.

Even when there are backward paths from a node to the boundary, the existence of cycles can be a source of semantic difficulties. Consider a sentence of the form used in Löb's paradox, γ: $T(\gamma) \supset B$, where B is a boundary sentence. The graph of the relevant part of the language is

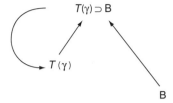

which obviously contains a cycle.

Once the graph of a language has cycles, not every backward path from a node will reach the boundary. And so once a graph has cycles, there is no guarantee that all of the nodes will be assigned truth values, or even that there is any global assignment of truth values which will simultaneously satisfy all the constraints demanded by the truth-functional connectives in the graph. Further, there is no guarantee that if such a global assignment exists it will be unique, even when the truth values of the boundary points are fixed.

Examples of each of the problems are well known, and are illustrated by our two examples above. The original Liar sentence, $\sim T(\lambda)$, creates an unsatisfiable cycle if the only truth values available are truth and falsity, and if every sentence must have a truth value. The time-honored strategy for avoiding this result is to insist (1) that not every meaningful sentence need be either true or false, so there are other truth values and (2) the connective $\sim$ maps true sentences to false and false to true, but also maps non-classical truth values to other non-classical values. The Kleene negation has exactly this feature. If the negation in the Liar is so construed, then the cycle is no longer unsatisfiable: both $\sim T(\lambda)$ and $T(\lambda)$ can be given non-classical values. But the fan of the Liar can respond with justice that one can also *refuse* to so construe the negation sign. One can admit to understanding the Kleene negation, but insist that the Kleene negation is not what one has in mind: one rather has in mind the Strong negation. No matter how many extra truth values are added, there will always be a Strong negation which maps truth into falsity and every other truth value into truth. And having insisted upon this, the cycle is unsatisfiable. Although cycles can consistently be admitted to a language and Strong negation can consistently be admitted to a language, they cannot *both* be admitted without constraint, else the boundary value problem becomes insoluble.

The Truthteller undermines not the existence but the uniqueness of the boundary-value problem. If *all* that is demanded is that the global assignment of truth values satisfy all of the local constraints imposed by the truth-functional semantics, then the Truthteller can consistently be held to be true or false or undetermined. So if we are to restore uniqueness, some constraint beyond local consistency must be found.

Our task now is to see how these problems can be avoided. We have seen that unsatisfiable cycles result if certain truth-functional logical particles (including the truth predicate as such a particle) are admitted. Solutions of this problem can be classed into two general sorts: those that restrict the logical connectives and semantic predicates available in the language so that cycles in the graph of the language can always be satisfied (the local semantic constraints can always be met) and those that restrict the semantic predicates so that cycles in the graph never arise in the first place. The first sort of theory requires abandoning a bivalent semantics, while the second does not. Kripke's theory is an archetype of the former strategy (although he does not put it this way) while Tarski's division into language and metalanguage is an example of the latter. And, as we will see, mixed strategies are possible: theories which constrain the logical connectives and semantic predicates in some parts of the language so that cycles are always satisfiable, and constrain them in other parts so cycles never arise there.

Before starting on our analysis, a bit more terminology will be of use. We have said that a sentence of the language is of rank n if all of the backward paths from that sentence terminate at the boundary, and if the maximal path length is n. In a language with quantifiers, a new possibility presents itself. Since a quantified sentence can have an infinite number of immediate semantic constituents, there can be sentences such that every backward path from the sentence terminates at the boundary, but there is no path of maximal length. Such a sentence cannot generate any paradoxes: we will call it *safe*. Every backward path from a safe sentence eventually reaches the boundary. Safe sentences will therefore be assigned a unique truth value once the boundary values are fixed, with no constraints on the sorts of logical connectives the language may contain. Sentences with backward paths that never reach the boundary are *unsafe*. Sentences that have no backward paths which reach the boundary, like the Liar and the Truthteller, are *completely unsafe*.

How to Accommodate Semantic Cycles

Let us begin with a theory like Kripke's. In this theory, cycles can arise because the domain in which the truth predicate functions as a semantic predicate includes all of the sentences of the language. By "functions as a semantic predicate", I mean that the truth value of $T(n)$ is a function of the truth value of $\mathscr{F}(n)$. In a language in which there are singular terms that denote things other than sentences, or quantifiers that range over things other than sentences, the truth predicate cannot always be a semantic predicate: the truth value of "The table is true" is not a function of the truth value of the table, since the table has no truth value. In any ordinary language, provision must be made for such "category mistakes", presumably by making them all false boundary sentences. We have finessed these obvious complications by only allowing singular terms to denote sentences and only allowing quantifiers to range over sentences. In Kripke's theory, there is a *single* truth predicate which always works the same way: whenever $\mathscr{F}(n)$ is a sentence, $\mathscr{F}(n)$ is an immediate semantic constituent of $T(n)$. That is, the *semantic value* of $T(n)$ always depends on the semantic value of $\mathscr{F}(n)$. This feature allows for cycles in the graph of the language. Use of arbitrarily specified singular terms allows for the Liar and Truthteller cycles, the quantification permits similar cycles achieved by quantification. Suppose, for example the only starred sentence in appendix A of *Truth and Paradox* is "Every starred sentence in Appendix A of *Truth and Paradox* is not true", and we translate this as $\forall x(S(x) \supset \sim T(x))$. Then part of the graph of the language is as follows:

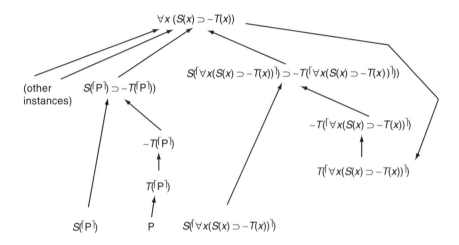

The three sentences at the bottom are boundary sentences, and the cycle which leads back to $\forall x(S(x \supset \sim T(x))$ is obvious. If that sentence happens to be the only starred sentence in Appendix A, then a form of the Liar results. (The reasoning pattern that reveals this paradox is discussed in Appendix A.)

If we are to allow such cycles, then the interpretation of the logical connectives and the truth predicate must be restricted or else the boundary-value problem has no solution. To be concrete, consider the graph above, with the following boundary values: $S(\ulcorner P \urcorner)$ and P are false, and $S(\ulcorner \forall x(S(x) \supset \sim T(x)) \urcorner)$ is true. Suppose that all of the other immediate semantic constituents of $\forall x(S(x) \supset \sim T(x))$ are true. And suppose that this much of the semantics is specified: $T(n)$ is true if $\mathscr{F}(n)$ is true, false if $\mathscr{F}(n)$ is false, and undetermined if $\mathscr{F}(n)$ is undetermined; $X \supset Y$ is true if both the antecedent and consequent are true, false if the antecedent is true and the consequent false, and undetermined if the antecedent is true and the consequent undetermined; a universally quantified sentence is true if all of its instances are true, false if at least one instance is false, and undetermined if some are undetermined and none false. All that is left is the semantics for negation. If one specifies it as Kleene negation, and one allows the three Kleene truth values, then the graph has a consistent solution (which happens to be unique): every sentence in the cycle is undetermined. But if the semantics for negation is the Strong semantics, so the negations of both false and undetermined sentences are true, then the graph has no solution at all.

This example is suggestive, but as yet proves nothing. What one would like, to begin with, is a proof of the following: if one restricts the logical connectives in a language to the Kleene connectives (or connectives appropriately like the Kleene connectives) then every boundary-value problem has at least one solution. This is easily proven.

First, we need to specify what it is for a connective to be appropriately like a Kleene connective: what makes a truth function safe for use in cycles? A generalized characterization will be useful. First, let us call any truth value which can be assigned to a boundary sentence a *primary* truth value. We have been assuming that the only primary truth values are truth and falsity, but if one would like to expand the list, so be it. Let us further assume that, beside the primary values, there is one other truth value, which we will call, for the moment, *undetermined*. A truth-functional logical connective is a function from the truth values of a set of sentences to the truth value of another sentence. The set of sentences are the immediate semantic constituents of the sentence whose truth value is determined by the function. The function is *Kleenesque* if it has the following property: changing the truth value of an immediate semantic constituent from undetermined to a primary value never results in changing the truth value of the sentence from one primary value to another, or to the undetermined value. We will say that a connective is a *normal* connective if it also has the following property: when all of the immediate semantic constituents of a sentence have primary truth values, so does the sentence containing the connective.

The Weak and Strong Kleene connectives are obviously normal Kleenesque, as is the truth predicate. The strong negation ¬ is not Kleenesque since changing A from undetermined to true changes ¬A from true to false. Similarly, ⇒ is not Kleenesque since A ⇒ B is true when A is undetermined and B is false and false when A is true and B is false. The quantifiers modeled after infinite Kleene conjunctions and disjunctions are normal Kleenesque.

The proof that a language with Kleenesque logical connectives always admits of global solutions to boundary-value problems is just Kripke's proof of the existence of a fixed point couched in a slightly different language. Begin with the graph of a language with arbitrary primary truth values assigned to the boundary sentences. Let all the other sentences be initially assigned the value *undetermined*. This will not be a global solution since, for example, all of the rank 1 sentences will be undetermined. Using that initial assignment of truth values, use the truth-functions associated with the logical connectives to assign truth values to every sentence on the basis of the values of its immediate semantic constituents. Since the boundary sentences have no immediate con-stituents, there is never call to change them, and they remain fixed. After this first iteration of the procedure, all rank 1 sentences will have primary values, as may others (if we are using the Strong Kleene connectives, for example). The only *change* in truth values that occurs at this first step is from undetermined to a primary value since the only sentences which are initially not undetermined are the boundary sentences, and they do not change.

We now apply a second iteration of the procedure, feeding the results of the first calculation back into the truth functions to calculate a new set of truth values. And it is here that the defining property of Kleenesque connectives is used: since the only change between the initial assignment of truth values and the results of the first iteration are changes from undetermined to primary, and since a change from undetermined to primary in an immediate semantic constituent never results in a change from one primary value to anything else, none of the primary values assigned at the first iteration are changed at the second. For such a change could only be due to a change in the truth value of an immediate constituent, and the only change which could have occurred to an immediate constituent is from undetermined to primary. So the primary values assigned in the first iteration cannot be changed in the second—or in any other—iteration. The extensions of the primary truth values therefore increase monotonically, as Kripke requires for his proof, entailing the existence of at least one fixed point in the sequence of iterations of the procedure (taking limits in the usual way). Such a fixed point is a global solution to the boundary-value problem.

All of this may seem a long way round back to Kripke's solution, but several features of his approach are now evident. First, *being a fixed point under this evaluation procedure is nothing but being a global assignment of truth values* (i.e. an assignment to all the sentences in the language) *which everywhere respects the truth-functional connections between a sentence and its immediate semantic constituents.* Let us call those truth-functional connections *local constraints* on the graph: they are the analogs of local differential equations in physics. Kripke's proof of the existence of fixed points then amounts to a proof of the existence of global assignments of truth values which satisfy all of the local constraints on a graph—no more and no less. Multiple fixed points indicate the existence of multiple global assignments of truth values (for fixed boundary values) that satisfy all of the local constraints. The fundamental *significance* of the fixed-point theorem is that it proves the existence of at least one such global solution that satisfies all local constraints.

Second, Kripke's choice of the Strong Kleene connectives in his initial discussion is not so casual as one might have thought. If one allows Strong negation, then there may be no fixed point for the language. In order for Kripke's solution to seem adequate to all natural language, then, one might argue that natural language cannot consistently contain the non-Kleenesque connectives such as Strong negation. But as yet we have no explanation of why natural language cannot contain such connectives: after all, they appear to be perfectly well defined, and seemingly one could just *stipulate* that one is using a non-Kleenesque connective. If so, then instead of forbidding non-Kleenesque connectives, one must rather insist that natural languages not contain semantic cycles.

Kripke would deny this: his view is that *obviously* one can use an individual term to denote any sentence, so *obviously* natural language can contain cycles such as one sees with the Liar. But one can equally argue that *obviously* one can intend, in a natural language, to use a non-Kleenesque connective, and so can construct the Liar with a Strong, rather than a Kleene, negation. But this would sink Kripke's project. Further, one can argue that one typically *does* use Strong negations in doing semantics, as when one intends something *true* when saying that the Liar sentence is not true. In forbidding non-Kleenesque connectives altogether, as he must to prove his theorem, Kripke seemingly jettisons the very language one needs to discuss the semantics of the Liar. And as we have seen, when Kripke tries to recover the intuition that it is true to say that the Liar is not true by "closing off" the truth predicate, he undercuts his entire project.

Indeed, closing off the truth predicate is really nothing more than introducing a non-Kleenesque truth predicate, one for which $T(n)$ is *false* when $\mathscr{F}(n)$ is either false or undetermined. Such a truth predicate is non-Kleenesque since changing $\mathscr{F}(n)$ from undetermined to true changes $T(n)$ from false to true. So Kripke's language cannot contain this truth predicate from the outset, otherwise he could not prove his fixed-point theorem.

The fan of Strong negation can keep non-Kleenesque connectives if some means is found to keep them out of vicious cycles. Tarski's way to do this is by distinguishing the object language from the metalanguage, and only allowing certain linguistic resources (e.g. the truth predicate) into the latter. While Kripke's approach is aimed at allowing us to live with cycles (and other unsafe sentences), the classical approach is to prevent them in the first place. Let us consider how this is done.

How to Avoid Semantic Cycles

We have already seen that the standard predicate calculus without any semantic predicates contains only safe sentences. This is because every immediate semantic constituent of any sentence in such a language always contains fewer grammatical symbols than the sentence of which it is a constituent. The graph of such a language can therefore contain no cycles. Let us envision that language as a two-dimensional network of nodes and arrows.

Now suppose we have another language, another two-dimensional network, which also contains no cycles. And let us suppose that this second network (which we may call a metalanguage) is literally above the first language, in the following sense: although there are immediate semantic constituents of the upper language in the lower language, there are no immediate semantic constituents of the lower in the upper. That is, all of the arrows that connect the two graphs run in the same direction: from lower sheet to upper sheet. Then it is obvious that if there are no cycles in the lower sheet alone and no cycles in the upper sheet alone, there are no cycles at all. For no cycle can be partially in the upper and partially in the lower sheet: there can be an arrow taking one from lower to upper but no return arrow from upper to lower.

This structural guarantee against cycles is exactly what the usual construction of metalanguages provides. We begin with a language that contains no semantic predicates. As we have seen, such a language can contain no cycles. Now we add a metalanguage with the following properties. The metalanguage does contain semantic predicates, but those predicates can only take as immediate semantic constituents sentences in the object language: either they can only be grammatically predicated of sentences in the object language, or when predicated of a sentence not in the object language, the truth value of the resulting sentence is *not* a function of the truth value of the sentence of which the predicate is predicated. (In particular, one may stipulate that when $\mathscr{F}(n)$ is not a sentence in the object language, $T(n)$ is always false.) The metalanguage on its own, then (i.e. the sentences now formulable which were not formulable in the object language), contains no cycles since it, in effect, has no semantic predicates. The metalanguage does contain semantic predicates, but they only take as immediate semantic constituents sentences in the *object* language. The topological situation described above therefore holds: the object language contains no cycles, the metalanguage alone contains no cycles, and the only arrows of semantic dependence run from the object language to the metalanguage. The whole comprising both the object and metalanguages therefore contains no cycles. No restriction need be put on the sorts of connectives allowed: non-Kleenesque connectives can be used with impunity. The price one pays, of course, is the inability to formulate informative claims about the semantic status of sentences in the metalanguage, since, for example, $T(n)$ is always false when $\mathscr{F}(n)$ is not in the object language. This can be remedied by use of a meta-metalanguage, with a corresponding new deficit being created.

That Kripke's approach is diametrically opposed to the metalanguage approach should now be obvious, although each strategy has exactly the same aim: eliminating vicious cycles. Tarski's approach achieves this by eliminating cycles altogether. No Liar or Truthteller sentence can be created in such a language since such sentences require a semantic predicate that can have as an immediate semantic constituent a sentence that belongs to the same "level" as the predicate itself. As a result, the language must always remain unfinished, even though one can always add yet another story to the structure. Kripke's slogan, in contrast, should be "Making Cycles Safe for Semantics". No language/metalanguage distinction is needed, since no attempt is made to eliminate cycles. There is only one truth predicate, and it can take any sentence in the language as an immediate semantic constituent. Given the use of arbitrary singular terms or quantifiers, it is obvious that cycles can exist: simply construct a sentence like the Liar. Kripke rather showed how to do semantics in the face of cycles, using the fixed-point construction. What Kripke does not highlight is that safety for cycles is only bought at a price: the elimination of all non-Kleenesque logical connectives. The problem is that such a restriction on the connectives seems completely *ad hoc*: why can I not understand and introduce into the language *any truth-functional connective at all*? Sentences constructed using those connectives are just *stipulated* to have the truth value assigned by the truth function, given the truth values of its immediate semantic constituents.

Both Kripke's approach and Tarski's metalanguage approach manage to forbid vicious cycles in the semantics, but also seem to contain gratuitous restrictions on language. This is, I suggest, the source of the perennial dissatisfaction with either solution. If one has been raised with metalanguages, then a prohibition against non-Kleenesque logical connectives will appear unfounded: they can be admitted without harm into a language without cycles.[5] And if one has become accustomed to Kripke's approach, a prohibition against cycles will appear Draconian: the fixed-point theorems show how some can be dealt with. But no language can abide vicious cycles, cycles such that no global assignment of truth values can satisfy all the local constraints on the graph. What is needed, then, is a *principled* curtailment of the language that prevents semantic disaster, a restriction on the language which arises *from the fundamental nature of the truth values themselves*.

It might occur to one that the advantages of Kripke's approach and the metalanguage approach can be combined. Begin with a language that contains only Kleenesque connectives, a truth predicate which functions as a semantic predicate for all sentences, and use of arbitrary singular terms. This language can contain cycles, but they are all benign. Now allow non-Kleenesque connectives, but only in the metalanguage. The metalanguage has the usual restrictions on the semantic predicates: when a semantic predicate is predicated of anything besides a sentence in the object language, the resulting sentence is always false. Since there are no cycles in the metalanguage alone, and no cycles partly in the object language and partly in the metalanguage, there are no cycles that contain non-Kleenesque connectives, ergo no vicious cycles. In this theory one can allow $\sim T(\lambda)$ in the object language (where it is undetermined), and

---

[5] I hope that the intent of this sentence is clear, even though it is technically inaccurate. That is: in a pure Tarskian approach, there can in a sense be no non-Kleenesque connectives since every sentence is safe, and so must receive a primary truth value (a truth value that a boundary sentence can take). So the question of what a logical particle does when an immediate semantic constituent fails to have a primary truth value is moot: the question never arises in fact.

also allow $\neg T(\lambda)$ in the metalanguage, where it is true. $\neg T(\lambda)$ cannot serve as the immediate semantic constituent of any semantic predicate, so one cannot yet truly say that $\neg T(\lambda)$ is true: $T(\ulcorner \neg T(\lambda)\urcorner)$ is automatically false. But this want can be provided for in the meta-metalanguage, with a new truth predicate $T_1(n)$. $T_1(\ulcorner \neg T(\lambda)\urcorner)$ will be true, but of course the meta-metalanguage will require its own metalanguage, and so on.

This hybrid system has some attractions, but it again abandons the shining virtue of Kripke's approach: the absence of the language/metalanguage distinction. Natural languages contain no such distinction, so we should do our best to avoid it. Fortunately, we are now in a position to construct a theory which demands no such distinction, and which contains no *ad hoc* restrictions on connectives. That theory drops out almost automatically from a single, simple observation about the directed graphs of languages.

The Semantics of Ungrounded Sentences

The standard semantic paradoxes are associated with the existence of cycles in the directed graph of a language. Any language with unrestricted use of quantifiers and proper names, and with unrestricted semantic predicates (i.e. semantic predicates which can take any sentence in the language as an immediate semantic constituent), is liable to cycles. But cycles also allow another striking phenomenon: the possibility of completely unsafe sentences. A completely unsafe sentence, recall, is represented by a node of the graph that has no backwards path that terminates at the boundary. There is therefore no way for the truth values at the boundary to "flow up" to such a sentence. Both the Liar and the Truthteller inhabit such cul-de-sacs on the semantic map of the language. These sentences, which are commonly used to illustrate semantic paradoxes, also contain the key to their resolution.

The semantic paradoxes can be resolved by the following principle: truth and falsity are always ultimately rooted in the state of the world. That is: if a sentence is either true or false, then either it is a boundary sentence, made true or false by the world of non-semantic facts, or it is semantically connected to at least one boundary sentence, from which its truth value can be traced. If we accept this as a constraint on our account of truth, then all of our problems dissolve.

The first obvious consequence of our principle is that *no completely unsafe sentence can be either true or false*. Since unsafe sentences, by definition, have no semantic connections (backwards paths) to the boundary, their truth values cannot be rooted in the boundary, and therefore cannot be rooted in the world. We therefore need a third truth value for such sentences. Let us call this truth value *ungrounded*.

Our attitude toward the notion of an ungrounded sentence is exactly the opposite of Kripke's attitude towards what he calls "undefined" sentences. Kripke writes:

"Undefined" is not an *extra* truth value, any more than—in Kleene's book—u is an *extra* number in Sec. 63. Nor should it be said that "classical logic" does not hold, any more than (in Kleene) the use of partially defined functions invalidates the commutative law of addition.   (Kripke 1975, in Martin 1984: 65 n.18)

In direct contrast, according to the approach we will develop, ungrounded *is* an extra truth value, and its existence *does* demand a revision of classical logic: exactly the revision needed to solve the inferential problem.[6] This difference in attitude motivates certain differences from Kripke in the construction of the semantics

If all completely unsafe sentences are ungrounded, then both the Liar and the Truthteller are ungrounded. This is already a significant difference from Kripke's theory. Kripke insists that the extension of the truth predicate be given by a fixed point, but there are multiple fixed points for any language such as we are discussing, in some of which the Truthteller is true, in others false, and in others "undefined" (in Kripke's sense). So we need some *additional* constraint to pin down the truth value of the Truthteller, beyond the constraint that the sentence have its truth value assigned to it at a fixed point. Since an assignment being a fixed point amounts to the assignment being a solution to all of the *local* constraints in a graph, the additional constraint must be determined by the *global* structure of the graph. Demanding that all completely unsafe sentences be ungrounded is exactly such a global constraint, since being completely unsafe is a matter of the global structure of the graph, not of the local truth-functional connections.

Since the Truthteller is completely unsafe, it is, on our approach, a paradigm ungrounded sentence. If the Truthteller could possibly be either true or false, where could either of those truth values have come *from*? Not from the boundary, whence we postulate all truth and falsity to originate. Therefore even though there are fixed points in Kripke's construction that assign the Truthteller the value true, and fixed points that assign it the value false, we have to reject those as legitimate candidates for correct truth-value assignments. Legitimate candidates have to be *more* than just fixed points in Kripke's construction.

---

[6] It is unclear to me on exactly what grounds Kripke denies that his undefined is a truth value. The analogy to Kleene's u is weak in the following way: there is a large collection of mathematical functions and relations whose domain ought to include all numbers. We expect that numbers can be added, multiplied, divided by one another, and so on. We also expect that they can be compared, so that any number is either greater than, less than, or equal to any other (at least in magnitude). But u seems not to be admissible to the domain of these operations. Is u greater than, less than, or equal to 1, for example? But the functions of truth values seem to be much more restricted: in semantics, the truth values of sentences function largely to determine the truth values of sentences of which they are immediate semantic constituents. So if u is added to the truth tables of the logical particles, and a clear account is given of the conditions under which a sentence is assigned u, it is unclear what else needs to be done to render u a truth value. In any case, the emendations to classical logic are unavoidable, as the inferential paradox shows.

Another immediate consequence of this approach is that, along with the Liar, the sentence which says the Liar is true, the sentence which says the Liar is false, and the sentence which says the Liar is ungrounded are all un-grounded, because they are all completely unsafe. We observe immediately that although the Liar is ungrounded, the sentence that says it is ungrounded is not true. Furthermore, although the Liar is not true, any sentence that says of it that it is not true is itself ungrounded (and hence not true). These results seem to fly in the face of truisms about truth, and much of the burden of our metaphysical analysis of truth will be to reveal them instead as natural and intrinsically plausible. Since all of these pronouncements about the truth value of the Liar are themselves completely unsafe, the controlling intuition should lead us to ask: if any of them were true (or false), where would the truth (or falsity) *come from*?

An obvious answer presents itself. We have already seen that in certain three-valued languages, two forms of negation must be distinguished: Kleene negation and Strong negation. The Kleene negation of a sentence with the third truth value has that truth value, while the Strong negation of such a sentence is true. So why not add Strong negation to our language, as a means of truly saying that the Liar is not true? $\sim T(\lambda)$ would be ungrounded, as would be $T(\ulcorner \sim T(\lambda) \urcorner)$ (or equivalently $T(\lambda)$) and $\sim T(\ulcorner \sim T(\lambda) \urcorner)$, but $\neg T(\ulcorner \sim T(\lambda) \urcorner)$ would be true.

But this is to reject the governing intuition about ungroundedness: every completely unsafe sentence is ungrounded, since there is no boundary sentence from which truth or falsity can reach them. *Any* unary truth-functional connective, then, must map ungrounded input into ungrounded output, since the connective applied to a completely unsafe sentence yields a com-pletely unsafe sentence. Similarly, any binary truth-functional connective must be such that when both the immediate semantic constituents of a sentence are ungrounded, so is the sentence. And in general, when all of the immediate semantic constituents of a sentence are ungrounded, so must the sentence be. For it is a straightforward matter of *graph-theoretic structure* that when all of the immediate semantic constituents of a sentence are completely unsafe, so is that sentence. The absence of Strong negation from this language, rather than being *ad hoc*, is a direct consequence of the fundamental postulate. Strong negation is ruled out by the global constraint that all completely unsafe sentences be ungrounded, and the demand that all connectives be truth-functional. Classical truth values cannot simply be conjured out of thin air: they must originate always at the boundary of a language, where the language meets the world.

Just as there can be only one negation in this language, so too can there be only one truth predicate. This provides our response to the suggestion at the end of Kripke's paper that one "close off" the truth predicate in order to make it true to say that the Liar is not true. Kripke has provided no grounds to reject any well-defined semantic predicate. He has in fact, up until the end, always employed what we may call the *Kleene* truth predicate: the predicate so defined that $T(n)$ always has the same truth value as $\mathscr{F}(n)$. But why could there not be another semantic predicate, call it the *Strong* truth predicate, such that $T_S(n)$ is *false* when $\mathscr{F}(n)$ is anything other than true? Kripke cannot, of course, admit such a predicate at the beginning of the game: since it is non-Kleenesque, the proof of the existence of a fixed point will be destroyed. Indeed, just as there is a *negation-strengthened* Liar $\neg T(\lambda')$ (where λ' denotes the very sentence $\neg T(\lambda')$), so there is a *truth-strengthened* Liar $\sim T_S(\lambda'')$ (where λ'' denotes $\sim T_S(\lambda'')$), for which there is no fixed point at all. Kripke's gambit of "closing off" the truth predicate is really the gambit of *adding the Strong truth predicate to the language after the fixed point* (for the language *without* such a predicate) *has been calculated.* But if the predicate is meaningful, why should it not be part of the language under study from the beginning? The only available answer for Kripke is the *ad hoc* one: if it were part of that language then the fixed-point theorem could not be proved. For if the language contains the truth-strengthened Liar, no fixed point exists.

Kripke does admit at this point that if we add the closed-off truth predicate "we still cannot avoid the need for a metalanguage". The metalanguage could presumably contain all the non-Kleenesque connectives, as long as their immediate semantic constituents were restricted to the object language. So Kripke is pursuing the "mixed" strategy we examined above. But then it is an understatement to say that a metalanguage is needed: a whole Tarskian infinite hierarchy of metalanguages will be needed. And it becomes less and less clear exactly what has been accomplished.

Kripke's option of closing off the truth predicate is simply not available once we accept the governing intuition. Just as our language cannot contain Strong negation, because of the nature of ungrounded sentences, so it cannot contain Strong truth. There can be only one truth predicate, and if it is predicated of an ungrounded sentence the result is an ungrounded sentence, for inescapable graph-theoretic reasons.

If an ungrounded sentence is one whose truth value cannot be generated by successive local calculations beginning at the boundary, then it is also obvious that there can be no ungrounded sentence all of whose immediate semantic constituents are boundary sentences. Since everything semantically relevant to such a sentence is fixed at the boundary, local calculations (i.e. calculations of truth values from given boundary values and local truth-functional connections) determine its truth value. Just as classical truth values cannot be conjured out of thin air, so too they cannot spontaneously evaporate. If no input to a connective is ungrounded, neither can the output be. (This is not to say that every safe sentence must be either true or false. One could have a semantics that allows other primary truth values for the *boundary* sentences, and those additional truth values could migrate up to any safe sentence. No safe sentence or boundary sentence can be *ungrounded*.) So any sentence all of whose immediate semantic constituents have primary truth values will also have a primary value (in the terminology introduced earlier, all of the connectives are normal).

These constraints on connectives, which arise from the very meaning of ungroundedness, radically reduce the number of possible truth-functional connectives. Naively, one would expect that a three-valued logic would admit 19,683 different binary connectives, corresponding to all of the ways the three truth values can be distributed among the nine entries on a truth table. But since any sentence all of whose immediate semantic constituents have primary values (true or false) must itself have a primary value, we are first restricted to *extensions* of the standard two-valued connectives. Even so, one would again naively expect every standard connective to have 243 distinct extensions, corresponding to the possible ways of distributing three truth values among the five new entries on the table. Extending conjunction, for example, would begin with the following truth table:

&	T	F	U
T	T	F	?
F	F	F	?
U	?	?	?

If we can replace the question marks with any truth value, there are 243 possible completions.

But since any sentence all of whose immediate semantic constituents are ungrounded must be ungrounded, the entry in the lower right-hand corner must be U. Now consider the entries for the conjunction of a true and an ungrounded sentence. If the truth value of a sentence cannot be calculated starting from the boundary and using the local constraints on the graph, then that sentence is ungrounded. And if we have been able to calculate that one conjunct is true, but unable to calculate the other conjunct, we cannot be sure what the truth value of the conjunction is (if the other conjunct should turn out to be true, the conjunction is true, if it should happen to turn out to be false, the conjunction is false). The upper right-hand and lower left-hand entries on the truth table must therefore be U. (In general, if any row or column in the truth table contains different truth values, then the entry at the end of the row or column must be U.)

This leaves only two entries: what if one conjunct is false and the other ungrounded? In these two slots, it is consistent to put either F or U. If one puts F, the truth value of the conjunction is indeed calculable from a single false input, so a sentence with a single false input is not ungrounded. If one puts a U, then the truth value is not calculable from the single false input, so a sentence with a single false input is ungrounded. So from our original stock of 243 possible extensions of conjunction, we are left with only four, corresponding to putting either F or U in each of the two open slots. One of these connectives is the Strong Kleene conjunction, the other the Weak Kleene, shown below:

&	T	F	U		$\&_W$	T	F	U
T	T	F	U		T	T	F	U
F	F	F	F		F	F	F	U
U	U	F	U		U	U	U	U

The other two "Medium Kleene" conjunctions can be defined from these: one is logically equivalent to (A & B) $\&_W$B, the other to (A & B) $\&_W$A.

The constraints are even more severe for the biconditional: there is only one consistent extension, which must be ungrounded when either of the immediate semantic constituents is ungrounded. In sum, despite the fear of an explosion of new three-valued connectives, one can make do with just negation and the Weak and Strong Kleene conjunctions: all the other consistent connectives can be reduced to these. The semantic predicates truth and falsity, of course, have a unique consistent extension. An atomic sentence containing the falsity predicate, $\Phi(n)$, is false when $\mathscr{F}(n)$ is true, true when $\mathscr{F}(n)$ is false, and ungrounded when $\mathscr{F}(n)$ is ungrounded. (Again, $\Phi(n)$ is automatically false when $\mathscr{F}(n)$ is not a sentence.) Since there is a third truth value, there should be a third semantic predicate, $Y(n)$, but there are complications. Intuitively, one would like $Y(n)$ to be false if $\mathscr{F}(n)$ is either true or false, and true if $\mathscr{F}(n)$ is ungrounded. The first condition can be met, but if $\mathscr{F}(n)$ is ungrounded, so is $Y(n)$ willy-nilly. We will introduce the predicate nonetheless, for reasons that will become apparent in time. $Y(n)$ is logically equivalent to $\sim T(n)$ & $\sim\Phi(n)$, which is intuitively pleasing: to say that a sentence is ungrounded is to say that it is not true and not false.

These strong constraints on the allowable truth-functional connectives and semantic predicates must be held in mind. There is always a temptation to insist that one can add to the language connectives that have whatever truth-functional properties one likes *by stipulation*. But given the *meaning* of "ungrounded" as "not calculable from the boundary values and the local constraints", one cannot simply stipulate that a sentence with given logical form and given truth values for its immediate semantic constituents be ungrounded, or, more importantly, fail to be ungrounded. No matter how much one *wants* there to be a Strong negation such that the Strong negation of an ungrounded sentence is true, such a connective is incoherent.

The idea that logical connectives can be stipulated to have whatever truth tables one likes is encouraged if one reflects only on languages whose graphs are acyclic. In such a case, placing values along the boundary yields a unique calculation of the values of all other sentences, no matter what connectives are introduced. One is allowed to say, in such a case, that a conjunction is true when both conjuncts are true simply because conjunction is *defined* as a connective with exactly that property.[7] As an analogy, imagine an acyclic directed graph with a boundary, and suppose that *numbers* are assigned to the boundary nodes. One can then simply *stipulate* that the value of a non-boundary node be whatever function one likes of the values of their inputs (i.e. the nodes with arrows leading into it), so long as the function be broadly enough defined to have a value for every possible input. One could stipulate that a given node be half the value of its single input, or the sum of the values of its two inputs, or the maximum of the values of all its inputs, etc. One could even stipulate that a node remain empty if its input is greater than zero, i.e. that the node *have no number at all*, so long as all the nodes for which it is an input have defined outputs for such a case. It is obvious that on a graph where every backward path leads to the boundary, the boundary-value problem will be well posed. One could then categorize each node by the function which relates the input to the output. One sort of node, for example, could have a single input and the following output: empty if the input is the number one, and the number one otherwise.

But if such a mathematical graph has cycles, one can no longer simply *stipulate* what value a node will have as a function of its inputs. One cannot, for example, stipulate that a node be empty if its input is the number one, and one if its input is anything else *if it can be its own input*. To insist that such a node *must* have a value, and that the value must, by stipulation, be the stated function of the input, is absurd. This is, of course, the mathematical version of the Liar paradox: the source of the *technical* problem of assigning truth values to sentences is really no more puzzling.

We are now in a position to give the complete semantics for our language. We first need two definitions:

> Definition 1: Given a partial assignment of truth values (true, false, and ungrounded) to the sentences in a language, the truth value of a sentence which is not directly assigned a value is *determined by the assignment* iff there is only one truth value it can have which is consistent with the truth values assigned to its immediate semantic constituents. Any sentence is determined by an assignment if the assignment assigns truth values to all of its immediate semantic constituents. Some sentences may be determined by an assignment even though not all of their immediate semantic

---

[7] At least this is so for the classical truth values, true and false. If one were to introduce, e.g., a new primary semantic value for sentences that fall in the borderline region of a vague predicate, then one might again argue that the very meaning of the semantic value precludes certain truth-functional connectives. It seems plausible, for example, that no unary logical connective could be such that, when applied to a true or false sentence, it yields a vague sentence. See Appendix C for more details.

constituents are assigned values; e.g. a Strong disjunction is determined to be true if one disjunct is true, even if the other is assigned no value.

Definition 2: A set of sentences is *ungrounded on an assignment* if (a) no member of the set is assigned a truth value by the assignment; (b) no member of the set is determined by the assignment; (c) every immediate semantic constituent of a member of the set that is not assigned a truth value is itself a member of the set.

The idea behind an ungrounded set is fairly simple: if an assignment does not determine the truth value of any member of a set, and if the only unsettled immediate semantic constituents of members of the set are in the set itself, then the set is impervious to truth or falsity flowing into it from outside. The Truthteller by itself forms an ungrounded set on any assignment which does not give it a truth value, as does the set $\{\sim T(\lambda), \; T(\lambda)\}$, if neither is assigned a truth value. The set $\{T(\gamma), \; T(\gamma) \supset B\}$ is ungrounded if B is false (and neither member is assigned a truth value), but not ungrounded if B is true (since then $T(\gamma) \supset B$ is determined to be true).

The semantics is now easy to describe. Begin with a partial assignment that assigns truth values *to all and only the boundary sentences*, all of whose truth values are by definition primary values (in our case true or false). Call this original assignment A_0. Now define a new assignment, A_1, which extends the original in the following way: if the truth value of a sentence is determined by A_0, let A_1 assign it the value so determined, and if a set of sentences is ungrounded on A_0, let A_1 assign every member of the set the value *ungrounded*. Repeat the process using A_1 to generate A_2, and so on, taking limits in the usual way. In other words, just follow Kripke's construction at this point, using three truth values rather than two and the algorithm just defined.

Kripke's proof of the existence of a fixed point relies only on the monotonicity of the changes in the extension and the anti-extension of the truth predicate. In our construction, the sets of true sentences, false sentences, and ungrounded sentences similarly increase monotonically. There will therefore be a fixed point of the hierarchy, and the fixed point will be a global solution which everywhere respects the local constraints of the truth-functional connections.

But unlike Kripke's construction, ours has a *single* fixed point, in which *every* sentence has been assigned one of the three truth values. The proof is by *reductio*. Suppose there is a fixed point in which not every sentence is assigned a truth value. Choose any such sentence. The sentence must not be determined by the truth values assigned to its immediate semantic constituents, otherwise it would be assigned a truth value on the next iteration of the evaluation procedure, and so the assignment would not be a fixed point. Since the sentence would be determined if all of its immediate semantic constituents were assigned truth values, at least one of its immediate semantic constituents must also be assigned no truth value. And that constituent must also not be determined by the assignment, and so it must have at least one constituent not assigned a truth value. Now consider the set which consists of the original sentence which is not assigned a truth value together with all of its immediate semantic constituents which are not assigned truth values, together with their semantic constituents which are not assigned truth values, etc. This set has the following features. First, no member of the set is assigned a truth value by the assignment. Second, none of the elements are determined by the assignment, else the assignment is not a fixed point. And lastly, every immediate semantic constituent of a member of the set which is not assigned a truth value is a member of the set. The set is therefore ungrounded on the assignment, and so every member will be assigned the value *ungrounded* on the next iteration of the evaluation procedure. So the assignment is not a fixed point. Hence no fixed point can fail to assign a value to a sentence. The fixed point of the procedure is unique and exhaustive: it assigns a truth value to every sentence. There is only one global solution which both respects all the local constraints and also global constraints imposed by the definition of ungroundedness.

We have now eliminated every vestige of arbitrariness from Kripke's approach. There are no longer multiple fixed points to choose among, nor multiple truth-functional connectives, nor multiple evaluation schemes. The semantic theory is perfectly determinate and unique.

The extensions of the truth and falsity predicates are exactly those yielded by the minimal fixed point in Kripke's construction, save that in our language we do not choose between the Weak and Strong Kleene connectives: the language can contain both, as well as the "Medium" connectives. But the understanding of the remainder of the sentences is quite different from Kripke's. For Kripke, the "undefined" sentences are merely those left over without truth values once a fixed point has been chosen. Sentences are never, on Kripke's view, *assigned* the value "undefined", they are just left without any value. This comports with Kripke's assertion that "undefined" is not a truth value. On our approach, sentences are ungrounded for definite reasons, and some can be recognized as such immediately. The Liar and Truthteller are determined to be ungrounded at the very first iteration of the evaluation procedure: they are necessarily ungrounded. Other ungrounded sentences are only determined to be such later in the process. The positive nature of ungroundedness is what puts unavoidable constraints on the sorts of connectives and semantic predicates which can be defined.

It is worthy of note that other sorts of ungrounded sets can be recognized at the first iteration: namely infinitely descending sets of sentences each of which has those below it as immediate semantic constituents. Such sets have been discussed by Steven Yablo in his (1993), where he shows that some give rise to paradoxes similar to the Liar. Consider, for example, an infinite set of sentences each of which says that at least one of those below it is false. Such a set is classically unsatisfiable: no assignment of truth and falsity to its members can respect all of the local truth-functional constraints. Nonetheless, the graph of the set contains no cycles, no direct or indirect self-reference. They are therefore a bit anomalous: the sentences all manage to be completely unsafe without the use of cycles. But it is obvious that the set of sentences is an ungrounded set relative to A_0, so our theory dispatches it immediately. Every member of the set is assigned the value *ungrounded* at the first iteration.

While our evaluation procedure deals with the Liar immediately, in contrast to Kripke's, which just leaves it over at the end, Kripke's scheme assigns truth values to other sentences much more rapidly than ours. On Kripke's scheme, every non-semantic sentence is either in the extension or the anti-extension of the truth predicate after the first iteration. In ours, truth values have to crawl up the graph from the boundary over many iterations before some non-semantic sentences are determined. The end result is the same, but the picture of the articulated dependence of the truth values of non-boundary sentences on the values at the boundary is slightly different. In particular, in our scheme the truth predicate is treated just like a unary truth-functional connective: an atomic sentence containing the truth predicate is just a sentence with a single immediate semantic constituent. The truth predicate appears on an equal footing with the other logical particles.

The technical problem of semantics—at least insofar as the non-boundary sentences are concerned—is now complete. A few relevant results ought to be mentioned immediately, although our final treatment of them must be delayed. Some of these results are pleasing, others extremely unintuitive. The Liar and Truthteller are ungrounded, which seems correct, but so are the sentences which ascribe any truth value—true, false, or ungrounded—to those sentences. The T-sentences of all ungrounded sentences are ungrounded, rather than, as Tarski would prefer, true.

Many universally quantified sentences are ungrounded even though they intuitively seem to be true. All of the instances of a universally quantified sentence must be true for the sentence to be true, a single false instance renders it false, and otherwise it is ungrounded. The sentence which translates "All true sentences are true", $\forall x(T(x) \supset T(x))$, is ungrounded since it has no false instances and the instance

$$T(\ulcorner \forall x(T(x) \supset T(x)) \urcorner) \supset T(\ulcorner \forall x(T(x) \supset T(x)) \urcorner)$$

cannot be assigned the value true at any iteration. For it is not determined to be true unless $T(\ulcorner \forall x(T(x) \supset T(x)) \urcorner)$ has been assigned true or false, and this cannot be done until $\forall x(T(x) \supset T(x))$ has been assigned true or false, completing the cycle of semantic dependence. Furthermore, if the language contains the Liar, the instance $T(\lambda) \supset T(\lambda)$ will be ungrounded rather than true.

This last problem can seemingly be avoided if one adopts a supervaluation technique, as Kripke occasionally suggests (1975: 76). In such a regime, every sentence of the form $X \supset X$ is true because it comes out true if X is either true or false. But the *technique* of supervaluation, which is entirely clear-cut, cannot be adequately *justified* as a means of assigning truth values in a language which can contain the Liar. Given the truth function associated with $\supset$, it is uncontroversial that $T(\lambda) \supset T(\lambda)$ would come out true if $T(\lambda)$ were either true or false. But the reason we worried about the Liar in the first place was that it apparently cannot be consistently maintained to be either true or false, so the relevance of the counterfactual is obscure. In a three-valued logic, supervaluation techniques should take account of all three truth values, not just truth and falsity. But then they become ineffective for the problems we are concerned with.

Here is another problem case. Maxwell utters only two sentences: "One plus one equals two" and the Liar, while Clio utters only "One plus one equals two". It seems true to say that every true sentence uttered by Maxwell was uttered by Clio. Let $M(x)$ stand for "Maxwell said x", $C(x)$ stand for "Clio said x", and let v denote the atomic sentence N, which translates "One plus one equals two". As usual, λ denotes the Liar sentence $\sim T(\lambda)$. If $\sim T(\lambda)$ and N are the only sentences in the domain (they are the only relevant ones here), then "All of the true sentences uttered by Maxwell were uttered by Clio" gets translated in the usual way as $\forall x((T(x) \ \& \ M(x)) \supset C(x))$, and this in turn becomes logically equivalent (in this context) to

$$((T(\lambda) \ \& \ M(\lambda)) \supset C(\lambda)) \ \& \ ((T(v) \ \& \ M(v)) \supset C(v)).$$

$C(\lambda)$ is false, $T(\lambda)$ is ungrounded, and the rest of the atomic sentences are true. The second conjunct is therefore true, but the first ungrounded, so the whole becomes ungrounded rather than true. Even supervaluation techniques using only truth and falsity could not save this case, since the universally quantified sentence does not come out true if one assigns $T(\lambda)$ the value true.

Since such universally quantified sentences will often come out ungrounded when we intuitively take them to be true, we will pause for a rather lengthy excursus on quantification. It will be important to convince ourselves that these problems cannot be avoided.

A Digression on the Formal Representation of Quantification

What has gone wrong with the semantic evaluation of "All of the true sentences uttered by Maxwell were uttered by Clio"? If translated as $\forall x((T(x) \ \& \ M(x)) \supset C(x))$, it comes out not to be true because Maxwell uttered the Liar, and Clio did not, and so $((T(\lambda) \ \& \ M(\lambda)) \supset C(\lambda))$ is not true. But the fact that Maxwell uttered the Liar sentence, which *is not a true sentence*, ought to be *irrelevant* to the semantic evaluation of "All of the true sentences uttered by Maxwell were uttered by Clio". The latter claim concerns only the *true* sentences uttered by Maxwell: how could the fact that Maxwell uttered the

Liar sentence preclude the truth of a claim about the true sentences he uttered? We must return to essentials and consider how Maxwell's utterance of the Liar comes into play when evaluating the claim that every true sentence uttered by Maxwell was uttered by Clio.

The story is straightforward, but we should not let its familiarity blind us to the substantive assumptions that are being made. The first move is translating "All of the true sentences uttered by Maxwell were uttered by Clio" into the formal language as $\forall x((T(x)\ \&\ M(x)) \supset C(x))$. Already, it seems, something has been lost in translation. The original English sentence appears to be only *about* the true sentences uttered by Maxwell. It says *of them* that they were uttered by Clio, and says of *other* sentences, sentences which were not uttered by Maxwell, or sentences which are not true, *absolutely nothing*. That is, the original English sentence appears to use a *restricted quantifier*: it quantifies only over the true sentences uttered by Maxwell. Since the Liar sentence is not a true sentence uttered by Maxwell, it would seem to lie outside the domain of that quantifier, and therefore to be completely irrelevant to the truth conditions of the sentence. But the standard translation of "All of the true sentences uttered by Maxwell were uttered by Clio" into the formal language employs a universal quantifier, which ranges over *all* sentences (indeed, over all things), whether true or not, whether uttered by Maxwell or not. The translation, $\forall x((T(x)\ \&\ M(x)) \supset C(x))$, says of *every* sentence that if it was uttered by Maxwell and is true, then it was uttered by Clio. The properties of being true and being uttered by Maxwell, which are intended to delimit the domain of discourse, do not play that role in the translation, and so arises the possibility that the Liar sentence may play a role in the semantic evaluation of the translation, even though it appears to be semantically irrelevant to the original.

The idea that restricted quantification ought to be translated as universal quantification over a conditional sentence is so deeply ingrained in the classical predicate calculus that it takes some effort to recover the sense of how peculiar it is. Classical predicate calculus does not recognize restricted quantification as fundamentally new: there are only the unrestricted quantifiers, and restrictions are imposed in the rendering of the instances. Thus, in classical logic, "All of the moons of Jupiter are rock" is rendered $\forall x(MJ(x) \supset R(x))$, an unrestricted quantifier over a conditional sentence. As we have taught generations of skeptical students, when we say that all of the moons of Jupiter are rock, we are really covertly making a claim about everything in the universe, saying of each thing that if it is a moon of Jupiter it is rock, that is, that either it is not a moon of Jupiter or it is rock. Particularly stubborn students may insist that they are doing no such thing, that they are making claims only about the moons of Jupiter and nothing else. Such students are argued into submission or quiescence by means we will examine shortly. But on reflection it should be clear that the students really have a perfectly valid point, that "All of the moons of Jupiter are rock" really does not seem to be a cryptic statement about

Peruvian rodents and white swans, and, indeed, about every last thing in the universe. It seems to be a statement *about the moons of Jupiter* and nothing else.

How do we convince students to accept the universal quantification $\forall x(MJ(x) \supset R(x))$ as a decent translation of the restricted claim about the moons of Jupiter? We do so by a logical sleight-of-hand. We argue that the expansion of the restricted quantifier to a universal quantifier is harmless because it is compensated for by the addition of the restriction as the antecedent of the conditional. The implicit argument runs as follows. The universal quantifier ranges over absolutely everything, but absolutely everything divides into those things that are moons of Jupiter and those that are not. But everything that is not a moon of Jupiter, all of that extra junk we have admitted into the domain of quantification, is something that does not satisfy the predicate "moon of Jupiter". Therefore, to say of any such item that it is a moon of Jupiter is not true. That is, if an interpretation assigns such an item as the denotation of the variable x, $MJ(x)$ is not, on that interpretation, true. Therefore (WARNING! OBSERVE CAREFULLY!) for any such interpretation $MJ(x)$ is false. Hence, on any such interpretation, $MJ(x) \supset R(x)$ is true. *But if $MJ(x) \supset R(x)$ is true for any interpretation which assigns one of the extra objects to the variable, then quantifying over the extra objects cannot possibly prevent the universal claim from being true.* The extra objects are rendered harmless by the conditional: they are *guaranteed* to yield true instances. So the truth value of the original sentence will be determined only by the character of objects which *are* moons of Jupiter (i.e. whether they are rock or not): the non-moons cannot be decisive one way or another, no matter what else happens to be true of them.[8]

The sleight-of-hand tacitly employs two principles. The first is that any interpretation that fails to make a sentence true must make it false. The second is that any conditional with a false antecedent is true. But the first supposition holds *only in a language whose semantics guarantees that every wff is either true or false. So if one is forced to abandon a bivalent semantics then the justification for translating restricted quantification as universal quantification over conditional sentences is undercut.* And since sentences like the Liar force us to abandon universal bivalent semantics, they force us to reconsider, for the very foundations, the treatment of quantification in formal language.

It is obvious that the existence of the Liar is interfering with the semantics of "All of the true sentences uttered by Maxwell were uttered by Clio" exactly because of the failure of bivalence. The Liar sentence ought not to fall within the domain of quantification since it is not true. But when translated as $\forall x((T(x) \,\&\, M(x)) \supset C(x))$, the Liar sentence, as well as every other sentence,

---

[8] Unless, of course, there are no moons of Jupiter at all. Then the non-moons are decisive, and render the claim true—again in conflict with naive intuition. Offhand, the untutored tend to think that if there are no moons of Jupiter, then it is not true to say that all the moons of Jupiter are made of rock.

does fall within the domain of the quantifier. And further, the argument that letting them into the domain is harmless fails: the Liar sentence yields the instance $((T(\lambda)\ \&\ M(\lambda)) \supset C(\lambda))$, which fails to be true even though the sentence denoted by λ is not true. Similar considerations show why "All true sentences are true" fails to be true: the existence of sentences which are neither true nor false gums up the works, even though one would have thought that they would be *irrelevant* to the sentence.

The dependence of the usual translation of restricted quantification on a universal bivalent semantics is clear, so the main source of our trouble has been identified. We might think that the problem lies in translating the sentence using the Kleene connective $\supset$. What one wants instead is a connective like $\Rightarrow$ defined above: a conditional that is automatically true if its antecedent is anything other than true. *But we have already seen that no such connective can exist in our language: any binary connective must yield an ungrounded sentence when both of its inputs are ungrounded.*

The second approach to solving these problems takes a quite different tack. Rather than changing the *connective* used in the translation of, e.g., "All the moons of Jupiter are rock", this approach insists that there is no connective at all in that sentence, and so none should appear in any translation into a formal language. The "if... then" construction is not employed in the original English, and its appearance in the formal translation is an awkward attempt to remedy a mistake which has already been made. That mistake is using the *unrestricted* quantifier in the first place. The original uses a quantifier whose domain is restricted to the moons of Jupiter, and if the formal language contained an equivalent device, no connective would come into play at all. Let us call this the *quantifier analysis* of the conundrum.

The quantifier analysis insists that the formal language be expanded to contain many restricted quantifiers in addition to the completely unrestricted one already available. We need quantifiers whose domains contain only the moons of Jupiter, only the true sentences, only the true sentences uttered by Maxwell, etc. Each such quantifier is associated with a restriction, which is specified by a predicate. Only objects that satisfy the predicate are to be quantified over. We must therefore abandon the standard representation of the predicate calculus in favor of a new formalism.

Instead of representing "All of the moons of Jupiter are rock" as $\forall x(M\mathcal{J}(x) \supset R(x))$, let us represent it as $[\forall M\mathcal{J}(x)]R(x)$. And instead of representing "All true sentences are true" as $\forall x(T(x) \supset T(x))$, let's use $[\forall T(x)]T(x)$. The quantifiers in the square brackets should be interpreted as different quantifiers in each case: in the first sentence, the quantifier has as its domain only those items that satisfy $M\mathcal{J}(x)$, and in the second only those items that satisfy $T(x)$. "All true sentences are true" thus has the same fundamental logical structure as "All sentences are true", or "Everything is true", which, in the standard approach, contains no horseshoe. "Everything is true" says of everything in the domain of the quantifier that it is true, and we happily render this as "All sentences are true" if only sentences are allowed in the domain. Similarly, "All true sentences are true" says unconditionally that everything in its domain is true, but the domain is restricted to the true sentences.

The semantics for restricted quantifiers is now exactly parallel to the semantics for unrestricted quantifiers: a universal claim is true if all of the instances are true, false if at least one is false, ungrounded if not all are true but none are false. Restricted existential claims such as "Some moon of Jupiter is rock" can be defined in the usual way from the restricted universal quantifiers.

Having eliminated the horseshoe from our analysis of restricted quantification, all of our problems about connectives evaporate. "All true sentences are true" comes out, unsurprisingly, as true, even in the face of the Liar. Similarly for "Every true sentence uttered by Maxwell was uttered by Clio", which would be represented as $[\forall(T(x) \ \& \ M(x))]C(x)$.

The introduction of restricted quantifiers alters our former picture of the semantic structure of the language in a fundamental way. In that picture, once one is given the function $\mathscr{F}(x)$ one can determine completely *a priori* (i.e. without reference to the truth values of any boundary sentence) what the immediate semantic constituents of any sentence are. The graph of the language is fixed, and the methods of semantic evaluation describe how truth values flow along the edges of the graph. But if restricted quantifiers are allowed into a language with semantic predicates, *the very structure of the graph changes as the truth value assignments are altered*. When a sentence is assigned the truth value true, for example, it *becomes* an immediate semantic constituent of "All true sentences are true", and the structure of the graph must be altered. The analytical problem becomes correspondingly complex: as the truth-value assignment changes, so does the structure on which the truth values are entered. Some such scheme may be able to get "All true sentences are true" and "Every true sentence uttered by Maxwell was uttered by Clio" to come out true, but one must wonder whether there is not a deep price to pay for the complexity.

Indeed there is. The problem with this scheme is exposed by a third test case. Clio utters one sentence, viz. "One plus one equals two". Maxwell utters one sentence, viz. "All of the true sentences uttered by either Clio or Maxwell were uttered by Clio". What have our different analyses to say of this case?

If we translate the sentence as $\forall x((T(x) \ \& \ (M(x) \lor C(x))) \supset C(x))$, then the sentence is ungrounded just like the Liar. Using a restricted quantifier, one would translate the sentence $[\forall(T(x) \ \& \ (M(x) \lor C(x)))]C(x)$, and a vicious cycle results. The cycle is rather different from the ones we have studied so far, since *the topology of the graph changes as the truth values of sentences change*. The fundamental issue, of course, is whether the problematic sentence itself falls within the domain of its own restricted quantifier. It is certainly a sentence which was uttered by either Clio or Maxwell, but is it a *true* sentence? If it is, it falls within the domain of the quantifier, and so the quantified sentence turns out to be false. And if the sentence is false, then it no longer falls in the domain of the quantifier. But rejected from the domain, only the sentence "One plus one equals two" remains in the domain, and so the quantified sentence is true. The apparatus of restricted quantification, then, suffers a deadly defect: it is not free of paradox. Our semantics may fail to make "All true sentences are true" and the like true, but it is guaranteed to assign to every sentence a unique truth value in a consistent way. Much as we would like "All true sentences are true" to be true, we still are better off regarding it as ungrounded if the alternative is to land us back in the problems we began with. In essence, a restricted quantifier with a semantic predicate in the restriction can act like a non-Kleenesque connective. For changing the truth value of a sentence from ungrounded to true can change the domain of the quantifier in such a way that other sentences switch from one primary value to another.

This evaluation of the situation seems quite depressing: the ungroundedness of "All true sentences are true" must be paid as the price for consistency and uniform treatment of the quantifiers.[9] Fortunately, the situation is not so dire. As we will see, we can live with the ungroundedness of many sentences we took to be true and lose almost nothing. But before presenting this therapy for ungrounded sentences, we should step back and answer the metaphysical question. The foregoing chapter contains an answer to the technical problem: how are truth values assigned to sentences which have immediate semantic constituents? The precise result is already familiar as the minimal fixed point in Kripke's theory of truth. We have offered a different way of arriving at that fixed point and a different understanding of the third semantic value, and these elaborations have allowed us to argue that only the minimal fixed point will do. These arguments have precluded us from trying to "close off" the truth predicate, as Kripke suggests, and there are several apparent infelicities in the theory to attend to. But at least we have a single, unique method for assigning truth values to sentences in a language, using a trivalent rather than bivalent semantics. With this in hand, we need to review the definitions of some basic semantic notions.

Implication, Logical Equivalence, Tautologies, and All That

In any standard logic text, once the semantics of a language has been described various logical notions can be defined. Having outlined our semantics, we are now in a position to provide these definitions. They will generally follow, in an

---

[9] The clause "uniform treatment of the quantifiers" must be added since not all uses of restricted quantifiers lead to trouble. Indeed, "All true sentences are true" can always be translated using a restricted quantifier as $[\forall(T(x))]T(x)$, and will then come out true. But one cannot determine *a priori* whether an arbitrary restricted quantifier allows for a consistent assignment of truth values.

obvious way, the standard definitions for a bivalent semantics, but due to the extra truth value, certain implications of these definitions no longer hold. It turns out that these divergences are of signal importance for some central arguments in metalogic, so we need to attend to them with care.

Given a language, together with the function $\mathscr{F}(x)$, the graph of a language is well defined. Every graph will have a boundary, and assigning primary truth values (in our case true and false) to the boundary sentences will induce a unique assignment of true, false, and ungrounded to all of the sentences of the language. Such an assignment is an *interpretation* of the language. (One can get more sophisticated: an interpretation can assign a set of objects in the domain to every non–semantic predicate, and so on . . . these obvious embellishments will not concern us here.) Interpretations are therefore in one-to-one correspondence with assignments of primary truth values to the boundary sentences.

A sentence in the language is a *tautology* iff it is assigned truth by every interpretation. We indicate a tautology with a double turnstile: $\models S$ means that S is a tautology. An argument from some set of premises to a conclusion is *valid* iff every interpretation which makes all of the premises true also makes the conclusion true. If Δ is the set of premises and C the conclusion, we represent this as $\Delta \models C$. We also say in this case that Δ *entails* C. Two sentence S_1 and S_2 are *logically equivalent* iff every interpretation assigns them the same truth value: we represent this relation by $S_1 \cong S_2$. These definitions are the standard ones.

But in the context of our semantics, these definitions do not have the usual implications. For example, in the standard bivalent logic,

$$S_1 \cong S_2 \text{ iff } \models S_1 \equiv S_2,$$

since if every interpretation assigns S_1 and S_2 the same truth value, then every interpretation either makes both true or both false, and hence every interpretation makes $S_1 \equiv S_2$ true. But this argument no longer holds: if, for example, every interpretation makes both S_1 and S_2 *ungrounded*, then $S_1 \cong S_2$, but $S_1 \equiv S_2$ is *never* true. The Liar is logically equivalent to the Truthteller, and the Liar is obviously logically equivalent to itself, but neither $\sim T(\lambda) \equiv T(\beta)$ nor even $\sim T(\lambda) \equiv \sim T(\lambda)$ is a tautology. Of course, logically equivalent sentences are always intersubstitutable *salva veritate* (and *salva falsitate* and *salva ungrounditate*) since the semantics is truth-functional. Similarly $S_1 \models S_2$ does not imply $\models S_1 \supset S_2$, as it does in a bivalent logic. Nor need S_1 and S_2 be logically equivalent just because $S_1 \models S_2$ and $S_2 \models S_1$. A classical contradiction, such as $A \& \sim A$ entails every sentence since no interpretation makes it true. Similarly, the Liar $\sim T(\lambda)$ entails every sentence since no interpretation makes it true. So we have both $A \& \sim A \models \sim T(\lambda)$ and $\sim T(\lambda) \models A \& \sim A$. But $A \& \sim A$ is not logically equivalent to $\sim T(\lambda)$; indeed, *no* interpretation assigns them the same truth value.

These divergences from classical bivalent logic are extremely important. For example, the standard proofs of the incompleteness of arithmetic and the undefinability of a truth predicate for arithmetic use a technique which shows (in the context of a *bivalent* semantics), that for any open formula $B(y)$ with only the variable y free, there is a sentence of the form $G \equiv B(\ulcorner G \urcorner)$ which is entailed by a particularly weak arithmetic theory called Robinson arithmetic. So if Robinson arithmetic is true, so is $G \equiv B(\ulcorner G \urcorner)$. Why is this important?

Suppose that the language (like ours) has a truth predicate $T(x)$. Then for $B(y)$ above we may use $\sim T(y)$, and the procedure would show that there exists a sentence G such that Robinson arithmetic entails $G \equiv \sim T(\ulcorner G \urcorner)$. And *that* would mean that if Robinson arithmetic is true, so is $G \equiv \sim T(\ulcorner G \urcorner)$. And that result is plainly at odds with the semantics we have developed: no sentence of the form $G \equiv \sim T(\ulcorner G \urcorner)$ can be true. If G is assigned truth by an interpretation, $\sim T(\ulcorner G \urcorner)$ will be false, if G is assigned falsehood, $\sim T(\ulcorner G \urcorner)$ will be true, and if G is ungrounded, so will $\sim T(\ulcorner G \urcorner)$ be. Therefore, $G \equiv \sim T(\ulcorner G \urcorner)$ may be false, or it may be ungrounded, but it is never true.

Logicians are tempted to draw the conclusion that no predicate like our $T(x)$ can exist, but that is plainly false. (More on this below.) $T(x)$ is a perfectly well-defined predicate in our language, albeit one which forces the semantics to be trivalent rather than bivalent. And equally clearly, there is no true sentence of the form $G \equiv \sim T(\ulcorner G \urcorner)$. And surely we have not somehow shown that Robinson arithmetic is not true! So what exactly has happened?

The problem is quite straightforward: the proof that for any open formula $B(y)$ with only the variable y free, there is a sentence of the form $G \equiv B(\ulcorner G \urcorner)$ which is entailed by Robinson arithmetic itself *presupposes a bivalent semantics*. Here is the critical passage from George Boolos and Richard Jeffrey's classic *Computability and Logic* (there is a lot of technical terminology here which will not concern us):

Let G be the expression $\exists x(x = \mathbf{n}\ \&\ \exists y(A(x,y)\ \&\ B(y)))$. As $\mathbf{n} = \ulcorner F \urcorner$, G is the diagonalization of F and a sentence of the language T. Since G is logically equivalent to $\exists y(A(x,y)\ \&\ B(y))$, we have

$\vdash_T G \leftrightarrow \exists y(A(x,y)\ \&\ B(y))$.   (Boolos and Jeffrey 1989: 173)

(Boolos and Jeffrey use $\leftrightarrow$ for the biconditional we call $\equiv$. $\vdash_T$ means "T entails". T is a theory that includes a certain amount of mathematics: the details are not important for us.) The key move in the proof is the inference from the *logical equivalence* of two sentences to a corresponding biconditional being *entailed*. But that is precisely the inference that one is *not* entitled to given our semantics. $T(\lambda)$ is logically equivalent to $\sim T(\lambda)$, but $T(\lambda) \equiv \sim T(\lambda)$ is not entailed by any consistent theory. So the standard results in metatheory have to be re-evaluated from the ground up once one accepts a third truth value. In particular, the Diagonalization Lemma no longer holds.

Another divergence from standard approaches deserves note, although this is just a matter of a terminological convention. Consider the following exercise from Boolos and Jeffrey: "A formula $B(y)$ is called a truth-predicate for T if for any sentence G of the language of T, $\vdash_T G \leftrightarrow B(\ulcorner G \urcorner)$. Show that if T is a consistent theory in which diag is representable, then there is no truth-predicate for T (ibid. 180)."

This problem *sounds* as if it is of critical importance to our enterprise: it seems to say that no consistent theory can contain its own truth predicate. And *given the definition of a truth predicate above*, this is so. But our truth predicate, $T(x)$, is not a truth predicate according to the above definition: not every sentence of the form $G \equiv T(\ulcorner G \urcorner)$ is true, so we should not expect them all to be entailed by any consistent theory. But the question is: even if $T(x)$ is not a "truth-predicate" according to the given definition, why should we accept that it is not a truth predicate? Why should we accept the definition (which obviously focuses on the Tarski biconditionals) as constitutive of truth? Our theory simply rejects the standards for a truth predicate offered in the problem and argues for other standards in their place. So we have to ask a foundational question about the standards of success for the project of analyzing truth. What sort of a project is it to produce a theory of truth, and what are the criteria by which we can judge such a theory? It is to these questions that we next turn.

3 What is Truth, and What is a Theory of Truth?

We now have a theory of the determination of truth values in a language. In what sense does all of this constitute a *theory* or *explication* of truth (and falsity)?

We need to distinguish three tasks. First, we want a theory to clearly explicate the *nature of the truth predicate*. Second, we want it to give an account, for any individual sentence, of *what would make the sentence have any given truth value*. Third, we want an account, for any given concrete situation, of *what ultimately gives any sentence the truth value it has*.

The first task has been easily, and completely, accomplished. We need only explicate the semantics of atomic sentences containing the truth predicate. In such a sentence, (1) the truth predicate binds to a term which denotes an object (2) if the object so denoted is a sentence, then the sentence denoted is the sole immediate semantic constituent of the atomic sentence (otherwise the atomic sentence is automatically false) (3) the function which defines the predicate is the *identity map* from the truth value of the immediate semantic constituent to the truth value of the atomic sentence: the atomic sentence has the same truth value as its immediate semantic constituent. It is because the function that defines the truth predicate is the identity map that truth can seem to be trivial. This triviality motivates the "redundancy" theories of truth.

There is a deep connection between the observation that the truth predicate is defined by the identity map and Tarski's claim that any acceptable theory of truth must yield the truth of the T-sentences. Tarski demanded this as a necessary material condition for a theory of truth, and there has ever since been a line of thought suggesting that the T-sentences, if true, also provide a *complete explication* of truth. But, on the other hand, Tarski's desideratum seems to be in jeopardy as soon as one admits that there are sentences that are neither true nor false. In our theory, the T-sentence for the Liar, $T(\lambda) \equiv \sim T(\lambda)$ is ungrounded rather than true. Does this, as Tarski suggests, render our theory unfit as theory of truth?

The answer to this question is not so obvious as it might seem, for Tarski only considered a bivalent semantics in which every sentence is either true or false. In such a case, the truth of all the T-sentences entails and is entailed by the fact that every sentence of the form $T(n)$ has the same truth value as $\mathscr{F}(n)$. So it is arguable that what Tarski was trying to *get at* with his material adequacy condition was not so much the truth of the T-sentences but the triviality of the truth predicate: that a sentence which says another sentence is true must have the same truth value as that other sentence.

What happens when one moves to a three-valued semantics? If Tarski's material condition is really trying to guarantee that the truth predicate is defined semantically by the identity map, then the T-sentences *should not be of the form* $T(n) \equiv \mathscr{F}(n)$, where $\equiv$ is the Kleene biconditional, and where we replace n by a singular term which denotes a sentence and $\mathscr{F}(n)$ by the sentence it denotes. What Tarski would need instead is what we might call the *Tarski biconditional* $\equiv_T$:

$\equiv$	T	F	U		$\equiv_T$	T	F	U
T	T	F	U		T	T	F	F
F	F	T	F		F	F	T	F
U	U	F	U		U	F	F	T

Both of these biconditionals are extensions of the classical two-valued connective, but only $\equiv_T$ expresses Tarski's real concern. For only according to the last *is the biconditional true if and only if the sentences on either side have the same truth value*. The Kleene biconditional is wrong because the sentence is not true when both sides are ungrounded. So the failure of a T-sentence constructed with the Kleene biconditional to be true is no mark against a three-valued theory of truth. One would be concerned if a T-sentence constructed using the Tarski biconditional were not true, *but given the meaning of U, the Tarski biconditional cannot exist*. Any biconditional both of whose immediate semantic constituents are ungrounded must be ungrounded, not true as the Tarski biconditional would require.[1]

---

[1] The slide from the claim that the T-Inferences are valid to the claim that the T-sentences must be true is amply illustrated in the literature. Consider the following from Gupta (1982): "It is a fundamental intuition about truth that from any sentence A the inference to another sentence that asserts that A is true is warranted. And conversely: from the latter sentence the inference to A is also warranted. It is this intuition which is enshrined in Tarski's famous Convention T. Tarski requires, as a material adequacy condition, that a definition for truth for a language L imply all sentences of the form (T) x is true iff p, where 'p' is replaced by an object language sentence (or its translation, if the sentence is not homophonic) and 'x' is replaced by a standard name of the sentence" (in Martin 1984: 181).

After discussing the Liar, Gupta concludes: "The Liar paradox shows, then, that in the case of a classical language that has its own truth predicate the fundamental intuition cannot be preserved under all conditions (i.e. in all models). This leads to the question whether there are any conditions under which the intuition can be preserved" (ibid. 183). From our present position, it is easy to see that the switch from talk of certain inferences being warranted to talk of certain sentences being true distorts the problematic. The "fundamental intuition" was that the T-Inferences are warranted. Indeed they are: they are valid, truth-preserving inferences in all

Tarski was getting at this central property of the truth predicate with his material condition, but in a roundabout, and somewhat ham-handed, way. The defining property of the truth predicate is that it is the identity map from the truth value of $\mathscr{F}(n)$ to the truth value of $T(n)$. It is, of course, exactly because of this defining property of truth that the T-Inferences must always be valid. In our language we cannot use Tarski's shift of expressing this defining property in terms of the truth of the T-sentences, but we have no need to. The truth predicate in our theory is defined by the identity map, just as Tarski would have wanted.

Our first question, viz. "What is the truth predicate?", has been answered completely and without remainder. There is nothing more about it to be known, just as there is nothing more to know about conjunction once one has the truth table which shows how the truth value of a conjunction is determined by the truth values of its immediate semantic constituents.

The second question, asked of a particular sentence, is what its truth conditions are, or more widely, what its semantic conditions are. What would make it have one truth value or another?

With respect to all non-boundary sentences, the *local* answer to this question is given by specifying the immediate semantic constituents of the sentence and the truth function that defines the relevant connective or semantic predicate. One understands all there is to understand about the logical connectives and semantic predicates by knowing the truth functions that define them. The specific case of the truth predicate discussed above is just an instance of this. So the local semantic conditions of all non-boundary sentences, the way they depend on their immediate semantic constituents, has been laid open to view.

What of the boundary sentences? We obviously do not understand their truth conditions in terms of their immediate semantic constituents: they have none. It is here that a second tradition, that of using the T-sentences as a *theory* of truth (rather than a *criterion of adequacy* of a theory of truth) comes into play. For every boundary sentence there is a T-sentence of the form $T(n) \equiv \mathscr{F}(n)$. Those T-sentences, all of which are true, specify non-semantic necessary and sufficient conditions for the boundary sentence to be true. (We here assume that every boundary sentence is either true or false.) Hence they provide a reduction of the truth of the boundary sentence to some purely non-semantic condition. The redundancy theory of truth is based in the observation that this is a completely adequate explanation of what it is for a boundary sentence to be true.

Thus, when it comes to a boundary sentence such as "France is hexagonal", if someone asks under what conditions that sentence is true, a perfectly

---

circumstances, even for languages with the Liar. Gupta, having fallen for Tarski's bait-and-switch, ends up worrying about the truth of the T-sentences rather than the very intuition he starts with.

appropriate response is that it is true just in case France is hexagonal. If one understands what it is for France to be hexagonal, then one understands the conditions under which "France is hexagonal" is true. End of story.

Of course, one might *not* understand what it is for France to be hexagonal. One might not know, for example, how close an approximation to a geometrical hexagon the border of France must be to count, in this context, as hexagonal. Or one might not know what a hexagon is. Or one might not know what France is. Or there might be a dispute over the legal territorial boundaries of France. All of these things might need to be explained or clarified, and the relevant concepts might even be so confused as to support no clarification. But none of this has anything at all to do with the notion of *truth*; it has instead to do with the notions of hexagonality and of France. The point is that in explaining what it is for France to be hexagonal we are no longer concerned with *the general theory of truth*: the obscurities left over are not obscurities about truth *per se*.

For boundary sentences, then, the T-sentences do play a central role in the explication of truth conditions. The T-sentences for the boundary sentences (which, again, are all true) provide a completely non-semantic explication of what it is for each boundary sentence to be true. The problem with the so-called redundancy theory of truth is mistaking this role of the T-sentences in explicating what it is for a *boundary* sentence to be true for an adequate general theory of what it is for *any* sentence to be true. One understands the truth conditions of a non-boundary sentence not in terms of its T-sentence, but, as explicated above, in terms of its immediate semantic constituents and the relevant truth function.

The hopelessness of the idea that the T-sentences could *in general* provide an adequate explication of truth is made strikingly obvious in the case of the Truthteller, whose T-sentence is $T(\beta) \equiv T(\beta)$. How could *this* sentence, even if it were true, provide any useful insight into what it is for the Truthteller to be true? If someone is enlightened by being told that the Truthteller is true just in case it is true, then that person will certainly be easy to satisfy on all sorts of seemingly deep and difficult issues. But to be told that the Truthteller sentence has one immediate semantic constituent, and that that constituent is the sentence denoted by β, and that the truth predicate maps the truth value of the immediate semantic constituent to the truth value of the sentence of which it is a constituent by the identity map, and that the denotation of β is the sentence $T(\beta)$ itself, is to be told something informative. It is not yet to be told *everything* relevant about the Truthteller, but it does illuminate the nature of the local constraints imposed on it by the semantics of the truth predicate.

Since boundary sentences can be false as well as true, explicating what it is for a boundary sentence to be false is also necessary. One needs, in addition to T-sentences for the boundary sentences, F-sentences. These can be of the form $\Phi(n) \equiv \sim T(n)$, or of the form $\Phi(n) \equiv \mathcal{NF}(n)$ where $\Phi(n)$ stands for "n is false" and $\mathcal{NF}(n)$ is the function which maps every individual term n which denotes a sentence to the negation of $\mathscr{F}(n)$. Like the T-sentences, these F-sentences for boundary sentences are all true. These sentences tell us, e.g., that "France is hexagonal" is false just in case France is not hexagonal. Again, if someone does not understand what it would be for France not to be hexagonal, this residual confusion has nothing to do with the notion of falsity.

If one wants there to be other primary truth values (i.e. other values for boundary sentences) than truth or falsity, then one needs to specify analogs of the T- and F-sentences which explicate, in non-semantic terms, what it is for boundary sentences to have these other truth values. The most obvious candidate for such a truth value would be something associated with borderline cases of vague predicates, since there intuitively seem to be sentences which are neither true nor false on account of the vagueness of the terms. An account of vagueness is required, and presents a *prima facie* case for non-classical *primary* truth values, but it is one of the contentions of our account of truth that vagueness plays no role in the Liar or other semantic paradoxes. The problem of vagueness is taken up in Appendix C.

Our second question, what locally constrains the truth value of any given sentence, has been answered. The answer for boundary sentences is different than for non-boundary sentences, reflecting the dependence of the truth values of non-boundary sentences on the truth values of other sentences. The T-sentences and F-sentences provide perfectly adequate accounts of what determines the truth value of any boundary sentence (assuming the only primary values are true and false), and we have diagnosed the source of a long-standing but futile attempt to use the T-sentences as a complete theory of truth.

There is, still, a third useful question that can be asked in any particular case when a sentence has a truth value. We may ask what, ultimately, the source or ground of that truth value is. This may not seem like a completely clear question, but its import will grow sharper when we see what sort of answers are available.

Consider, for example, the sentence "Either the Earth is more massive than the Sun or the Earth is not more massive than the Sun". That sentence is true. What, exactly, *makes* it true? The correct *proximate* answer is this: the sentence is true because it is a disjunction whose first disjunct is false and whose second disjunct is true, and disjunction is a function which maps that pair of inputs into truth. That is, to understand what proximately makes the sentence true, one must know not only which sentences are the immediate semantic constituents of it, and what the relevant truth function is, but also *what truth values the immediate semantic constituents have*. In a straightforward sense, in this case, it is in particular *the truth of the second disjunct* which makes this disjunction true. And the second disjunct is true because it is a negation whose immediate semantic constituent is false. And its immediate semantic constituent, viz. "The Earth is more massive than the Sun", is false because *the Earth is not more massive than the Sun*. And now we have traced the truth of our original sentence back to its ultimate ground: the sentence is true because the Earth is not more massive than the Sun.

While the foregoing account of the truth of "Either the Earth is more massive than the Sun or the Earth is not more massive than the Sun" may seem like a verbose triviality, it stands in direct opposition to a long and powerful tradition in semantics. According to that tradition, the sentence above, which we may render $(M(e,s) \lor \sim M(e,s))$ is *true in virtue of its logical form*. This doctrine, perhaps most evident in the logical positivists, finds a clear expression in Tarski's seminal paper on truth. Having rejected, because of problems with the Liar sentence, the *semantic* definition of truth based on the T-sentences, Tarski then tries another route, which he calls a *structural definition* of truth. As this second idea of Tarski has received considerably less attention than the first, an extensive citation is in order:

The general scheme of this definition would be somewhat as follows: *a true sentence is a sentence which possesses such and such structural properties* (i.e. properties concerning the form and order of succession of the individual parts of the expression) *or which can be obtained from such and such structurally described expressions by means of such and such structural transformations*. As a starting-point we can press into service many laws from formal logic which enable us to infer the truth or falsehood of sentences from their structural properties; or from the truth or falsehood of certain sentences to infer analogous properties of other sentences which can be obtained from the former by means of various structural transformations. Here are some trivial examples of such laws: *every expression consisting of four parts of which the first is the word "if", the third is the word "then", and the second and fourth are the same sentence, is a true sentence; if a true sentence consists of four parts, of which the first is the word "if", the second a true sentence, the third the word "then", then the fourth part is a true sentence.* (Tarski 1956: 163)

Tarski admits that such definitions may be of great help in *extending* a partial definition of truth to cover more of a language which contains the logical connectives, but abandons the strategy as adequate for a *general* definition of truth in a natural language because in the constantly expanding texture of a natural language there will be too many unforeseeable forms for there to be a set of "sufficiently numerous, powerful and general laws for every sentence to fall under one of them" (ibid. 164). Of course, as a *general* definition of truth the attempt fails miserably even for a circumscribed formal language: surely no *structural* definition can determine whether, e.g., "Neutrinos have a non-zero rest mass" is true, no matter what other expressive resources the language has.

Although the structural theory cannot be a complete theory of truth, something like it has had a long-standing appeal as a theory of the truth of certain tautologous sentences. The idea, as expressed by Tarski, is that some sentences containing logical connectives are true not in virtue of any compositional semantics, but solely in virtue of their structural form. The idea is expressed in even more detail by Rudolph Carnap:

(Meaningful) statements are divided into the following kinds. First there are statements that are true solely by virtue of their form ("tautologies" according to Wittgenstein; they correspond approximately to Kant's "analytic judgments"). They say nothing about reality. The formulae of logic and mathematics are of this kind. They are not themselves factual statements, but serve for the transformations of such sentences. Secondly there are the negations of such sentences ("*contradictions*"). They are self-contradictory, hence false by virtue of their form. With respect to all other statements the decision about truth or falsity lies in the protocol sentences. They are therefore (true or false) *empirical statements*, and belong to the domain of empirical science. (Carnap 1959: 76)

Note that Carnap postulates two completely different *kinds* or *sources* of truth: truth conferred by syntactic form alone, and truth conferred, ultimately, by the world.

The appeal of this approach may be in explaining how, e.g., mathematical claims can be true without postulating a realm of mathematical objects to make them true. But the idea that sentences like "Either the Earth is more massive than the Sun or the Earth is not more massive than the Sun" are true in some fundamentally different way than true sentences such as "Either snow is black or the Earth is not more massive than the Sun" (which is not true in virtue of its logical form) is mistaken, misleading, and pernicious.

Of course, the former appears to be *a priori* while the latter is *a posteriori*, but that is, in any case, an *epistemic* matter, not a *semantic* one. We may *know* that the first sentence is true in virtue of knowing its logical form (and, say, knowing that "The Earth is more massive than the Sun" is not ungrounded since it is a boundary sentence), while we can't *know* the truth value of the second by inspection. But the theory of truth is nowhere couched in terms of what we can know, or how. Our knowing, in virtue of knowing only its logical form, that a sentence is true is not the same as the sentence being made true by its logical form alone: it is rather a matter of our being able to know *that* a sentence is true without knowing exactly *what makes it true*, e.g. whether the truth of the first or second disjunct (or both) makes it true.

Some might object that it is wrong to say that the truth of the second disjunct makes "The Earth is more massive than the Sun or the Earth is not more massive than the Sun" true, since it would remain true even if the second disjunct were false (and hence the first disjunct true). But this observation is not about what makes the sentence true, but about how it would remain true under certain counterfactual variations in the world. It is plausible that some sentences are *necessarily* true in virtue of their logical form (i.e. their *necessity* is explained by their logical form), but it does not follow that they are *true* in virtue of that form. The point, again, is that *truth conditions are articulated by the semantics*, and a compositional semantics gives general rules for how the truth values of molecular sentences depend on the truth values of their components. The truth value of the molecular sentences is determined by the *truth values of the components and the function associated with the connectives*, not, in any other sense, by the "logical form" of the sentence.

This erroneous view about tautologies sometimes derives from a confusion between what makes a sentence true and what the truth of the sentence informs us of. The truth of "Either the Earth is more massive than the Sun or the Earth is not more massive than the Sun" carries no information about the world, since it remains true no matter how the world is (i.e. no matter what boundary values are assigned to the language). In this sense, as Carnap writes, the sentence "say[s] nothing about reality". But even so, it is the world, and particular facts about the world, which make it true. Just because one cannot *infer* from its truth which boundary value makes it true does not mean that one doesn't. The explanation of the truth of the disjunction proceeds by observing the truth of one disjunct, which is ultimately explained by observing facts about the relative masses of the Sun and the Earth. And the explanation need not stop there: there may well be an explanation of why the Earth is less massive than the Sun—but that is no longer a matter of *semantics*.

Of course, the truth value of some sentences is overdetermined, in which case it would be incorrect to attribute the truth to a single set of boundary values. "Either the Earth is more massive than Mercury or the Earth is not more massive than the Sun" is not made true by the truth of one disjunct rather than the truth of the other. But still, some informative things may be said about its truth. The truth of that disjunction is guaranteed by the truth of each of its disjuncts taken individually, so its truth is *rooted* in the truth value of each of the relevant boundary sentences. The idea of *rooting* is explicated by the directed graph of a language. Let *semantic constituent* denote the ancestral of the relation of immediate semantic constituent. In general, we can say that the truth value of one sentence is rooted in the truth values of some set of its semantic constituents if the truth value of the one is guaranteed by the values of the others and the nature of the semantic paths which connect them. So the truth of "Either the Earth is more massive than Mercury or the Earth is not more massive than the Sun" is rooted in the truth of "The Earth is more massive than Mercury" and in the falsity of "The Earth is more massive than the Sun", and these truth values in turn are explained by the Earth's being more massive than Mercury and by its being less massive than the Sun.

Any non-boundary sentence that is either true or false ultimately owes its truth value to one or more boundary sentences. The ultimate account of truth or falsity for such sentences involves reconstructing the section of the language that connects that sentence back to the boundary, and seeing how the truth values at the boundary, together with the truth-functional connections, entail the truth value of the given sentence. Such an account of the truth or falsity of a sentence is complete.

The problem of explaining the ultimate source of the truth value of un-grounded sentences, though, is somewhat trickier. One can, of course, always explain the truth value of any non-boundary sentence in terms of the truth values of its immediate semantic constituents. But since such an explanation either ends up going in a circle (as with the Liar and Truthteller), or never reaches a boundary because of an infinite regress, there is still something left to be explained, namely why the cycle as a whole, or the infinite chain as a whole, contains the truth values that it does.

The problem is reminiscent of Kant's antinomies about the world as a whole. Kant claimed that even if the world is deterministic, so every state can be explained by a previous state, and even if the world is infinite in time, there is still an explanatory gap if other infinite sequences of states are possible. Why *this* sequence rather than any other?

(Kant also argues that there is an explanatory gap if the world is finite in time: why *this* initial state rather than any other? In the case of language, this amounts to asking why the boundary sentences have one set of truth values rather than another, and is answered by citing the nature of the world. If one is asking a similar question about the world itself, the explanatory resources seem to run dry.)

One could similarly ask about a cycle, each of whose truth values is determined by the one before it, but which could equally consistently admit of a different distribution of truth values, why there should be just *this* distribution rather than another? In Kripke's theory, this problem arises for the Truthteller, since the *only* semantic constraint is that its truth value be part of a fixed point. The same problem appears in the *local* account of the Truthteller offered above: at the end of the day, one is still left with the conclusion that the Truthteller has the same truth value as its immediate semantic constituent, i.e. itself, and the local structure of the language goes no further.

If one adopts Kripke's theory, which admits multiple fixed points, then the explanation of the truth value of the Truthteller in terms of the truth value of its immediate semantic constituent (i.e. itself) fails to be adequate. Since there are other consistent attributions of truth value to it (on Kripke's theory), one wants to know why the sentence should have one rather than another. This is evidently not a *contingent* matter: two distinct possible worlds cannot agree on everything save for the truth value of the Truthteller. So there must be some necessary fact which determines that the Truthteller has the value it does. It is just very hard to see, if one adopts Kripke's theory, what that fact could be.

But on our theory, the explanation of the truth value of the Truthteller is straightforward. Ultimately, the Truthteller is ungrounded not because its immediate semantic constituent is, but because it is *completely unsafe*: no backward path leads from it to the boundary. Since all completely unsafe sentences are ungrounded, one understands why the Truthteller *must* be ungrounded when one understands the structure of the graph of the language. The truth value "ungrounded" did not "migrate up" the graph to the Truthteller from elsewhere, as truth and falsity do, but there is a complete explanation for it nonetheless. The explanation is global rather than local, and adverts to the very nature of ungroundedness.

In the end, then, ultimate explanations of truth values come in four flavors. The truth values of boundary sentences are explained in completely non-semantic terms: boundary sentences are made true or false by the world. The truth values of completely unsafe sentences, like the Liar and the Truthteller, are explained *a priori* by appeal to the structure of the graph of the language. The truth values of non-boundary sentences which are either true or false are explained by the truth-functional connectives within them, and the truth values of their immediate semantic constituents. Truth and falsity migrate up the graph in virtue of the truth-functional relations between sentences. And lastly there are ungrounded sentences that are not completely unsafe (i.e. which have some backward paths which lead to the boundary). Their ungroundedness is a more complicated matter: an ungrounded set is formed by a combination of graph-theoretic and of semantic features: either because of the particular truth values at the boundary or because of the detailed structure of the truth-functional connections, truth and falsity are unable to infiltrate such a set from the boundary. One understands why these sentences are ungrounded when one appreciates all of these factors.

Every sentence is either a boundary sentence, a true or false non-boundary sentence, a completely unsafe sentence, or an ungrounded sentence which is not completely unsafe. Depending on the category it falls into, there is a different sort of ultimate explanation for the truth value of the sentence. If the sentence is not completely unsafe, that explanation will advert at some point to boundary sentences, and hence to the world. At that point, explanations may continue, but semantics ends. We have understood all there is to know about truth, falsity, and ungroundedness as such.

The theory we have presented is therefore, in a certain sense, complete. Unlike Kripke's theory, with multiple fixed points to choose between, there are no loose ends to tie up or further choices to be made. If the world makes every boundary sentence either true or false, then the structure of the language and the nature of ungroundedness explain the truth value of every sentence in the language.

But the completeness of the theory in this sense is not likely to convince anyone of its adequacy. Although the theory is formally complete, in a certain sense, it may nonetheless be deemed materially inadequate. It certainly yields some quite unexpected results. "All true sentences are true", for example, turns out to be ungrounded, as does "All of the true sentences uttered by either Clio or Maxwell were uttered by Clio" in the test case discussed above. Surely we would all happily *assert* these ungrounded sentences. Does this not imply that we regard them as *true* rather than anything else?

Even worse, one might think, both the Liar $\sim T(\lambda)$ and $T(\lambda)$ are ungrounded, as is the Truthteller $T(\beta)$ and its negation $\sim T(\beta)$. Yet when describing the semantics, we happily say that the Liar is not true, and the Truthteller is not true. We would deny that the Liar is true and that the Truthteller is true. Do not these assertions and denials indicate that we regard the first two claims as true and the last two as false? But the first two claims just are $\sim T(\lambda)$ and $\sim T(\beta)$, the last two are $T(\lambda)$ and $T(\beta)$. Even the claims that the Liar and Truthteller are ungrounded can be translated into the formal language as $Y(\lambda)$ and $Y(\beta)$ respectively, and these sentences are ungrounded rather than true. By what right, then do we assert them? Do we not implicitly contradict ourselves by asserting and denying sentences which, by our own lights, are neither true nor false? These are serious difficulties. But before directly addressing them, let us make them seem a little bit worse.

4 A Language That Can Express Its Own Truth Theory

We originally formulated the Liar paradox in the little language L, which supplements the unquantified propositional calculus only with the truth predicate and arbitrary proper names for sentences. We later expanded the language to include quantifiers, arbitrary non-semantic predicates, and a falsity predicate. We also have the function $\mathscr{F}(x)$ which maps individual terms to the sentences they denote. We have presented a semantic theory for this language, but have not attempted to do so in the language itself. Since one of the primary questions facing the theory of truth is whether any language can serve as its own metalanguage, it seems worthwhile to pause to ask whether the semantics of our expanded language can be expressed in the language itself.

We begin by specifying some of the non-semantic, purely syntactical predicates of the expanded language. Let *Conj(x)* be a predicate that is satisfied by all and only grammatical strings whose main connective is a conjunction. Similarly, let *Univ(x)* be satisfied by all and only grammatical strings whose main connective is a universal quantifier, *Neg(x)* by strings whose main connective is a negation, *Tau(x)* by atomic sentences that contain the truth predicate, and *Phi(x)* by atomic strings that contain the falsity predicate. (We will provide the semantic theory for negation, conjunction, universal quantification, and the truth and falsity predicates: other connectives can be defined in the usual ways from these.) In addition, let *Bound(x)* be satisfied by all and only boundary sentences, i.e. non-semantic atomic sentences. We will in addition need the relation *ISC(x,y)*, which holds just in case *x* is an immediate semantic constituent of *y*. Since the immediate semantic constituents can be determined by completely syntactical means (given $\mathscr{F}(x)$), this is not a problematic relation. (We continue to assume that every item in the domain of quantification of the language has a name, and that every sentence has at least its quotation name.) The language also contains the functions $\mathscr{F}(x)$ and $\mathscr{N}\mathscr{F}(x)$. The argument of $\mathscr{F}(x)$ and $\mathscr{N}\mathscr{F}(x)$ in any well-formed sentence is a variable. For convenience, we again assume that all singular terms denote sentences, and the domain of all quantifiers is the well-formed sentences of the language: the complications which arise in dealing with the more general case are just distractions.[1] We can therefore treat quantification substitutionally, where we replace $\mathscr{F}(n)$ and $\mathscr{NF}(n)$ by the image of n under the relevant function. Grammatically, $\mathscr{F}(n)$ and $\mathscr{NF}(n)$ are sentences. So

$$\forall x(T(x) \equiv \mathscr{F}(x))$$

is now a grammatical sentence of the language, whose instances are sentences like $T(\lambda) \equiv {\sim}T(\lambda)$, $T(\beta) \equiv T(\beta)$, $T(\ulcorner \forall x(T(x) \supset T(x))\urcorner) \equiv \forall x(T(x) \supset T(x))$, $T(\ulcorner {\sim}T(\lambda)\urcorner) \equiv {\sim}T(\lambda)$, and so on.

Next we specify the truth theory for boundary sentences. Here we can follow Tarski directly:

$$\forall x(Bound(x) \supset (T(x) \equiv \mathscr{F}(x))).$$

We have a completely deflationary theory of truth for the boundary sentences. Since the Liar and its ilk are never boundary sentences, paradoxes cannot arise here.

We can also provide a theory of falsity for the boundary sentences, in either of the two ways discussed above. We can add as a postulate:

$$\forall x(Bound(x) \supset (\Phi(x) \equiv {\sim}T(x)))$$

or

$$\forall x(Bound(x) \supset (\Phi(x) \equiv \mathscr{NF}(x))).$$

The truth theory for boundary sentences is now complete.

The truth theory for non-boundary sentences is given, in part, by the local constraints on the graph. Interestingly, the semantics for conjunction,[2] universal quantification, and the truth predicate all turn out to be identical, viz.:

$$\forall x(Conj(x) \supset (T(x) \equiv \forall y(ISC(y,x) \supset T(y))))$$
$$\forall x(Univ(x) \supset (T(x) \equiv \forall y(ISC(y,x) \supset T(y))))$$
$$\forall x(Tau(x) \supset (T(x) \equiv \forall y(ISC(y,x) \supset T(y)))).$$

Theories of falsity for these sorts of sentences are similarly identical:

$$\forall x(Conj(x) \supset (\Phi(x) \equiv \exists y(ISC(y,x) \,\&\, \Phi(y))))$$
$$\forall x(Univ(x) \supset (\Phi(x) \equiv \exists y(ISC(y,x) \,\&\, \Phi(y))))$$
$$\forall x(Tau(x) \supset (\Phi(x) \equiv \exists y(ISC(y,x) \,\&\, \Phi(y)))).$$

---

[1] As an example of how to deal with wider domains of quantification, one could introduce restricted quantifiers which range only over well-formed sentences in our language. There is no difficulty in having such restricted quantifiers, and one could demand that if the argument of $\mathscr{F}(n)$ or $\mathscr{NF}(n)$ is a variable, the variable be so restricted. The truth theory would then be given using such restricted quantifiers.

[2] The falsity condition given is for the Strong Kleene conjunction. The condition for the Weak Kleene conjunction would be: $\forall x(\text{Weakconj}(x) \supset (\Phi(x) \equiv (\exists y(ISC(y,x) \,\&\, \Phi(y)))) \,\&\, \forall y(ISC(y,x) \supset (T(y) \vee \Phi(y)))).$

Negation and the falsity predicate also have similar treatments:

$\forall x(Neg(x) \supset (T(x) \equiv \exists y(ISC(y,x) \ \& \ \Phi(y))))$
$\forall x(Phi(x) \supset (T(x) \equiv \exists y(ISC(y,x) \ \& \ \Phi(y))))$
$\forall x(Neg(x) \supset (\Phi(x) \equiv \forall y(ISC(y,x) \supset T(y))))$
$\forall x(Phi(x) \supset (\Phi(x) \equiv \forall y(ISC(y,x) \supset T(y))))$.

In what sense do all of the above postulates constitute a theory of truth and falsity for the language? Not in the sense of being a recursive definition that allows for the truth and falsity predicates to be "analyzed away" in any given circumstance. That does occur for the boundary sentences, but the truth and falsity of non-boundary sentences is always explicated by reference to the truth or falsity of their immediate semantic constituents, and there is no guarantee that the attempt to analyze these latter will ever bottom out into non-semantic terms. Of course, in a language with a non-cyclic graph and with no infinite descending chains (i.e. in a language in which every sentence is safe) the truth and falsity conditions for every sentence will eventually resolve into truth and falsity conditions for boundary sentences, and thence into non-semantic terms. But all of our effort has been directed toward languages that lack that structure, so we have not provided a recursive definition of truth and falsity.

Even worse, we have not yet pinned down the semantics that has been advocated heretofore. The problem, of course, is that beyond the local constraints on the graph of a language, we have been insisting on certain global constraints, and those have not yet been formulated. It is, for example, consistent with the postulates above that the Truthteller be true, or that it be false. The basic idea that truth and falsity must "flow up" from the boundary of the graph has found no expression.

In order to put constraints on the global distribution of truth values, we first need to define the ancestral of the Immediate Semantic Constituent relation. We introduce the notion of a Semantic Constituent in the obvious way, by two definitional postulates:

$\forall x \forall y(ISC(x,y) \supset SC(x,y))$
$\forall x \forall y \forall z((SC(x,y) \ \& \ SC(y,z)) \supset SC(x,z))$

We can now try to add postulates that will specify exactly the theory of truth we want.

For example, we can easily write down conditions that forbid any completely unsafe sentence from being either true or false:

$\forall x(T(x) \supset \exists y(SC(y,x) \ \& \ Bound(y)))$
$\forall x(\Phi(x) \supset \exists y(SC(y,x) \ \& \ Bound(y)))$.

These conditions imply that the Truthteller is neither true nor false, since none of its semantic constituents is a boundary sentence.

But dealing with completely unsafe sentences is not the whole story. Consider the sentence $\xi\colon T(\xi)$ & X, where X is a true boundary sentence. According to our semantics, this sentence is ungrounded, even though it has a boundary sentence as a semantic constituent and even though assigning it the value true or the value false satisfies all the local constraints on the graph. We could write down complex conditions forbidding this, e.g.

$\forall x((Conj(x)$ & $T(x)) \supset \sim\exists y((ISC(y,x)$ & $ISC(x,y)$ & $Tau(y)))$ and
$\forall x((Conj(x)$ & $\exists y((ISC(y,x)$ & $ISC(x,y)$ & $Tau(y)))$ & $\Phi(x))) \supset$
$\exists y((ISC(y,x)$ & $\sim(y = x))$ & $\Phi(y))$,

but this condition will not cover more complicated cases which can easily be constructed.

Indeed, although a condition can be written down which will secure the right result for any case that involves only a finite part of the graph of a language, new conditions will have to be constructed for each different structure, and furthermore even then not every possible case will be covered. Consider, for example, the following infinitely descending tree. Each node is a conjunction, one of whose conjuncts is a true boundary sentence while the other conjunct asserts the truth of the next node down:

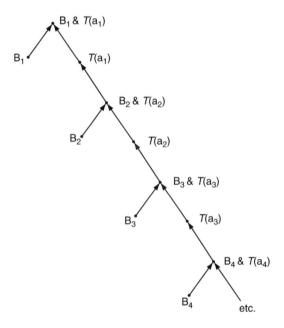

$\mathscr{F}(a_1) = B_2$ & $T(a_2)$, $\mathscr{F}(a_2) = B_3$ & $T(a_3)$, $\mathscr{F}(a_3) = B_4$ & $T(a_4)$, and so on. If all of the boundary sentences are true (they could all be the same sentence), then it is consistent with the local constraints on the graph that all of the sentences running along the spine be true, or that they be false, or that they be ungrounded. What one needs is, as it were, a boundary condition "at infinity" for the spine, but since the spine never terminates, there is no boundary to it.

The semantics we have developed entails that the sentences on the spine are all ungrounded, since they form, in totality, an ungrounded set. And the intuition that they ought to be ungrounded is borne out by the facts of the case: the totality of truth values assigned to boundary sentences (i.e. the totality of truth values determined directly by the world) together with the local constraints do not force truth values on the sentences along the spine. Hence the truth values of sentences on the spine are not determined by the world and the semantics of the connectives. Hence they are all ungrounded.

It may seem incorrect that all of the sentences along the spine are ungrounded if one considers the top sentence, B_1 & $T(a_1)$ to be nothing but the infinite conjunction of all of the boundary sentences, each of which is true. But the semantic structure of this graph is not the same as that of that infinite conjunction. The conjunction of all of the boundary sentences is semantically equivalent to $\forall x(Bound(x) \supset T(x))$, which is, indeed, true.[3] For every instance of $\forall x(Bound(x) \supset T(x))$ is true, since every boundary sentence is true. The semantic structure of our infinitely descending tree is analogous not to an infinite conjunction, but rather to the mathematical structure of an infinitely continued fraction. Infinitely continued fractions also have surprising mathematical properties: for example, although every finitely continued fraction denotes a unique real number, an infinitely continued fraction can ambiguously denote several real numbers. Further, an infinitely continued fraction constructed solely from positive numbers and addition can (ambiguously) denote a negative real number. These curious results are presented in Appendix B.

The problem is to write down a condition in the language itself that disallows assigning truth or falsity to the sentences on the spine. No obvious candidates for such a condition present themselves, since no finite portion of the graph reveals the problem. No sentence in the graph is completely unsafe, nor is any a semantic constituent of itself (i.e. there are no cycles in the graph). One could, perhaps, jerry-rig a condition to fit this particular case because of the symmetry of the graph, but it is fairly clear that the general case poses a very difficult problem. The question is how one can capture, in formal terms, the idea that truth and falsity in the interior

---

[3] Note that the truth predicate here plays one of the roles commonly required of it: to make possible infinite conjunctions.

of the graph must always migrate in from the boundary in accord with the local constraints. What we need is a formal condition expressible in the language that guarantees interior truth or falsity to be grounded at the boundary in this way.

The picture of truth values migrating in from the boundary is obviously a metaphor, but it is a useful one. The idea of flow is exactly the idea of an ordering of the truth values assigned to the nodes, an ordering which reflects the metaphysical dependence of truth values. Truth values are assigned to the boundary "first", and then can be assigned to some interior nodes at one remove from the boundary, and then two removes, and so on. What we need is a formal condition that obtains only when the truth values on the graph could have been assigned in such an ordered way.

To write down such a condition requires that the language be somewhat stronger than we have needed heretofore. In particular, we need for the language to contain a quantifier over functions, i.e. we need a second-order language. The functions will assign an ordinal to each of the sentences, and the ordinals will represent one way that truth values can have "flowed" from sentence to sentence. For example, if a conjunction is to come out true, then there must be some way of assigning ordinals to it and to its immediate semantic constituents such that the ordinal assigned to the conjunction is greater than those assigned to its immediate semantic constituents: i.e. the constituents must have been made true "before" the conjunction was. Similarly, if an atomic sentence containing the truth predicate is true, then it must be assigned an ordinal greater than that of its immediate semantic constituent: the sentence which it refers to must have been made true "before" it was determined to be true. The conjunction of these two conditions rule out assigning truth to the sentence $T(\xi)$ & X discussed above: if the conjunction $T(\xi)$ & X were true, then $T(\xi)$ would have to be true and be assigned a lower ordinal than $T(\xi)$ & X, but if $T(\xi)$ were true, then its immediate semantic constituent, viz. $T(\xi)$ & X, would have to both be true and have a lower ordinal assigned to it than is assigned to $T(\xi)$. Thus $T(\xi)$ & X would have to be assigned a lower ordinal than itself, an impossibility.

Similarly, if a conjunction is false, then it not only must have a false immediate semantic constituent, but that constituent must be assigned a lower ordinal: the conjunction is false *because* the conjunct is false, so in the "order of being" the falsity of the conjunct precedes the falsity of the conjunction. Collecting together all of these conditions in an obvious way, we can finally write down the complete semantics for the language, if the language contains a variable which ranges over functions from the sentences of the language onto the ordinals. Let us denote that variable by Ξ. The whole semantic theory then becomes (being cavalier with parentheses):

$\forall x(Bound(x) \supset (T(x) \equiv \mathscr{F}(x))) \,\&\, \forall x(Bound(x) \supset (\Phi(x) \equiv \mathscr{N}\mathscr{F}(x))) \,\&$
$\exists\Xi((\forall x(Conj(x) \supset (T(x) \equiv \forall y(ISC(y,x) \supset (T(y) \,\&\, (\Xi(y) < \Xi(x)))))) \,\&$
$(\forall x(Univ(x) \supset (T(x) \equiv \forall y(ISC(y,x) \supset (T(y) \,\&\, (\Xi(y) < \Xi(x)))))) \,\&$
$(\forall x(Tau(x) \supset (T(x) \equiv \forall y(ISC(y,x) \supset (T(y) \,\&\, (\Xi(y) < \Xi(x)))))) \,\&$
$(\forall x(Neg(x) \supset (T(x) \equiv \forall y(ISC(y,x) \supset (\Phi(y) \,\&\, (\Xi(y) < \Xi(x)))))) \,\&$
$(\forall x(Phi(x) \supset (T(x) \equiv \forall y(ISC(y,x) \supset (\Phi(y) \,\&\, (\Xi(y) < \Xi(x)))))) \,\&$
$(\forall x(Conj(x) \supset (\Phi(x) \equiv \exists y(ISC(y,x) \,\&\, (\Phi(y) \,\&\, (\Xi(y) < \Xi(x)))))) \,\&$
$(\forall x(Univ(x) \supset (\Phi(x) \equiv \exists y(ISC(y,x) \,\&\, (\Phi(y) \,\&\, (\Xi(y) < \Xi(x)))))) \,\&$
$(\forall x(Tau(x) \supset (\Phi(x) \equiv \exists y(ISC(y,x) \,\&\, (\Phi(y) \,\&\, (\Xi(y) < \Xi(x)))))) \,\&$
$(\forall x(Neg(x) \supset (\Phi(x) \equiv \forall y(ISC(y,x) \supset (T(y) \,\&\, (\Xi(y) < \Xi(x)))))) \,\&$
$(\forall x(Phi(x) \supset (\Phi(x) \equiv \forall y(ISC(y,x) \supset (T(y) \,\&\, (\Xi(y) < \Xi(x))))))))).$

One could add further conditions so that the function would more nearly mimic the intuitive order in which sentences get truth values by, e.g., requiring that boundary sentences all be assigned the first ordinal, and that a true conjunction be assigned the ordinal one greater than the maximum ordinal assigned to its immediate semantic constituents, etc., but the resulting complication would make no material difference. So long as any function exists which meets the requirement above, truth and falsity in the interior can ultimately be traced back to the boundary using the local constraints. That is, from any interior sentence with a classical truth value, one can find a set of backward paths such that (1) every arrow on every path goes from a node assigned a lower ordinal to one assigned a higher ordinal and (2) the truth value of every non-boundary node is determined by the truth values of some of its immediate semantic constituents and the local constraints (truth functions). Every such backward path must terminate at the boundary, where the primary truth values originate.

The demand for such a function from sentences to the ordinals also rules out assigning truth or falsity to the spine of the infinite tree above. It is important, in this respect, that the function be to the ordinals, and not, say, to the reals. If the function were to the reals, one could easily assign numbers so that every sentence higher along the spine is assigned a number greater than its immediate semantic constituents. But one cannot assign *ordinals* to such an infinitely descending chain such that each node higher on the chain has a higher ordinal than those below it. If, for example, the top element, $B_1 \,\&\, T(a_1)$, were assigned the ordinal ω^2, then $T(a_1)$ would have to be assigned $N\omega + M$, for some finite integers N and M. After M downward steps, we would reach a node whose assigned ordinal is at most $N\omega$, and the next one down could be assigned at most $(N - 1)\omega + L$ for some finite L. Again, after L steps one would have to drop to $(N - 2)\omega$, and so on until one reaches $(N - N)\omega + K$ (i.e. K), and after K steps one runs out of ordinals. The key feature of the ordinals, in this context, is that every set of ordinals has a least member. This is why infinitely descending chains cannot be assigned ordinals such that each member of the chain has a lower ordinal than those above it. So our condition rules out assigning truth or falsity to problematic infinitely descending chains, even though they contain no cycles.

If one has a formal language with the truth and falsity predicates, various grammatical predicates, the function $\mathscr{F}(x)$, and a variable over functions from sentences in the language into the ordinals, the language can serve as its own metalanguage. Or at least, one can write down sentences in such a language that express the semantic theory which we have been considering.

The good news that one can write down the theory in the language is, however, matched by a piece of bad news. For the theory so expressed is, by its own lights, not true. That is, if one applies the method of semantic evaluation to the very sentences that express the semantic theory, those sentences mostly turn out to be ungrounded.

The theory of truth and falsity for boundary sentences, the theory modeled on Tarski's convention T, is not problematic. If every boundary sentence is either true or false, the sentence

$$\forall x(Bound(x) \supset (T(x) \equiv \mathscr{F}(x))) \ \& \ \forall x(Bound(x) \supset (\Phi(x) \equiv \mathscr{N}\mathscr{F}(x)))$$

will be true: the antecedent of the conditionals will be true for all boundary sentences and false for all other sentences, and the boundary sentences all satisfy the T-sentences. Therefore every instance of the universally quantified sentence is true, and hence it is true also.

The semantic theory for the non-boundary sentences, though, does not fare so well. Consider, for example,

$$\forall x(Tau(x) \supset (T(x) \equiv \forall y(ISC(y,x) \supset T(y))))$$

(we leave aside the clause concerning assignment of ordinals as it is not relevant here). Suppose the language contains the Truthteller sentence $T(\beta)$, where β denotes $T(\beta)$. Then one immediate semantic constituent of the sentence above is

$$Tau(\beta) \supset (T(\beta) \equiv \forall y(ISC(y,\beta) \supset T(y))).$$

Since $Tau(\beta)$ is true, the truth value of this instance is the same as the truth value of the consequent

$$T(\beta) \equiv \forall y(ISC(y,\beta) \supset T(y)).$$

Now consider the right-hand side of the biconditional. Since $T(\beta)$ has exactly one immediate semantic constituent, viz. itself, $ISC(n,\beta)$ is true when n is β and false otherwise. The only instance of $\forall y(ISC(y,\beta) \supset T(y))$ which could fail to be true is therefore $ISC(\beta,\beta) \supset T(\beta)$. Since $ISC(\beta,\beta)$ is true, the truth value of $ISC(\beta,\beta) \supset T(\beta)$ is just the truth value of $T(\beta)$, viz. ungrounded. It follows that the truth value of $\forall y(ISC(y,\beta) \supset T(y))$ is ungrounded, since none of its immediate semantic constituents are false and one is ungrounded.

$$T(\beta) \equiv \forall y(ISC(y,\beta) \supset T(y))$$

is therefore ungrounded, as a biconditional both of whose immediate semantic constituents are ungrounded.[4] It follows that

$$\forall x(Tau(x) \supset (T(x) \equiv \forall y(ISC(y,x) \supset T(y))))$$

cannot be true, since at least one of its immediate semantic constituents is ungrounded.

Similar arguments can be made for all of the other clauses of the semantic theory: take, for example, $T(\beta)$ & $T(\beta)$ and test the clause for conjunctions.

The semantic theory does not, at least, end up false. Again, take as a clinical example

$$\forall x(Tau(x) \supset (T(x) \equiv \forall y(ISC(y,x) \supset T(y)))).$$

In order to be false, one of its immediate semantic constituents would have to be false. All of its immediate semantic constituents are conditionals, and to be false a conditional must have a true antecedent and a false consequent. This requires that there be a sentence n whose main logical particle is the truth predicate such that

$$T(n) \equiv \forall y(ISC(y,n) \supset T(y)))$$

is false. The sentence n will have exactly one immediate semantic constituent, call it m. The truth value of the sentence cited above is then equivalent to the truth value of

$$T(n) \equiv T(m).$$

But given the semantics, this sentence cannot be false, since each side of the biconditional is assigned the same truth value. The sentence is either true (if n is either true or false) or ungrounded (if n is ungrounded), but never false. So the clause of our semantic theory concerning the truth predicate, viz.

$$\forall x(Tau(x) \supset (T(x) \equiv \forall y(ISC(y,x) \supset T(y)))),$$

turns out to be ungrounded if any sentence in the language is ungrounded.

The situation is now quite clear. In presenting the semantic theory we make claims whose natural translation into the formalized language yields sentences like the one we just analyzed. The theory itself implies that those sentences are not true. We cannot, therefore, be justified in making those claims because they are true. But we also, it seems, cannot be criticized for making the claims on the

---

[4] One could more swiftly prove that $T(\beta) \equiv \forall y(ISC(y,\beta) \subset T(y))$ is ungrounded by noting that $T(\beta)$ is ungrounded, and if either side of a biconditional is ungrounded, so is the biconditional. But it seems best to determine the semantic values of all of the relevant sentences here.

grounds that they are false. This raises a pivotal question, viz. *when is it permissible and when impermissible to assert ungrounded sentences.* By a judicious choice of rules governing such cases, we will be able to claim back almost everything that our analysis seems to have lost. Sentences like "All true sentences are true" and "All conjunctions are true just in case both their conjuncts, are true" (or the obvious translations of these into the formalized language), although not themselves true, can still come out to be what one is allowed to say.

Appendix B: On Ungrounded Sentences and Continued Fractions

We have seen that the sentence B_1 & $T(a_1)$ whose graph is

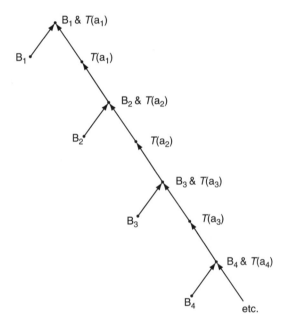

turns out to be ungrounded when all of the boundary sentences in the graph are true. (Again, a_1 denotes B_2 & $T(a_2)$, a_2 denotes B_3 & $T(a_3)$, a_3 denotes B_4 & $T(a_4)$, and so on.) This is because the truth value of B_1 & $T(a_1)$ is not fixed by the values of the boundary sentences and the local truth-functional constraints: making all the sentences on the spine true satisfies the local constraints, but so does making all of the sentences along the spine false. This conclusion may seem somewhat unpalatable: it is a common reaction to expect that the sentence B_1 & $T(a_1)$ should be true, thinking of it roughly as an infinite conjunction all of whose conjuncts are true. Perhaps the unpalatable conclusion can be made more attractive by noting a curiously analogical result that occurs in the theory of continued fractions.

Consider the "infinitely descending" continued fraction

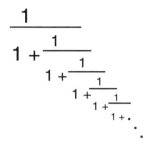

The structural similarity between this fraction and the graph above is evident. What is the value of this fraction? Since it does not have a bottom, we cannot calculate its value from the bottom up, as we would a normal fraction, but we have other techniques available. The simplest way to arrive at a value begins with the observation that the part of the fraction enclosed in square brackets below is just the same fraction again:

$$\cfrac{1}{1 + \left[\cfrac{1}{1 + \cfrac{1}{1 + \cfrac{1}{1 + \cfrac{1}{1 + {}_{\displaystyle \cdot_{\cdot_{\cdot}}}}}}}\right]}$$

If we call the continued fraction X, then, we get the equation

$$X = \frac{1}{1 + X}.$$

Multiplying both side by $1 + X$ yields

$$X + X^2 = 1,$$

or equivalently

$$X^2 + X - 1 = 0.$$

This quadratic equation is easily solved to get the two solutions

$$X = \frac{-1 \pm \sqrt{1 + 4}}{2},$$

so

$$X = \frac{\sqrt{5}-1}{2} \text{ or } X = -\frac{\sqrt{5}+1}{2}.$$

Finally, the obvious thing to do is to discard the negative solution as incorrect: the continued fraction must equal $\frac{\sqrt{5}-1}{2}$ (which happens incidentally to be the reciprocal of the golden mean). There is a puzzle about why we came up with two solutions rather than one, but the negative solution cannot possibly be right, so we seem to have satisfactorily determined the value of X. So speaks Common Sense.[5]

But suppose a voice rises up in opposition to Common Sense. The correct solution, says the Contrarian, is the negative root, $-\frac{\sqrt{5}+1}{2}$ (which happens to be the negative of the golden mean). The Contrarian asserts that Common Sense has blindly ignored the correct solution: infinite continued fractions have deep, counterintuitive properties, and by simply discarding the negative solution in favor of the positive Common Sense has chosen the shallow thinking of the mob over the subtle insights of the initiated.

Is there any way to justify the last step of the derivation and to prove to the Contrarian that the correct value is the positive rather than the negative one?

One might simply assert that since the continued fraction is constructed entirely from positive numbers using only the mathematical functions of addition and division, and since the sum of positive numbers is always positive, and any fraction with a positive numerator and denominator is positive, there is no way that the result could possibly be negative. Where, one wonders, could the negativity *come from*? The Contrarian, however, rejects this reasoning out of hand. *Finite* sums of positive numbers are positive, and *finite* fractions composed from positive numbers are positive, but (as the example shows, he insists) *infinite* compositions of these mathematical operations have other properties. Infinity has the power of producing the negative from the positive.

Common Sense next tries the following argument. Let us approach X by a series of better and better approximations C_i:

$$C_1 = \frac{1}{1}$$

---

[5] As Jim Pryor has very helpfully pointed out, just as a proper part of the continued fraction is identical to the whole fraction, allowing the substitution of X on the right above, so a proper part of the infinitely descending graph is *semantically isomorphic* to the whole, allowing a similar substitution. Let all of the boundary sentences in the graph be same sentence, viz. B_1. Then the part of the graph from what would now be the node B_1 & $T(a_2)$ on down has the same semantic structure as the whole graph. It is not identical to the whole graph, since each individual term a_n has been replaced by $a_{(n+1)}$, but that substitution could not reasonably affect the truth values in the graph. So the original sentence B_1 & $T(a_1)$ is the conjunction of B_1 with a sentence that says that a sentence semantically isomorphic to B_1 & $T(a_1)$ is true. We have, as it were, effective self-reference without literal self-reference. So we need only ask ourselves how we would semantically evaluate a sentence like η: B_1 & $T(\eta)$, when B_1 is true. But this is evidently just a form of the Truthteller, which is intuitively ungrounded!

$$C_2 = \cfrac{1}{1 + \cfrac{1}{1}}$$

$$C_3 = \cfrac{1}{1 + \cfrac{1}{1 + \cfrac{1}{1}}}$$

etc.

X is then claimed to be the limit of C_i as $i \to \infty$. Simple calculation shows that $C_1 = 1$, $C_2 = \frac{1}{2}$, $C_3 = \frac{2}{3}$, and then a bit of insight reveals how we go on. In general,

$$C_{n+1} = \frac{1}{1 + C_n}.$$

If we write C_n as $\frac{p}{q}$, then

$$C_{n+1} = \frac{1}{1 + \dfrac{p}{q}} = \frac{1}{\dfrac{p+q}{q}} = \frac{q}{p+q}.$$

In short the algorithm which takes us from C_n to $C_{(n+1)}$ is just the algorithm which takes us from $\frac{p}{q}$ to $\frac{q}{p+q}$, generating the sequence $\frac{1}{1}$, $\frac{1}{2}$, $\frac{2}{3}$, $\frac{3}{5}$, ... Since we get each successive denominator by taking the sum of the previous numerator and denominator, it is now easy to see that the sequence of C_is are closely related to the Fibonacci sequence 1, 1, 2, 3, 5, 8, ... Indeed, the sequence of C_is is nothing but the sequence of ratios of successive Fibonacci numbers $\frac{F_n}{F_{n+1}}$.

But it is well known that the limit as $n \to \infty$ of $\frac{F_{n+1}}{F_n}$ is the golden mean, so the limit of C_i as $i \to \infty$ must be the reciprocal of the golden mean, proving that X is in fact the very positive solution which Common Sense identified.

"Further", states Common Sense in an uncharacteristic display, "the deep connection between X and the Fibonacci sequence reveals the underlying unity of mathematical structure, a unity which would be lost if the correct value for X were the negative solution".

The Contrarian, however, is not cowed. "Of course the limit of C_i as $i \to \infty$ is the reciprocal of the golden mean, but the sequence generated by your 'successive approximations' has nothing to do with the value of X. Every member of the sequence is produced by mutilating X: the very infinite structure which is characteristic of X is simply cut off. It doesn't matter whether the cut is made sooner or later; the stump that remains once the infinite chain has been amputated is just a common everyday fraction, and an infinite sequence of such fractions gives us no insight into the nature of the sublime X. Each of your 'approximations' is fatally flawed, and they don't get any closer to being adequate simply by being made longer. The gap between the finite and the infinite is no closer to being bridged.

"Furthermore, your grasp of the Fibonacci sequence is as shallow and pedestrian as your grasp of continued fractions. The Fibonacci sequence is just one of an infinite number of Fibonacci-like sequences, and not by any means the most interesting one. Consider all normalized Fibonacci-like sequences, that is, sequences which begin with a 1, followed by some other number, and such that every other number in the sequence is the sum of the previous two. The generic normalized Fibonacci-like sequence, then, is

$$1,\ p,\ 1+p,\ 1+2p,\ 2+3p,\ 3+5p,\ \ldots$$

If the nth member of the regular Fibonacci sequence is denoted by F_n, then the nth member of the Fibonacci-like sequence is $F_{(n-2)} + F_{(n-1)}p$. In this universe of Fibonacci-like sequences, *all but one* diverge (as does the Fibonacci sequence) and in *all but one* the ratio of successive members of the sequence limits to the reciprocal of the golden mean. The Fibonacci sequence, then, is just a common, garden-variety member of the universe. There is, however, a single, unique *converging* Fibonacci-like sequence. This is the special mystical sequence, understood only by the initiated.

"If we want a Fibonacci-like sequence to converge rather than diverge, then the members of the sequence must always alternate between negative and positive numbers. For if there are two positive numbers in a row, the next in the sequence will be another positive number, larger than the first two. The rest of the sequence will grow without bound. Similarly, if there are two negative numbers in a row, the rest of the sequence will become ever more negative, without bound. So to get the sequence to converge, we must keep it perfectly balanced, alternating between positive and negative.

"It follows that for the sequence to converge, p must be negative, $1+p$ positive, $1+2p$ negative, $2+3p$ positive, and so on. Collecting together these requirements we have

$$p < 0$$
$$p > -1$$
$$p < -\tfrac{1}{2}$$
$$p > -\tfrac{2}{3}$$

And in general $p > -\frac{F_n}{F_{(n+1)}}$ for n odd, $p < -\frac{F_n}{(F_{n+1})}$ for n even. So the unique p which yields a convergent sequence is $p =$ the limit as $n \to \infty$ of $-\frac{F_n}{(F_{n+1})}$, and p must be the negative reciprocal of the golden mean. And in this single case and no other, the ratio of successive members of the sequence is always the negative of the golden mean. The ratio does not limit to the reciprocal of the golden mean, as it does for the Fibonacci sequence and all other Fibonacci-like sequences.

"Now consider the generic sequence of fractions

$$D_1 = \frac{1}{p}$$

$$D_2 = \cfrac{1}{1+\cfrac{1}{p}}$$

$$D_3 = \cfrac{1}{1+\cfrac{1}{1+\cfrac{1}{p}}}$$

etc.

By the same argument as was given above, D_n is just the ratio of the nth and the $n + 1^{\text{st}}$ member of the Fibonacci-like sequence which begins $1, p, \ldots$. If p happens to be the negative reciprocal of the golden mean, then $D_1 = D_2 = D_3 = \ldots = $ the negative of the golden mean. In that case, the limit of D_i as $i \rightarrow \infty$ is obviously the negative of the golden mean. But X could just as well be considered the limit of the sequence of Ds as the limit of the sequence of Cs. So the argument that X is the positive solution to the quadratic equation is not stronger than the argument that it is the negative solution."

"That's ridiculous" objects Common Sense. "Every member of your sequence of Ds contains the negative reciprocal of the golden mean, but X is composed only of ones! How can a number which contains only ones be considered the limit of a sequence of numbers each of which contains the negative reciprocal of the golden mean!?"

"But look at your sequence of Cs", rejoins the Contrarian. "Each one contains a part which is $1 + \frac{1}{1}$. X has no part that looks like that! So how can X be considered to be the limit of your sequence?"

"The part which is $1 + \frac{1}{1}$ is at the bottom of each C. In the limit, there is no bottom, so that just disappears."

"Yes, and in my sequence of Ds the negative reciprocal of the golden mean is always at the bottom, so it disappears in the limit as well, leaving just X. Your argument is still no better than mine."

"This is ridiculous!" expostulates Common Sense. "The continued fraction X is just a way of indicating the limit of the sequence of Cs. Its value is *by definition* the limit of the value of the Cs.

"Whose definition is that?" replies the Contrarian. "We started with a perfectly good mathematical demonstration which gave the negative golden mean as a solution, and you just decided to discard that solution with no justification. The original argument didn't make any mention of your sequence of Cs. And besides, if continued fractions are just ways of indicating sequences of regular fractions, then which continued fraction other than X represents my sequence of Ds?"

Let's leave Common Sense and the Contrarian to fight and consider the moral. The only reasonable conclusion, I think, is that the continued fraction X *is not a number at all*. It is more akin to a description like "square root of 4": there are two equally good square roots of 4, viz. 2 and -2, and neither has a better claim to be called *the* square root of 4. Or, to take a Russellian line about the definite article, there is no such thing as the square root of 4, although there are square roots of 4. Similarly, there is no such number as X, but there are two numbers which, as it were, *satisfy* X: $\frac{\sqrt{5}-1}{2}$ and $-\frac{\sqrt{5}+1}{2}$. X cannot properly be said to be either positive or negative: the continued fraction ambiguously represents each of two different numbers. X is, as it were, an indeterminate number, which is to say that it isn't a number at all, even though all of the Cs (and all of the Ds) are perfectly good, unproblematic, determinate numbers.

Normal fractions are evaluated "from the bottom up". Continued fractions, which have no bottom, therefore can become problematic, and display quite surprising behavior, even if every finite part of them looks perfectly ordinary. There is no principled way to impose a "top down" evaluation procedure on them, which is essentially what the use of the Cs and Ds was trying to do. Ultimately, we have to concede that continued fractions aren't really numbers at all.

Similarly, semantics is meant to be a "bottom up" procedure: start at the boundary and work your way in. Sentences with infinite graphs like B_1 & $T(a_1)$ can fail to have a classical truth value even though every finite portion of the graph looks ordinary and unproblematic. Just as the mathematical structure of X does not impose a unique mathematical value on it, so the semantic structure of the graph of B_1 & $T(a_1)$ (supposing that all of the boundary sentences are true) does not impose a truth value on it. B_1 & $T(a_1)$ is therefore ungrounded.

5 The Norms of Assertion and Denial

It is, in some sense, always appropriate to assert truths and deny falsehoods, or at least to assert claims one takes to be true and deny those one takes to be false. The sense in which this is appropriate *per se* and without regard to other circumstances is *sui generis*: surely no broadly moral or ethical or practical considerations could entail that to say what one takes to be true and deny what one takes to be false is always morally or ethically justified, or certain to maximize one's own, or humanity's, chances for success or happiness in various practical endeavors (unless the endeavor is just to assert the true and deny the false). There is certainly something *dissonant* about asserting a sentence one takes to be false, or denying a sentence one takes to be true, and a theory of these *sui generis* norms of assertion and denial which recommends asserting false sentences and denying true ones would face a considerable burden of explanation.

Furthermore, if one asserts that a sentence is true, one ought to be willing to assert the sentence, and if one asserts that a sentence is false one ought to be willing to deny the sentence and assert its negation. Without further explanation, one would not really know what to make of someone who asserts that a sentence is true but refuses to assert the sentence, or asserts its negation. *Prima facie*, such behavior would be incomprehensible, and the assertions made would have no claim to be taken seriously. These norms of assertion and denial should not be abrogated without reason.

These norms, however, are not broad enough to cover all possible cases. They tell us what to do with sentences we take to be true or false, but not what to do with those sentences, if any, which we take to be neither. These norms are silent about whether it is appropriate to assert or deny sentences that are taken to be ungrounded. If we come to recognize some well-formed, meaningful sentences as neither true nor false, then we must *expand* the usual rules governing the appropriateness of assertion and denial. We must lay down rules for when we should and should not assert ungrounded sentences. In the ideal case, those rules will be simple, complete, and will yield intuitively satisfactory results.

The project of formulating prescriptive rules for the assertion and denial of sentences is fundamentally different from the project that we have pursued so far. We have offered an *analysis* of truth: a complete account of the semantic structure of the truth predicate (the identity map from the truth value of $\mathscr{F}(n)$ to the truth value of $T(n)$) plus the additional constraint that all primary truth values be rooted in the truth values at the boundary. The T- and F-sentences then explicate the non-semantic state of affairs that must obtain for the boundary sentences to have the various primary values. Insofar as those non-semantic conditions are precise, the world induces a unique assignment of truth values to all of the sentences in the language.

But the project of formulating rules governing the assertion and denial of sentences will not offer an *analysis* but rather an *ideal*. The ideal specifies properties that we would like our rules to have: it remains uncommitted about whether those ideals can, in fact, be achieved. Rules can be *criticized* insofar as they fail to fulfill the ideal, and one would rationally replace a set of rules with another if the second does sometimes better and never worse with respect to satisfying the ideal. But it may be that no rules, or alternatively that several sets of rules, satisfy the ideal. And it may be that no set of rules can do better than all others with respect to satisfying the ideal. Our problem now is to articulate the ideal as clearly as possible.

As argued above, there are two obvious aspirations in the ideal:

- We would like the rules to be *truth-permissive*: they should allow the assertion of any true sentence.
- We would like the rules to be *falsity-forbidding*: they should prohibit the assertion of any false sentence.

If the language were bivalent, then it appears that we would be done: if every sentence is either true or false, then every sentence would be either permitted or forbidden.[1] But having abandoned bivalence, we need to add criteria by which we can evaluate rules for asserting ungrounded sentences. Since we are not representing that all of these desiderata can be *met*, there is no harm in listing whatever properties we would like the rules to have.

In addition to being truth-permissive and falsity-forbidding, then

- We would like the rules to be *complete*: they should render a decision about every sentence, either permitting or forbidding that it be asserted.
- We would like the rules to be *pragmatically coherent*: they should not have as a consequence that the assertion of any sentence is both permitted and forbidden.
- We would like the rules to *mimic the logical particles*: if a sentence is permitted, then its negation ought to be forbidden, if a conjunction is permitted, then both conjuncts should be, and so on. Considering (as

---

[1] In fact, the situation is not so simple. Even if a language were bivalent, it might not be possible to meet the desiderata of being truth-permissive and falsity-forbidding. We will confront this problem when we take up the permissivity paradoxes in Ch. 8.

we do) the truth predicate as a logical particle, we would similarly like it to be the case that if $\mathscr{F}(n)$ be permitted, so should $T(n)$.

- We would like the rules to be *simple*.
- We would like the rules to *harmonize with the statement of the semantic theory*: they should permit the assertion of those sentences which we use to convey the theory of truth.

Perhaps unsurprisingly, it is impossible to simultaneously satisfy all of the criteria listed in the ideal. If we could, then we could presumably revert to a bivalent semantics: let all of the sentences permitted by the rules be true and all of those forbidden be false. But no bivalent semantics is adequate to deal with the Liar and other paradoxes. So we will have to give up something when formulating our rules for assertion and denial. The question is what we should give up.

The simplest rules are blanket prescriptions: one ought to assert *all* true sentences and deny *all* false ones. If we are to meet the criterion of coherence with the statement of the semantic theory no such blanket prescription is adequate to ungrounded sentences. The Liar, I claim, is ungrounded, it is not true and it is not false. It would be incorrect to say that the Liar is not ungrounded, that it is true, or that it is false. *All* of these claims are ungrounded, according to my theory, so I deem it correct to assert some ungrounded sentences and not others. Indeed, I *believe* what is expressed by some ungrounded sentences and not others. I believe that all true sentences are true, and (in the test case discussed above in Chapter 3) that every true sentence uttered by Maxwell was uttered by Clio. I do not believe that not all true sentences are true. I also believe that all of these sentences are ungrounded. So whatever rules there may be for the appropriate assertion or denial, or belief or disbelief, of ungrounded sentences, they are not simple blanket rules advising the same attitude toward all ungrounded sentences.

Extremely simple and adequate rules are, however, available. Given the language that we have so far, only one of the criteria listed above needs to be relaxed: the desire to mimic the logical structure of the truth predicate when we are concerned even with ungrounded sentences. The key to formulating the relevant rule can be found in a single observation: when a sentence is ungrounded, it can be appropriate to assert the sentence, but not to assert that the sentence is true. It is, for example, appropriate to assert that the Liar is not true, i.e. to assert $\sim T(\lambda)$, i.e. to assert the Liar itself. It is not appropriate to assert that the Liar is true, i.e. $T(\lambda)$. So even though $T(n)$ is always *true* when $\mathscr{F}(n)$ is true, it is not the case that $T(n)$ is always *appropriate to assert* when $\mathscr{F}(n)$ is appropriate to assert. The T-Inferences always preserve truth, but they do not always preserve appropriateness.

If a sentence is ungrounded, then it is not appropriate to assert that the sentence is true or that the sentence is false. The claim that an ungrounded sentence is either true or false, such as $T(\lambda)$ or $\Phi(\lambda)$, is, we shall say, *impermissible*.

If a sentence is ungrounded, then it is appropriate to say that it is ungrounded. So a sentence such as $Y(\lambda)$, although itself ungrounded, is *permissible*. If the truth, falsity, and ungroundedness predicates are the only semantic predicates in the language (as they should be, if there are only three truth values), then we have just given exhaustive rules for the permissibility or impermissibility of atomic ungrounded sentences. Furthermore, since we demand that it be appropriate to assert all true sentences and deny all false sentences, once the truth values of the sentences of a language are settled, the permissibility or impermissibility of *all* the atomic sentences of our formal language has been settled.

And once the permissibility or impermissibility of all atomic sentences has been settled, the permissibility or impermissibility of all the rest of the sentences is easily defined. Permissibility and impermissibility for non-atomic sentences behave just like truth and falsity with respect to all logical particles save the truth predicate. A conjunction is permissible just in case both conjuncts are, impermissible otherwise. A disjunction is permissible if either disjunct is, and impermissible otherwise. A negation is permissible if the sentence negated is impermissible, and vice versa. A universally quantified sentence is permissible if all of its instances are, and impermissible if any instance is. Once we have settled the permissibility or impermissibility of the atomic sentences (including the semantic atomic sentences) the rest of the language follows suit in the usual way.

The rule for permissibility and impermissibility of ungrounded sentences is so simple and obvious that it is almost impossible to avoid once the right question has been asked. And indeed, the rule given above has, in a certain sense, already been advocated by Saul Kripke. What we have done corresponds formally to what Kripke calls "closing off the truth predicate". That is, our permissible sentences are exactly those which are true if one uses the closed-off predicate, and the impermissible ones are false using the closed-off predicate. The problem with Kripke's presentation is not in the formal rule, but in the interpretation of what the rule is doing. Kripke saw that, at the end of the day, one wants to assert some sentences which, using the original truth predicate, have no truth value. *And he tacitly assumes that the only way one can make it appropriate to assert a sentence is to make it true.* He therefore has to replace the original truth predicate, whose extension and antiextension do not exhaust the set of wffs, with the "closed-off" predicate whose extension and antiextension do. And Kripke further asserts that "it is certainly reasonable to suppose that it is really the metalanguage predicate that expresses the 'genuine' concept of truth for the closed-off object language" (Martin 1984: 81). As we have already remarked, this wrecks the whole theory: the so-called Liar sentence which Kripke analyzes, since it *does not* use the closed-off predicate, evidently does not "genuinely" say of itself that it is not true. The problem Kripke solves is suddenly not the one we were interested in.

One can get just the effect Kripke wants without the complications by taking ungrounded sentences seriously as neither true nor false, and constructing rules of assertion that do not require that only true sentences can be appropriately stated. The rules given above achieve exactly this end.[2]

In the language we have constructed, no paradoxes or unsatisfiable cycles can arise in these judgments of permissibility and impermissibility since they are not required to follow the T-Inferences. Here is an exact image of what we have done. Take the graph of the language, assign truth values to all the nodes in accordance with our rules, then snip out the arrows which connect every atomic semantic sentence to its immediate semantic constituent. The resulting graph contains no cycles and no infinitely descending chains, since the remaining arrows always run from sentences with fewer grammatical parts to sentences with more. Every sentence in the resulting graph is safe: all backward paths terminate at a boundary (i.e. at an atomic sentence). Now assign the values P and I to the boundary of the new graph by these rules: if an atomic sentence is true, it gets assigned a P, if false it gets assigned an I, if ungrounded, then it is assigned an I if it contains the truth or falsity predicate, and a P if it contains the predicate for ungroundedness. Once the boundary values are set, the P and I values migrate up the graph according to the usual rules for truth and falsity.

This procedure for deciding whether a sentence is permissible or not is simple, unambiguous, and intrinsically plausible. Further, it yields a definite decision for every sentence in the language. Among these decisions are:

- If $\mathscr{F}(n)$ is an ungrounded sentence, one is permitted to assert $Y(n)$, $\sim T(n)$, and $\sim \Phi(n)$, and one is not permitted to assert $\sim Y(n)$, $T(n)$, or $\Phi(n)$.[3]
- If $\mathscr{F}(n)$ is a true sentence, one is permitted to assert $T(n)$, $\sim \Phi(n)$, and $\sim Y(n)$, and one is not permitted to assert $\sim T(n)$, $\Phi(n)$, or $Y(n)$.

[2] Given that the method for determining whether a sentence is permissible or not is technically identical to Kripke's method of closing off the truth predicate, it is perhaps appropriate to expand a bit on the relation between this theory and Kripke's. On the one hand, the formal machinery, including the use of fixed-point theorems, is obviously shared by the two approaches. On the other, the theories differ at a level of fine detail (e.g. whether one must choose between the Weak and Strong Kleene connectives or can include both in the language, whether supervaluational techniques are allowable), of technical outlook (e.g. whether there are global constraints in addition to the local constraints on a graph), and of broad metaphysical commitment (e.g. whether there are more than two truth values). I would not be upset if the reader regards this chapter as better entitled "Detailed Working Drawings of a Theory of Truth", i.e. as a specification of Kripke's "Outline of a Theory of Truth". But there are sufficient differences between the approaches for one reasonably to regard this as a repudiation, rather than a refinement, of Kripke's. I would not be upset if the reader took this attitude either.

[3] We are being sloppy about the use of n here, but in an obvious way. One can replace n with any singular term that denotes a sentence in the language.

- If $\mathscr{F}(\mu)$ is a false sentence, one is permitted to assert $\Phi(n)$, $\sim T(n)$, and $\sim Y(n)$, and one is not permitted to assert $\sim\Phi(n)$, $T(n)$, or $Y(n)$.
- No matter what the values of the boundary sentences are, one is permitted to assert $\forall x(T(x) \supset T(x))$: "All true sentences are true" is permissible *a priori*.
- Given the boundary values stipulated for the test case, $\forall x((T(x) \ \& \ M(x)) \supset C(x))$ can be asserted: one can properly say that every true sentence uttered by Maxwell was uttered by Clio, even though this sentence is ungrounded.

In short, most of the things that we originally want to say we can indeed appropriately say. It is appropriate to say that all true sentences are true, and that the Liar is not true and not false, and that (in the case described) all the true sentences uttered by Maxwell were uttered by Clio. It is also appropriate to *believe* these sentences, to defend them in argument, and so on. It is appropriate to assert and believe and defend these sentences even though they are not true. It is not, of course, appropriate to say, or believe, or defend the claim that these sentences are *true*: they are not. And this is a bit jarring: if we have to deal only with true or false sentences, then whenever it is appropriate to assert a sentence it is appropriate to assert that it is true. Once we consider ungrounded sentences, we find that this is no longer the case.

With respect to the Liar sentence, this comes as a great relief. The obvious thing one wants to say about the Liar is that it is neither true nor false. And it follows from this that it is not true. And it *logically* follows from that (i.e. it follows by a *valid, truth-preserving inference*) that it is true that the Liar is not true. And it follows from that by another valid inference that the Liar is true. That is, the sequence

$$\sim(T(\lambda) \vee \Phi((\lambda)) \rightarrow \sim T(\lambda) \rightarrow T(^\lceil \sim T(\lambda)^\rceil) \rightarrow T(\lambda)$$

is a sequence of valid inferences, since $^\lceil \sim T(\lambda)^\rceil$ and λ denote one and the same sentence (i.e. since $\mathscr{F}(\lambda) = \sim T(\lambda)$). But the *validity* of these inferences simply guarantees that they are *truth-preserving*: if the initial sentence is true, so are all of the rest. That is trouble if the initial sentence *is* true: both $T(\lambda)$ and its negation would then have to be true, which is inconsistent with the truth function which defines negation. But the initial sentence in this chain is not true: it, and all that follow it, are ungrounded. The initial sentence and the one that follows it (i.e. the Liar itself) are *permissible*, and the last two are *impermissible*, so one never ends up asserting both a sentence and its negation. The age-old source of the Liar paradox is that one wants both to assert the Liar and to assert that the Liar is not true: indeed, asserting one and the same sentence, the Liar itself, does both jobs. So it must sometimes be appropriate to assert a sentence and assert that it is not true. Our rules provide for exactly this result.

Concerning the Liar itself, then, one could not ask for a better result. Not all the results are so intuitively pleasing. We can properly say that all true sentences are true and properly deny that some true sentence is not true, but we cannot properly assert that either of these claims is itself true. No doubt, we pre-analytically take "All true sentences are true" to be true, and so we have to abandon some of our original opinions. But on the other hand, the semantic theory explains *why* "All true sentences are true" is ungrounded in a perfectly clear and comprehensible way: once it gets translated as $\forall x(T(x) \supset T(x))$, the cycle in the graph of the language is obvious, as is the fact that no instance will be false. Abandoning the belief that "All true sentences are true" is true is a reasonable price to pay for clarity and consistency in semantics; abandoning the belief that all true sentences are true would not be. Fortunately, the latter is not recommended by the theory.

The importance of recognizing that some ungrounded sentences are permissible and others impermissible cannot be overstated. In *Truth, Vagueness and Paradox*, Vann McGee begins his investigation of the Liar with two methodological criteria of adequacy for any theory of truth. These are:

(P1) A satisfactory theory should never make claims that manifestly contradict clear observations.

(P2) A satisfactory theory should never make claims that are, according to theory itself, untrue.

(McGee 1990: 5)

He further makes clear in an accompanying footnote that "untrue" means "not true" rather than false, so the Liar, and all other ungrounded sentences, count as untrue. Our own theory therefore fails to satisfy (P2). McGee makes use of this principle when discussing a three-valued interpretation of Kripke's theory. Such a theory, he says, cannot assert:

If a conjunction is true then both conjuncts are true.

Nor even:

Every true sentence is a true sentence. (Cf. Ibid. 102.)

But what McGee fails to do is motivate (P2). Our own theory satisfies the following principles:

(P2′) A satisfactory theory should never make claims that are, according to the theory itself, false.

(P2*) A satisfactory theory should never make claims that, according to normative rules that have been adopted for assertion and denial, it ought not to make.

In order to reject our theory for failing to satisfy (P2) one would have to argue that satisfying (P2′) and (P2*) is not sufficient. Of course, no such argument can be made without some actual theory in view, otherwise the way that (P2) fails and (P2′) and (P2*) hold cannot be understood. I hope that the sort of theory outlined here simply never occurred to McGee, and he would be willing to amend his principles. If not, we need a clear reason why.

The rules for permissibility entail that some predicates that are truth-functionally equivalent are not substitutable *salva permissibilitate*. This is particularly noticeable for the semantic predicates themselves. $\sim T(n)$ is truth-functionally equivalent to $\Phi(n)$: each is true if $\mathscr{F}(n)$ is false, false if $\mathscr{F}(n)$ is true, and ungrounded if $\mathscr{F}(n)$ is ungrounded. But one cannot always replace $\sim T(\dots)$ with $\Phi(\dots)$ in a sentence and retain permissibility. $\sim T(\lambda)$ is permissible while $\Phi(\lambda)$ is not. One can appropriately say that the Liar is not true, but not that it is false. One can appropriately (but not necessarily truly) say of any sentence that it is either true or not true, but one cannot appropriately say of any ungrounded sentence that it is either true or false. "False" does not mean the same as "not true", even though the two predicates are associated with the same truth functions. The notion of meaning must therefore take in more than just truth conditions: for two sentences to have the same meaning, they must not only be guaranteed to have the same truth value, but also guaranteed to be either both permissible or both impermissible.

The difference between "False" and "Not True" with respect to the rules for permissibility means that we need more than one semantic predicate. In order to be semantically complete, in order to be able to express all we wish to express, a language must contain more than just the truth predicate. Adding the falsity predicate to a language does not change its *truth-functional* power at all: every sentence containing the falsity predicate is logically guaranteed to have the same truth value as the sentence produced by substituting $\Phi(\dots)$ everywhere with $\sim T(\dots)$. But still, without the falsity predicate, the language is not *expressively complete*: one cannot appropriately say some things one would like to. (Adding the ungroundedness predicate on top of these two, however, does not increase expressive power: $Y(n)$ is both truth-functionally and expressively equivalent to $\sim T(n)$ & $\sim \Phi(n)$.)

The fact that $\Phi(\dots)$ and $\sim T(\dots)$ can be interchanged *salva veritate* but not *salva permissibilitate* puts an interesting light on one line of argument concerning the Liar paradox. Brian Skyrms, in "Intensional Aspects of Semantical Self-Reference" (1984), argues that discussions of the Liar sentence involve the sort of opaque contexts familiar from intensional locutions:

What would be required of a theory, for that theory to give the result that the Liar sentence is neither true nor false, and that we can say so truly and without equivocation? Let the Liar sentence in question be:

    (1) (1) is not true.

And consider:

    (2) "(1) is not true" is not true.

Intuitively, we want (1) to be neither true nor false, and (2) to be true. Since one can move between (1) and (2) by substitution of coreferential singular terms, such a theory must be *intensional*. (Skyrms 1984, in Martin 1984: 119)

On our theory, one can say *appropriately* but not *truly* that the Liar is not true, and one can say so using the Liar sentence itself. Furthermore, on our theory, there is never any change in either truth value or permissibility if one replaces a singular term with a coreferential term: that sort of intensionality is banished. Nor does the *truth value* of any sentence change if one replaces a predicate with a coextensive predicate. But the *permissibility* of a sentence can change on account of such a substitution, e.g. when replacing the $\Phi(\dots)$ in $\Phi(\lambda)$ with $\sim T(\dots)$. So the intuition that the Liar reveals intensional phenomena contains a grain of truth, but one must focus on predicates rather than singular terms and permissibility rather than truth value.

Recalling the three little quizzes with which Chapter 1 began, we can now begin to see a resolution. The first quiz invited the conclusion that "This sentence is false" is neither true nor false. That conclusion is correct: the sentence is obviously ungrounded. But the third quiz seemed to require that the sentence "This sentence is not true" be neither true nor not true: an impossibility. And indeed, it is never appropriate to say of any sentence that it is neither true nor not true, and is appropriate to say of some that they are neither true nor false. We can safely accept the conclusion of the first quiz, and must reject the conclusion of the last. Our semantics, and our rules of permissibility and impermissibility, allow this.

What of Kripke's claim that closing off the truth predicate reintroduces the language/metalanguage distinction? Presumably, he had in mind the fact that closing off the truth predicate really amounts to introducing a new truth predicate, one that did not exist in the original language. As we have seen, this leads to trouble since one then expects that a Liar sentence can now be constructed in the "metalanguage", with the closed-off predicate, and it is unclear how this Liar is to be analyzed. If the analysis of it requires a meta-metalanguage, then it is unclear that we have made any progress over Tarski.

We have not introduced a new truth predicate, so we do not immediately require any language/metalanguage distinction. We have, however, employed a new *concept*, viz. permissibility, and we have not yet introduced a corresponding predicate into our formal language. One naturally suspects that when we do, new Liar-like problems will arise. Indeed they will. But the nature of these problems is importantly different from the Liar paradox. We will defer discussion of the permissibility paradoxes for some time, until we have developed some of the formal tools needed to make the situation clear.

All of this may still leave the reader unconvinced. The fact that one cannot *truly* say that all true sentences are true is not the easiest consequence to swallow. But we still have one string left to our bow. Our investigation commenced with the observation that there is an inferential version of the Liar paradox and a semantic version, and that solutions to the semantic version (i.e. consistent recipes for attributing truth and falsehood to sentences, such as Kripke's scheme) may not obviously suggest any solution to the inferential version. We have now completed our account of the semantics of our language, and of the norms of assertion and denial. It is time to take on the inferential version of the paradox and examine inferential structure. We will find that the solution to the inferential problem strikingly reinforces our results—even the more unpalatable ones.

6 Solving the Inferential Liar Antinomy

The burden of the last four chapters has been to provide a theory of the nature of truth values and a semantic theory for a formal language that contains its own truth predicate. The problem of the inconsistency of standard logical inferences supplemented by the Upward and Downward T-Inferences has largely vanished from view. At long last, it is time to return to the problem with which we began. In the minimal language L, which supplements the standard propositional calculus with only a truth predicate and individual terms, the Liar can be constructed. But further, when the standard inference schemes for the propositional language are supplemented with the Upward and Downward T-Inferences, the whole becomes inconsistent. Proof Lambda allows one to derive both $T(\lambda)$ and $\sim T(\lambda)$ as theorems, and Proof Gamma, Löb's paradox, allows one to derive any sentence at all as a theorem using only the T-Inferences, Modus Ponens, and $\supset$ Introduction. One of the tests that our semantics faces is diagnosing the faults of these proofs, and suggesting the appropriate means to reform the inferential scheme. We will expand the solution to include a language with quantifiers once the key to the solution has become apparent.

When one examines proofs Lambda and Gamma of Chapter 1 for clues to solving the inference problem, one is struck, if anything, by an overabundance of suggestive features. What properties do these pathological proofs have in common that might be the key to mending the inferential structure? They both employ hypothetical arguments, i.e. inferences that use subderivations. They both begin those subderivations with hypotheses that turn out to be ungrounded (assuming the sentence X in Proof Gamma is false, which is the most problematic case). They both use the Downward T-Inference within the subderivation, and the Upward T-Inference outside the subderivation. So both proofs could be blocked by forbidding subderivations altogether, or forbidding them to begin with ungrounded sentences, or forbidding T-Inferences within subderivations, or forbidding derivations which use both Upward and Downward T-Inferences, etc.

This embarrassment of riches is, however, just an embarrassment. The availability of so many means of blocking these two problematic proofs leaves us without any clear guidance about how to proceed, without any plausible guess about which restriction will defeat exactly the problematic proofs while leaving the unproblematic part of classical logic intact. We must find a way to amend the inference schemes on a principled basis.

It is, I am told, something like folk wisdom among logicians that the problematic proofs are to be defeated by disallowing the T-Inferences in conditional proofs, i.e. within a subderivation. This diagnosis is made explicitly by McGee (1990: 216–22), albeit in the context of the full theory that he develops. (McGee makes a distinction between truth and definite truth, and demands rules of inference which are definite-truth preserving.) As we have seen, though, the T-Inferences are, on any view, valid (i.e. truth-preserving), so disallowing them looks unprincipled. If one can't use all valid rules in conditional proofs, why can one use some rather than others?

Furthermore, if our semantics is accepted then we can identify problematic proofs that don't use the T-Inferences at all. Consider the following trivial proof of $T(\lambda) \supset T(\lambda)$:

$$
\begin{array}{ll}
\quad T(\lambda) & \text{Hypothesis} \\
\quad T(\lambda) & \text{Reiteration} \\
T(\lambda) \supset T(\lambda) & \supset \text{Introduction}
\end{array}
$$

According to our semantics, this theorem is not true—it is ungrounded. So the rule of $\supset$ Introduction alone, without any use of the T-Inferences, is already invalid. The introduction of the truth predicate allows for the construction of problematic proofs, but the T-Inferences themselves are not the culprits. The weakness must lie already in the inference rules for the standard propositional logic.

Turning to Proof Lambda, if we remove the T-Inferences from suspicion, then we have hardly any choice but to blame the rule of $\sim$ Introduction for our troubles. If the Liar sentence is not true, then the application of that rule in Proof Lambda allows for the derivation of a theorem that is not true. But a wholesale rejection of the rule is not indicated: it works perfectly well in the context of classical propositional calculus. Let's consider why that is so.

The *justification* for $\sim$ Introduction from the point of view of classical logic is straightforward. Suppose one begins a subderivation with an hypothesis and subsequently reasons by means of valid (i.e. truth-preserving) rules of inference. Then if the hypothesis happens to be true, everything derived from it will also be true. But given that no sentence and its negation are both true, if the hypothesis is true one will not be able to derive (by means of valid rules) any sentence and its negation. So if one *can* derive a sentence and its negation, then the hypothesis is not true. *But since classical semantics is bivalent, and every wff gets assigned a truth value, any sentence that is not true is false, and its negation is true*. In classical settings, if one can reason from an hypothesis to a sentence and its negation using valid rules, the negation of the hypothesis is true. Hence one can assert the negation of the hypothesis.

In a semantics which admits a third truth value (such as ours) or truth–value gaps (such as Kripke's), this justification for the rule fails. The sentence $T(\lambda)$ is not true, yet its negation is not true either. Hence the use of the rule is not guaranteed to be valid. It will, of course, be valid if the hypothesis happens to be either true or false.

According to this diagnosis, it is a tacit presupposition of the rule of $\sim$ Introduction that the hypothesis of the subderivation is either true or false. If we are convinced that the Liar is neither, then the source of our difficulties is clear, although the solution is not yet to hand.

What we need is a sort of bookkeeping device to keep track of the sentences that must be either true or false for the inferences we have used to be valid. The most straightforward proposal is to keep the books explicitly, by writing next to every line in a derivation the relevant set of sentences. We will call this set the *index set* for the line, and will represent it as a set of sentences enclosed in curly brackets. So as a first approximation the rule for $\sim$ Introduction becomes:

$\sim$ Introduction

	A	Hypothesis
	•	
	B	
	•	(valid rules)
	•	
	~B	
~A$_{\{A\}}$		$\sim$ Introduction

We now indicate in the conclusion that we have assumed A to have a classical truth value.

This first approximation needs immediately to be amplified. The first problem is that we may have had to make similar assumptions when deriving B and ~B. If Δ is the index set for the line on which B is derived, and E is the index set for the line one which $\sim$ B is derived, then the rule becomes:

$\sim$ Introduction

	A	Hypothesis
	•	
	B$_\Delta$	
	•	(valid rules)
	•	
	~B$_E$	
~A$_{\{A\} \cup \Delta \cup E}$		$\sim$ Introduction

Proof Gamma does not use $\sim$ Introduction, so we have not yet solved the puzzle it poses. But a little reflection reveals that the rule of $\supset$ Introduction, just like $\sim$ Introduction, presupposes that the hypothesis of the subderivation has a classical truth value. If that value happens to be "true", and all of the rules used in the subderivation are valid, then every line derived will be true. Therefore any line derived by $\supset$ Introduction from that subderivation will be a conditional with a true antecedent and true consequent, and will therefore be true. On the other hand, if the hypothesis of the subderivation happens to be false, then any line derived by use of $\supset$ Introduction will be a conditional with a false antecedent, and will therefore be true no matter what the truth value of the consequent. But if besides true and false sentences there are others, such as ungrounded sentences, the justification of the rule is undercut. For suppose the hypothesis of the subderivation happens to have a non–classical truth value, or no truth value at all. Then the line derived by $\supset$ Introduction will be a conditional whose antecedent has a non–classical truth value, and whose consequent has an unknown truth value (valid rules of inference might lead from sentences that are not classically true to sentences that are true, or sentences that are false, or sentences that have no classical value). If, e.g., we derive an ungrounded sentence from an ungrounded sentence using valid rules (such as the simple rule of Reiteration in the little proof of $T(\lambda) \supset T(\lambda)$ above), then the result of applying $\supset$ Introduction will be an ungrounded sentence rather than a true one.

$\supset$ Introduction must therefore be treated just like $\sim$ Introduction: the hypothesis of the subderivation must be entered into the index set of the conclusion, along with the contents of the index set of the consequent. Schematically, the rule looks as follows:

$\supset$ Introduction

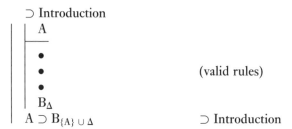

The intuition that the problems with Proofs Lambda and Gamma stem from the use of conditional proofs is correct: but it is not the appearance of T-Inferences within the conditional proofs which causes the problem. And on reflection, the problematic character of conditional proofs ought to have struck us even in the classical setting, for conditional proofs, and conditional proofs alone, *seem to enable us to validly infer sentences from no premises whatsoever.* If truth is ultimately grounded in the world, as we have claimed, how could we possibly establish with certainty that *any* sentence is true without at least tacitly employing suppositions about the nature of the world? The apparent ability of logic to conjure guarantees of truth out of absolutely nothing ought to be as puzzling as the apparent ability of geometry to reveal the nature of space *a priori* was to Kant.

That there may be valid inferences from one sentence to another is no surprise. The validity, for example, of both & Introduction and & Elimination can be read off from the truth table for &: If a conjunction is true, each conjunct is, and if both conjuncts are true, the conjunction is. Such valid rules of inference from a set of premises to a conclusion are not puzzling: they reflect how the truth of the premises, if they happen to be true, entail the truth of the conclusion in virtue of the truth-functional structure of the connectives. But the truth of some sentences *entailing* the truth of others is not the same as *establishing truth from scratch*. If an argument has *no* premises, if there is nothing going in, how can one possibly be assured of getting truth out?

This is particularly obvious in our semantics since there is no sentence whose truth is guaranteed by its logical form alone. Take any sentence and suppose that all of its immediate semantic constituents are ungrounded. Then the truth tables will imply that the sentence itself is ungrounded. If we somehow know that a sentence is true, we must somehow know that some other sentences have classical truth values. And if this further information has not been provided by any explicit premises, it must have been smuggled in as an assumption.

We have made that assumption and made it explicitly: we have assumed that every boundary sentence, i.e. every non-semantic atomic sentence, is either true or false. If that assumption should fail (as it might due to vagueness, ambiguity, etc.) then the foundations of classical logic are threatened as surely as if one admits ungrounded sentences. *The reliability of conditional proof is always tacitly based on assumptions about the world and the language, viz. that the world renders all boundary sentences either true or false.* It is now no longer a surprise that one can derive theorems from no explicit premises: the tacit premise about the world is inherent in the use of the inference rules themselves. We will explore this metaphysical presupposition of classical logic in some detail below. Let us first discuss the other inferential rules of L.

Given this analysis, the most problematic rules are rules that employ sub-derivations. The validity of other rules can be read off from the truth tables for the connectives, since the semantics is truth-functional. So, for example, the rules for & Introduction and Elimination are valid, as are Modus Ponens and Modus Tollens. Modus Tollens must be posited as a separate rule from Modus Ponens: the classical strategy for using Reductio and Modus Ponens to achieve the same effect as Modus Tollens fails, since the use of Reductio picks up an element in the index set:

$$
\begin{array}{ll}
\text{A} \supset \text{B} & \text{Premise} \\
\sim\!\text{B} & \text{Premise} \\[4pt]
\quad \text{A} & \text{Hypothesis} \\[4pt]
\quad \text{A} & \text{Reiteration} \\
\quad \text{A} \supset \text{B} & \text{Reiteration} \\
\quad \text{B} & \supset \text{Elimination} \\
\quad \sim\!\text{B} & \text{Reiteration} \\
\sim\!A_{\{A\}} & \sim \text{Introduction}
\end{array}
$$

The existence of the Weak as well as the Strong Kleene conjunctions, disjunctions, and conditionals also complicates the situation a bit. One cannot infer the negation of a Weak Kleene conjunction from the negation of a conjunct: as the truth table shows, this is not a valid inference. The same inference for the Strong Kleene conjunction is valid, but must be posited as a special rule. One can, however, introduce the same rule for the Weak Kleene conjunction if one also places the second conjunct in the index set: the rule is valid if the second conjunct is either true or false. Similarly, one cannot validly infer the Weak Kleene disjunction from one disjunct: the second disjunct must be added to the index set. Since the various Weak connectives (and "Medium" connectives) will not much interest us, we will not dwell on them: in general, the rules for them mirror those for the Strong connectives, with the additional constraint that in some cases the index set must be enlarged.

Similar remarks hold for the conditional: the inference from B to A $\supset$ B is valid for the Strong conditional, but must be posited as a separate rule, and similarly the inference from $\sim\!$A to A $\supset$ B. The rule for $\equiv$ Introduction requires subderivations in some systems, but we can adopt a system that eliminates those subderivations, instead using conditionals as premises. The rule of $\equiv$ Introduction runs as follows: if one has derived A $\supset$ B and B $\supset$ A, then one may write down A $\equiv$ B (with an index set which is the union of the sets of the premises).

The rule of $\vee$ Elimination deserves especial notice. In standard natural deduction systems, the rule runs as follows. If one has established a disjunction, and one has also constructed subderivations from each disjunct to a conclusion, one can write the conclusion next to the same derivation bar as the disjunction. Our system posits exactly the same rule, adding only that the index set of the conclusion must be the union of the index sets of the disjunction and the index sets which accompany the conclusion in the subderivations. The *hypotheses* of the subderivations, i.e. the two disjuncts, *are not* added to the index set of the conclusion.

This rule appears to violate our claim that hypothetical reasoning always presupposes that the hypotheses have classical truth values. But the rule for $\vee$

Elimination, unlike ∼ Introduction and ⊃ Introduction, *does not, in the stand-ard formulation, allow one to derive conclusions from no premises.* The disjunction itself must be established as a premise, and if the disjunction is true then at least one of the disjuncts is true. If the conclusion follows by valid reasoning from each disjunct, then the conclusion must be true, since one or the other disjunct guarantees it.

To justify the rule of ∨ Elimination, then, it is essential that a disjunction be true only if at least one disjunct is true. In some semantic theories, e.g. those using supervaluations, this is not so: in van Fraassen's system, for example, $T(\lambda) \vee \sim T(\lambda)$ is true even though neither disjunct is. If one decides to use such a semantics, then the rule for ∨ Elimination just given will no longer be valid. One could, for example, prove the Liar from the (supervaluationally) true premise $T(\lambda) \vee \sim T(\lambda)$ as follows:

$T(\lambda) \vee \sim T(\lambda)$	
$T(\lambda)$	Hypothesis
$T(\lambda)$	Reiteration
$\sim T(\lambda)$	Downward T-Inference
$\sim T(\lambda)$	Hypothesis
$\sim T(\lambda)$	Reiteration
$\sim T(\lambda)$	∨ Elimination

If one allows for true disjunctions neither of whose disjuncts are true, then one needs a different rule for ∨ Elimination: the rule would have to demand that both of the disjuncts be added to the index set of the conclusion. If each disjunct has a classical truth value, then at least one must be true for the disjunction to be true. This illustrates once again why the problem of inferential structure cannot be addressed without having a semantics at hand. It also illustrates a certain weakness with the supervaluational approach. Supervaluations allow one to *say* that $T(\lambda) \vee \sim T(\lambda)$ is true, but if the inferential system is consistent one will not be able to *reason from* $T(\lambda) \vee \sim T(\lambda)$ to any conclusion by using ∨ Elimination. Since both $T(\lambda)$ and $\sim T(\lambda)$ would enter the index set of any such conclusion, and since neither can ever be eliminated from an index set, no conclusion could be established with an empty index set (using that rule). So the "true" disjunction $T(\lambda) \vee \sim T(\lambda)$ would, *qua* disjunction, be inferentially impotent. The advantages of being able to *say* that it is true are therefore obscure: according to our semantics, that sentence, although it is a classical tautology, is not true. Our inference rules can therefore be kept simpler and more intuitive.

The inferential rules we have specified are therefore tightly tied to our semantics: other approaches to the Liar may not be able to adopt these very rules. The important point for solving the Inferential Liar paradox is to note that the rules for $\sim$ Introduction and $\supset$ Introduction, each of which uses a subderivation and each of which, in the standard systems, allows one to produce conclusions from no premises, both presuppose that the hypothesis of the subderivation has a classical truth value. The other rules come in two sorts: for the Strong Kleene connectives, the inference rules always *transmit* presuppositions, but never *create* them: the index set of the conclusion must be the union of the index sets of the premises (and, for $\vee$ Elimination, the index sets produced in the subderivations). If one wants similar rules for the Weak Kleene connectives, though, the rules must be modified. The index set of the conclusion must include not only those of the premises, but also any wff which is part of the conclusion but not the premises, such as the second disjunct introduced when using $\vee$ Introduction.

The Upward and Downward T-Inferences also create no new presuppositions: as we have seen, those inferences are valid even in a non-classical semantics or a semantics with truth-value gaps. The T-Inferences are to be completely unrestricted, although they too *transmit* the index set of the premise to the conclusion. If the language includes the falsity predicate, then we also need to add Upward and Downward F-Inferences. The Upward F-Inference allows one to infer $\Phi(n)$ from the negation of $\mathscr{F}(n)$ (which we have called $\mathscr{N}\mathscr{F}(n)$), and the Downward F-Inference allows one to infer $\mathscr{N}\mathscr{F}(n)$ from $\Phi(n)$. Since $\Phi(n)$ is true just in case the sentence denoted by n is false, and since the negation of the sentence denoted by n is true just in case the sentence denoted by n is false, these are valid inferences. They also transmit presuppositions but create none.

Using our new notation, we can now revisit Proofs Lambda and Gamma. Proof Lambda becomes:

$T(\lambda)$	Hypothesis
$T(\lambda)$	Reiteration
$\sim T(\lambda)$	Downward T-Inference
$\sim T(\lambda)_{\{T(\lambda)\}}$	$\sim$ Introduction
$T(\lambda)_{\{T(\lambda)\}}$	Upward T-Inference

We omit the index set on lines where it is null.

Proof Gamma also contains non-trivial index sets:

$T(\gamma)$	Hypothesis
$T(\gamma)$	Reiteration
$T(\gamma) \supset X$	Downward T-Inference
X	$\supset$ Elimination
$T(\gamma) \supset X_{\{T(\gamma)\}}$	$\supset$ Introduction
$T(\gamma)_{\{T(\gamma)\}}$	Upward T-Inference
$X_{\{T(\gamma)\}}$	$\supset$ Elimination

The conclusion of Proof Gamma is now not X *simpliciter*, but X conditional on the assumption that $T(\gamma)$ is either true or false. This is the correct result: If X is true, then $T(\gamma)$ is true, but if X is false or ungrounded, $T(\gamma)$ is ungrounded.

The definitions of validity and consistency for our system should be made explicit: the system is *valid* iff every sentence *with an empty index set* that can be derived from true premises (or no premises) is true. The system is inconsistent if some sentence and its negation are both theorems, *each with an empty index set*. It is the presence of non-trivial index sets in Proofs Lambda and Gamma which saves the system from inconsistency.

Deriving a conclusion we can safely regard as true demands deriving the sentence with an empty index set. The theorems of our systems are therefore the sentences with null index sets that can be derived from no premises. *Since the rules using subderivations all yield conclusions with index sets, and since every theorem requires use of a subderivation (all other rules require already established premises), if there are no rules for eliminating sentences from index sets, there are no theorems.* This is a welcome result, which answers the "Kantian" question of how we could have any *a priori* method for establishing the truth of sentences, given that truth and falsity are always rooted in the non-semantic world. The simple answer is: we cannot. Our inferential system only has theorems *if we add rules for eliminating sentences from index sets.* Such rules reflect a *presupposition* that certain syntactically specifiable sentences are either true or false. If we come to doubt that a class of sentences must have a classical truth value, we will revoke the relevant rules for reducing index sets, and correspondingly reduce the number of theorems. If we become skeptical enough to doubt that any boundary sentences must be true or false, we will simultaneously renounce any claims to *a priori* logical knowledge. In direct contrast to the Positivist dictum that logical truths are not about the world, we see that exactly because all truth is grounded in the world, without presuppositions about the world we will recognize no "logical" truths.

Rules for eliminating sentences from the index set are therefore extremely important: they reflect our assumptions about which sorts of sentences are guaranteed (somehow) to have classical truth values. Without such rules, the inferential system can play a role in deriving consequences from given premises, but none in establishing truth from no premises. Our fundamental assumption has been stated repeatedly: we assume that every boundary sentence is either true or false. We will therefore construct a system reflecting that assumption. If one raises doubts about that assumption, either because one takes some boundary sentences to be vague or meaningless or ill-formed, or because one doubts that there is any relevant non-semantic world to make the boundary sentence true or false (as one might doubt that there is any Platonic world of mathematical entities to make mathematical claims true or false), then the inferential system must be retooled to reflect that decision.

The first rule that we will admit allows us to change the index set, but not, in a deep sense, remove anything from it. This rule, which we call *Analysis*, permits one to replace any sentence in the index set with its immediate semantic constituents, if it has such constituents. The rule is justified by the truth-functional semantics: any sentence with immediate semantic constituents that fails to have a classical truth value, must have an immediate semantic constituent which fails to have a classical value. So if every member of the analyzed index set has a classical value, so does the original set. This rule is therefore permissible. (Note that the converse does not always hold: a sentence may have a classical truth value even though not all of its immediate semantic constituents do, e.g. $M(\lambda) \vee T(\lambda)$ when $M(\lambda)$ is true.)

The Rule of Analysis allows one to replace a negation in the index set with the sentence negated, a conjunction with the conjuncts, etc. It also allows one to replace any atomic semantic sentence such as $T(n)$ or $\Phi(n)$ with $\mathscr{F}(n)$. This single rule is therefore extremely serviceable. In L, it allows one to reduce any index set to a set all of whose members are atomic sentences. Furthermore, in our little language L (which has no quantifiers) a sentence is safe iff a finite number of repetitions of the Rule of Analysis on the unit set containing the sentence yields a set containing only non-semantic atomic sentences, i.e. boundary sentences. At that point, there is nothing left to analyze. So in L, a finite index set contains only safe sentences iff repeated use of the Rule of Analysis eventually gives out, leaving only boundary sentences.

The use of Analysis can never render a non-empty index set empty. It is founded on nothing more than the truth-functional character of the logical connectives and the semantic predicates. But we are now in a position to introduce a rule that reflects our main metaphysical presupposition that every boundary sentence is either true or false. The *Boundary Rule* permits one to *delete* any boundary sentence, i.e. any non-semantic atomic sentence, from the index set. We are allowed to do this without establishing that the sentence is true or that it is false: our substantive supposition is that every boundary sentence must be one or the other.

The Boundary Rule is, as one would expect, extremely powerful. Every safe sentence can eventually be reduced by Analysis to a set of boundary sentences. If those boundary sentences can be eliminated from the index set, then we can finally have theorems, and a rather powerful lot of them. If one restricts oneself to using Strong Kleene connectives, then the only way a sentence can get into an index set of a derivation is by being the hypothesis of a subderivation. And if those hypotheses are all safe sentences, then they can all be eliminated from the index sets by use of the two rules just introduced. Hence so long as one restricts oneself to safe hypotheses, one can ignore the index sets altogether: the rules of classical logic and the Upward and Downward T-Inferences can be used everywhere (including in subderivations) with impunity. Since almost all of everyday discourse consists in safe sentences, this explains why both classical logic and the T-Inferences should appear unobjectionable, and why the index sets can typically be ignored.

The Rule of Analysis and the Boundary Rule can be bundled together into a single *Expanded Rule of Analysis*: any sentence can be replaced by its immediate semantic constituents. Since boundary sentences have no immediate semantic constituents, the set of their constituents is the null set: boundary sentences can be deleted. We did not want to bundle these rules together initially, though, since the justifications of the two parts are so different: in the one case appeal to the compositional semantics, in the other appeal to an assumption about boundary sentences.

Unsafety, the impossibility of ever removing the semantic predicate by successive analysis, is the source of all ungroundedness. The simplest way to achieve unsafety is, of course, by direct self-reference, as with the Liar and Truthteller. Indirect self-reference will serve just as well, when a succession of analyses leads back to a sentence in the chain. Thus given the pair of sentences

ζ: $T(\eta)$
η: $\sim T(\zeta)$,

$T(\eta)$ analyzes into $\sim T(\zeta)$, which analyzes in turn into $T(\zeta)$, which gives back $T(\eta)$ again, and the process of analysis will obviously never end. But unsafety can also be achieved without any such cycles at all if one has an infinite set of semantic sentences, each of which analyzes into a sentence containing another member of the set.

Since the only way (given the rules as we have them, and restricting ourselves to the Strong connectives) for a sentence to get into an index set is for it to be a hypothesis of a subderivation, and since every safe sentence can be eliminated without remainder by repeated uses of the Expanded Rule of Analysis, that rule alone is as powerful as one could want if one restricts hypotheses to safe sentences. But even some unsafe sentences can be discharged from index sets, if they can be established as either true or false. We therefore also postulate the *Discharge Rule*: a sentence can be eliminated from an index set if it has been shown to be either true or false. To be precise, if one has derived $T(n) \vee \Phi(n)$ without an index set on a line, then one may discharge $\mathscr{F}(n)$ from the index set of any succeeding line. Since we have both the Upward T-Inference and the Upward F-Inference, as well as $\vee$ Introduction, this means that if we can establish either a sentence or its negation, we can dismiss that sentence from all succeeding index sets. And if we can manage to establish the disjunction $T(n) \vee \Phi(n)$ without establishing either disjunct, we can still eliminate $\mathscr{F}(n)$ from the index sets.

This completes our initial account of the inferential structure of L. We still have to enlarge L to include quantifiers, but before doing so, we should reflect on the metaphysical morals once more. The source of difficulty in Proofs

Lambda and Gamma is not the T-Inferences, which are perfectly valid, but the rules of ∼ Introduction and ⊃ Introduction, both of which use subderivations and both of which, in the classical regime, can be used to derive conclusions from no premises. Given that the difficulties with these proofs trace to the *classical* inference rules, rather than the rules that come with the addition of the truth predicate, one must pause to reflect why the problems do not show up in the classical propositional calculus. From one point of view, the answer is this: since the classical calculus has no semantic predicates, all of the wffs are safe sentences. Therefore the index set of every line derived can be reduced to the null set. In essence, the classical propositional calculus omits the repeated uses of Analysis and the Boundary Rule, which empty out the index sets, and writes the null index sets on the remaining lines in invisible ink. The rules of the classical propositional calculus are *abbreviated versions* of the rules of our system.

If this is correct, then even the classical propositional calculus presupposes the validity of the Boundary Rule, i.e. presupposes that all atomic propositions are either true or false. One does not notice the presupposition exactly because the use of that rule has been hidden in the abbreviation. One may then easily fall into the mistaken notion that classical logic allows one to establish the truth of certain sentences without any presuppositions about the world at all. This is not correct, and would be quite mysterious if it were. The irony, of course, is that the addition of the truth predicate to the language reveals the underlying presuppositions of the propositional calculus, and the content of those presuppositions. But the T-Inferences, like the messenger who brings bad news, have tended to be executed because of what they reveal rather than what they are responsible for. Those who respond to Proofs Lambda and Gamma by banning the T-Inferences, even if just from subderivations, have got the wrong culprit. The flaw lay in classical logic itself, so long as its presuppositions were not merely hidden but also unrecognized.

There is, of course, an irony in characterizing the question of how one could possibly use *pure logic* to establish truth *a priori* as "Kantian". Kant saw, quite correctly, that there was a deep puzzle about the contemporary notion that Euclidean geometry provides a system of *a priori* synthetic knowledge of space. Knowledge, Kant thought, requires a correspondence between our belief and the object of the knowledge, and if the object lay without the mind, there could be no way to be sure that the requisite correspondence held save through sensory contact with the world. In this, Kant was quite right. He then picked up the wrong end of the stick: instead of concluding that geometry is not *a priori* knowledge of the nature of space, and doing a service to both philosophy and science, he maintained that space could not exist without the mind, and led philosophy down one of the greatest cul-de-sacs of its history. Had he gone the other route, and cast doubt on the status of geometry as any sort of *a priori* knowledge, he might then have been led to another interesting question: viz. how is *a priori analytic* knowledge possible? If truth demands some substantive connection between the belief and the world, how could one know, merely by means of formal manipulations on sentences, that such a relation holds? And the obvious answer is: one cannot. Logic alone cannot establish the truth of any sentence. One needs in addition some substantive assumption, such as the Boundary Rule, about the relation between certain syntactically specified sentences and the world.

To complete our account of the inferential structure, we need to expand the little language L to include quantifiers. Having done so, the rule for ∃ Introduction is unchanged from standard approaches: from any sentence with an individual term one can validly infer a sentence which differs only by replacement of the individual term (in one or more spots) by a variable and appending the existential quantifier. If the premise has an index set, that index set must be carried down to the conclusion. Similarly, the rule for ∀ elimination is straightforward: if one has a universally quantified sentence on a line, one can derive any instance, again carrying the index set. This rule will be amended slightly in a moment.

The usual transformations between existential and universal quantifiers are obviously valid, and can be added to the rules.

The more problematic rules are those for ∀ Introduction and ∃ Elimination. The usual rule for ∀ Introduction has it that if one can derive a sentence with an individual term that does not appear in any premises, one can replace the term with a variable everywhere and append a universal quantifier. That basic rule still works fine, save that one also must require that the individual term not appear in the domain of the function $\mathscr{F}(x)$, otherwise particular information about the sentence that term refers to could be used in the derivation. There is also another complication. When one applies the rule of ∀ Introduction, the idea is to eliminate the "dummy" individual term entirely from the premise. The term must be replaced by a variable everywhere within the sentence. But what if the "dummy" term also appears in the *index set*? Then the derivation has presupposed that it has a classical truth value, and that presupposition must be reflected in the conclusion.

Here is a simple way to do that. When applying ∀ Introduction, the dummy individual term should be replaced by the variable everywhere, including in the index set. This may mean that the index set will contain formulae with unbound variables, but since the set is essentially only a bookkeeping device, that is not important. When one then *instantiates* the universal generalization, one again replaces the variable with an individual term *everywhere*, including in the index set. The relevant supposition is thereby represented.

It is easier to see how the rule works than to describe it, so let's examine the critical case: the image in our system of the classical derivation of "All true sentences are true":

	$T(\xi)$	Hypothesis
	$T(\xi)$	Reiteration
	$T(\xi) \supset T(\xi)_{\{T(\xi)\}}$	$\supset$ Introduction
	$\forall x(T(x) \supset T(x))_{\{T(x)\}}$	$\forall$ Introduction

Just as "All true sentences are true" turns out not to be true according to our semantics, so it turns out not to be a theorem of our inferential scheme. One cannot derive the sentence with an empty index set, and whenever one derives an instance of the universal claim the index set of the line derived will not be empty. Of course, if one instantiates using a term that denotes a safe sentence, then the index set can be emptied by Analysis and the Boundary Rule.

One can expand the Boundary Rule to include non-semantic atomic formulae with unbound variables. Thus, under our usual supposition, "All the sentences uttered by Maxwell were uttered by Maxwell" is a theorem even though "All true sentences are true" is not. The complete derivation would be:

	$M(\xi)$	Hypothesis
	$M(\xi)$	Reiteration
	$M(\xi) \supset M(\xi)_{\{M(\xi)\}}$	$\supset$ Introduction
	$\forall x(M(x) \supset M(x))_{\{M(x)\}}$	$\forall$ Introduction
	$\forall x(M(x) \supset M(x))$	Boundary Rule

The idea is that no matter what individual term is used to instantiate the variable, the result will be a boundary sentence, which can be eliminated by the Boundary Rule.

The only remaining rule is $\exists$ Elimination. The usual structure of that rule is to start a subderivation with an instance of the existentially quantified claim instantiated on a dummy term, and then derive a sentence in the subderivation from which the dummy term is absent. If so, then the relevant sentence follows validly from any instance, and hence can be written outside the subderivation. Again, the dummy term ought not to be in the domain of $\mathcal{F}(x)$ (else Analysis or the T-Inferences could be applied to sentences containing it). The dummy term must also be absent from the index set of the conclusion, and non-semantic atomic sentences with the dummy term can be removed by the Boundary Rule. Of course, the index set of the final conclusion must be the union of the index set of the existentially quantified premise and the index set of the last line of the subderivation.

Addition of quantifiers to the system is therefore tractable. It does entail one complication, though. Since quantified sentences can have an infinite number of immediate semantic constituents, the rule of Analysis cannot be applied to them in an index set. One could, however, add to the Expanded Rule of Analysis a clause that allows one to eliminate any sentence which contains no semantic predicates, since any such sentence must be safe. In essence, an infinite number of applications of the Expanded Rule, deriving an infinite number of boundary sentences and then eliminating them, can be telescoped down into a single step. With this addition, it becomes obvious that *every theorem of the classical predicate calculus (with no semantic predicates) is a theorem of our system.* For if one restricts oneself to sentences without semantic predicates, then no sentence in an index set can contain a semantic predicate, so every index set can be emptied by use of the amended Expanded Rule of Analysis. We can therefore construct an image of any derivation in the standard predicate calculus, which will differ only by the existence of index sets, all of which can be emptied out at the end. Again, the Expanded Rule is founded on both the compositionality of the semantics and the fundamental presupposition about boundary sentences.

As a final example of the consequences of our system, consider one of the "logical" puzzles mentioned above:

> Sam says "Sue is lying". Sue says "Joe is lying". Joe says "Both Sam and Sue are lying". Who is telling the truth?

The usual "solution" to this puzzle requires arguing first by *reductio* that Joe cannot be telling the truth, and then that Sue is telling the truth and hence Sam lying. We can formalize the puzzle in our language by naming the sentences used by Sam, Sue, and Joe σ, τ, and φ respectively. We then have for the function $\mathscr{F}(x)$,

$$\mathscr{F}(\sigma) = \sim T(\tau)$$
$$\mathscr{F}(\tau) = \sim T(\varphi)$$
$$\mathscr{F}(\varphi) = \sim T(\sigma) \ \& \sim T(\tau).$$

The "proof" in our system of the claims that Joe is not telling the truth and that Sue is runs as follows:

$T(\phi)$	Hypothesis
$T(\phi)$	Reiteration
$\sim T(\sigma) \ \& \sim T(\tau)$	Downward T-Inference
$\sim T(\sigma)$	& Elimination
$\sim T(\tau)$	& Elimination
$T(\sigma)$	Upward T-Inference
$\sim T(\phi)_{\{T(\phi)\}}$	$\sim$ Introduction
$T(\tau)_{\{T(\phi)\}}$	Upward T-Inference

If we didn't have the index sets, then $T(\tau)$ would be a theorem. But since the index sets can never be eliminated, our system does not allow one to "solve" this problem, as indeed it should not. According to our semantics, all three sentences are ungrounded: no one is telling the truth and no one is lying.

Again, the results of our examination of the Inferential Liar reinforce the results of the purely semantic analysis.

In Chapter 1, I claimed that consideration of the inference problem would allow us to triangulate on the correct account of the semantics for our language. It is worthwhile now to appreciate how strong these results are. Kripke's fixed-point method *per se* does not return a unique result for the extension of the truth predicate because there are multiple fixed points for his construction. Kripke himself mentions in a footnote that the minimal fixed point "certainly is singled out as natural in many respects" (Martin 1984: 77), but he does not propose to make any firm recommendation about which fixed point to accept. Familiarity with logic puzzles such as the one above breeds a natural attraction instead to the maximal intrinsic fixed point: in that fixed point, what Sue says is true and what Sam and Joe say is false. But once one is confronted with the inference problem, the situation reverses. If there are more than the two classical truth values, and one uses the Kleene valuation rules for the logical connectives, the standard rules of conditional proof become invalid. This is demonstrable even apart from any consideration of the T-Inferences: if one accepts that the Liar is neither true nor false, and adopts a Kleene valuation scheme for the horseshoe, then $T(\lambda) \supset T(\lambda)$ is not true even though it is a classical theorem. The method of index sets solves this problem in a perfectly principled way. But if we adopt the method of index sets to solve the inference problem, then we are in trouble if we try to hold on to the maximal intrinsic fixed point as an account of truth. Since Sue's statement is true in that fixed point, the inferential structure would be too weak to prove a necessary truth. Scaling back to the minimal fixed point is therefore recommended on grounds that are entirely independent of the graph-theoretic arguments with which we began.[1]

Having explained why the conclusions of many logic puzzles are not true, we might ask for the proper account of such puzzles. Vann McGee has pointed out (p.c.) that one can now understand the puzzles as demanding that one derive the *logical consequences* of the conditions for the puzzle, even though the conditions for the puzzle may be *metaphysically impossible*. For example, in the familiar "knights and knaves" type of puzzle, one is told that each inhabitant of the island either always lies or always tells the truth. This claim is naturally represented as

$$\forall x(\forall y(A(x,y) \supset T(y)) \vee \forall y(A(x,y) \supset \Phi(y))),$$

---

[1] In his discussion, Kripke recommends consideration of the nonminimal fixed points because "without the nonminimal fixed-points we could not have defined the intuitive difference between 'grounded' and 'paradoxical'" (Martin 1984: 77). As we will see below, the proper definition of "paradoxical" makes reference to the inferential structure, not to the semantics: a paradoxical sentence is a self-contradictory sentence (i.e. a sentence from which a contradiction can be validly derived) whose negation is also self-contradictory.

where $A(x,y)$ stands for "x asserts y". In the puzzle discussed above, the assumption is weaker: it is merely that everything said is either true or false, i.e.

$$\forall x \forall y (A(x,y) \supset (T(y) \vee \Phi(y))).$$

With either of these sentences given as a premise, one can, using the Discharge Rule, eliminate any asserted sentence from any index set, by deriving that the asserted sentence is either true or false. All of the classical inferences together with the T- and F-Inferences can therefore be used for asserted sentences and the index sets ignored. What escapes one's attention, though, is that the premises of the puzzle (i.e. the particular statements made together with the claim that every assertion has a classical truth value) are not metaphysically possible: if statements such as those in the puzzle above were in fact made, they would not have classical truth values. In a well-constructed puzzle, the premises are not self-contradictory, even though they are metaphysically impossible.[2] We will examine the notion of logical consequence further in Chapter 7.

The rules of inference are really rather obvious and straightforward generalizations of the rules of the classical predicate calculus, amended to take account of the possibility of ungrounded sentences. When we use a rule involving a subderivation (save for the rules of $\exists$ and $\vee$ Elimination), or one of the various rules for the Weak Kleene connectives, we tacitly presuppose that certain sentences are not ungrounded. The index sets simply keep track of those presuppositions. The Rule of Analysis allows those presuppositions to be replaced by others which entail them. The Discharge Rule can be used when the holding of a presupposition has been established, and the Boundary Rule reflects our generic presupposition that a certain class of sentences have classical truth values. In its final form, the Expanded Rule of Analysis subsumes both the Rule of Analysis and the Boundary Rule, and allows the immediate elimination of any non–semantic sentence from the index set. Doubtless there are other, more elegant, ways to construct an inferential scheme to reflect the semantics, but this will do to illustrate how the Inferential Liar antinomy can be solved in a principled way, and how that solution suggests the same counterintuitive consequences which appeared already in the semantics. In particular, the natural way to solve the Inferential antinomy has the consequence that "All true sentences are true" is no longer a theorem, which means either that the system must be incomplete or, as we have suggested, that "All true sentences are true" is not true.

---

[2] Of course, this account of logical puzzles is overly charitable. Since the valid rules of inference were not known when the puzzles were created, the intent cannot actually have been to use those valid rules of inference together with the metaphysically impossible presupposition. The intent, instead, was simply to use an incoherent set of rules, i.e. standard logic with the T- and F-Inferences, but without index sets. But at least we can now provide an adequate understanding of such puzzles as exercises in valid reasoning from metaphysically impossible premises.

Some Related Paradoxes

Proof Lambda and Proof Gamma are sterling examples of inferential paradoxes: employing only inferential rules that appear intuitively to be valid, they manage to derive contradictory, or evidently false, conclusions. According to our diagnosis, both of these paradoxes commit the same error and acquire their plausibility in the same way. They both rely on reasoning that uses a subderivation, and the subderivation begins with an hypothesis that, according to our semantics, is ungrounded. In such a case, the inference rule that discharges the subderivation ($\sim$ Introduction or $\supset$ Introduction) is no longer valid. The paradox is resolved when one amends the logic to include index sets. The initial plausibility of the argument is explained since the index sets do not become crucial to the inferences unless the language contains sentences that are neither true nor false.

There are other paradoxes that display somewhat analogous structures but turn on quite different errors. We will now turn to an examination of several of these. Some of these arguments employ premises that intuitively appear to be true but which (according to our semantics) are ungrounded. Some arguments replace the truth-functional connectives or semantic predicates in our original arguments with other connectives or predicates that seem to support similar inferences. For example, these arguments may replace the truth predicate with a predicate for *theoremhood* or the truth-functional horseshoe with a relation of *derivability*. Let's consider this latter move first.

Suppose one is using a system of inferential rules, which we will denominate Σ. And suppose that one regards these rules as truth-preserving. Then one will believe that any sentence which follows, according to the rules of Σ, from a true sentence is also true. Let us formulate this claim in a natural way within the formal language.

Let us use the predicate $Der_\Sigma(m,n)$ to denote the relation that holds just in case the sentence denoted by n can be derived from the sentence denoted by m in accordance with the inference rules in Σ. (Note that there is a slightly discordant inversion of order here: $Der_\Sigma(m,n)$ is true if n can be derived from m. The change in order helps to highlight the similarity to the horseshoe.) Then the natural way to translate the claim that the rules in Σ are truth-preserving is

$$\forall x \forall y((Der_\Sigma(x,y) \;\&\; T(x)) \supset T(y)).$$

Since we will be making extensive reference to this sentence, it will simplify things to give it a name. Let us call the sentence *Sigma-Validity*, since it expresses the claim that the inference rules in set Σ all preserve truth. If one regards the system of inferences contained in Σ as truth-preserving, then one would, it seems, naturally regard Sigma-Validity itself as a *true* sentence.

Furthermore, if one is using the set of inference rules Σ and one manages to correctly derive the sentence denoted by n from the sentence denoted by m (i.e. if $\mathscr{F}(n)$ is derived (with an empty index set) next to the main derivation bar in a proof which starts from $\mathscr{F}(m)$ as its sole premise), then $Der_\Sigma(m,n)$ is true. That being so, the following rule is certainly truth-preserving, for any set of rules Σ:

Der$_\Sigma$ Introduction: If a derivation begins with $\mathscr{F}(m)$ as sole premise, and uses only rules from the set Σ, and if the sentence $\mathscr{F}(n)$ is derived (next to the main derivation bar, and with a null index set), one may write $Der_\Sigma(m,n)$ on any subsequent line of the proof. Also, if one begins a subderivation with the sole hypothesis $\mathscr{F}(m)$, and one is able to derive $\mathscr{F}(n)$ with a null index set *without reiterating into the subderivation any premises or hypotheses from outside it*, then one may dismiss the subderivation and write $Der_\Sigma(m,n)$ on any subsequent line.

Since *Der*$_\Sigma$ Introduction divides into two different cases, we should comment on its structure. Let's begin with the second case first.

If one starts a subderivation on $\mathscr{F}(m)$ and can derive $\mathscr{F}(n)$ without any use of additional hypotheses or premises using only rules from Σ, then the sub-derivation *shows* or *displays* the fact that $\mathscr{F}(n)$ can be derived from $\mathscr{F}(m)$ by means of those rules. This use of a subderivation as a display must be sharply distinguished from its usual use in conditional proof, where a subderivation *adds an additional hypothesis* to those that are currently in play in an ongoing argument. In this latter case, the premises of the overall argument (or of any subderivation in which this one is embedded) are available for use in the reasoning. What is envisaged in *Der*$_\Sigma$ Introduction is rather a *demonstration* that one sentence can be derived from another in accordance with certain rules by so deriving it. This is a distinct—albeit perfectly legitimate—use of something that looks like a subderivation.

Once one sees the justification for the second clause of *Der*$_\Sigma$ Introduction, then the justification of the first clause is evident. If the proof one is constructing happens to start from a single premise, $\mathscr{F}(m)$, then the proof simultaneously can *derive $\mathscr{F}(n)$ from $\mathscr{F}(m)$*, and *demonstrate that $\mathscr{F}(n)$ can be derived from $\mathscr{F}(m)$*. That is, the proof itself can function as a display of what can be proven using the rules in Σ. Note that the use of the rule that appeals to the second clause, with a subderivation, looks suspiciously similar to the rule $\supset$ Introduction. There are, however, two salient differences. The first, as remarked above, is that *Der*$_\Sigma$ Introduction includes a restriction that $\supset$ Introduction does not: one cannot reiterate in premises or hypothesis from the outside. The second salient difference is that *Der*$_\Sigma$ *Introduction itself does not demand that anything be put in the index set of the conclusion*. If I can produce a subderivation from $\mathscr{F}(m)$ to $\mathscr{F}(n)$, then $\mathscr{F}(n)$ is derivable from $\mathscr{F}(m)$. This remains true no matter what *truth value $\mathscr{F}(m)$* happens to have. The validity of *Der*$_\Sigma$ Introduction, unlike that of $\supset$ Introduction, does not depend on the hypothesis of the subderivation having a classical truth value. This fact will be important in the sequel.

One final observation. In order for Der_Σ Introduction to count as a *formal* or *syntactically specifiable* or *computable* rule of inference, in order for it to be possible to check mechanically that the rule has been properly applied, there must be an effective mechanical procedure to determine that a given set of inferences can all be justified by application of rules from Σ. This means, of course, that each rule in Σ must be formally or syntactically specifiable, but it means more than that. It means also that one can check by some algorithm whether a given rule is in Σ. If Σ is finite this is straightforward, but if Σ is infinite, then there may be no effective procedure to enumerate the rules, and so no effective procedure to check if Der_Σ Introduction has been correctly applied. At the moment, this restriction on Σ will not affect us, since the relevant sets are quite small. But as we will see, the restriction to effectively enumerable sets of rules will eventually become important.

Since Der_Σ Introduction is obviously valid, one may add it to any set of valid rules and still have a valid set. Furthermore, one can use Der_Σ Introduction even if the set Σ includes Der_Σ Introduction itself.

The exact content of Der_Σ Introduction depends on the specification of the set Σ, and similarly the content of a sentence like

Sigma-Validity: $\forall x \forall y ((Der_\Sigma(x,y) \ \& \ T(x)) \supset T(y))$

depends on the rules which happen to be in Σ. Let us fix Σ to contain the rules of Hypothesis, Reiteration, $\forall$ Elimination, $\&$ Introduction, $\supset$ Elimination, Upward T-Inference, Downward T-Inference, $\sim$ Introduction, and the Boundary Rule. If one can derive $\mathscr{F}(n)$ from $\mathscr{F}(m)$ using only these rules, one is entitled to write $Der_\Sigma(m,n)$ on the next line of the proof. And if one regards this set of rules as truth-preserving, then one should believe Sigma-Validity. Since the rules of Σ (save the Boundary Rule, which I have invented) are standard rules of inference, it is hard to see how one can accept standard logic and not also accept Sigma-Validity.

Now the problem is this: if one regards $\forall x \forall y ((Der_\Sigma(x,y) \ \& \ T(x)) \supset T(y))$ as *true* and if one's set of inference rules includes the rules in Σ together with Der_Σ Introduction, then the deductive closure of one's beliefs is inconsistent. Furthermore, the inconsistency *cannot be solved by the use of index sets*.

Let us use χ to denote the sentence

$\forall x \forall y ((Der_\Sigma(x,y) \ \& \ T(x)) \supset T(y))$,

and further let the term ξ denote the sentence

$\sim Der_\Sigma(\chi,\xi)$.

That is, $\mathscr{F}(\chi) = \forall x \forall y ((Der_\Sigma(x,y) \ \& \ T(x)) \supset T(y))$ and $\mathscr{F}(\xi) = \sim Der_\Sigma(\chi,\xi)$. Then we have the following derivation from $\forall x \forall y ((Der_\Sigma(x,y) \ \& \ T(x)) \supset T(y))$ to a contradiction:

$\forall x \forall y((Der_\Sigma(x,y) \ \& \ T(x)) \supset T(y))$	Premise
$Der_\Sigma(\chi,\xi)$	Hypothesis
$\forall x \forall y((Der_\Sigma(x,y) \ \& \ T(x)) \supset T(y))$	Reiteration
$\forall y((Der_\Sigma(\chi,y) \ \& \ T(\chi)) \supset T(y))$	$\forall$ Elimination
$(Der_\Sigma(\chi,\xi) \ \& \ T(\chi)) \supset T(\xi)$	$\forall$ Elimination
$Der_\Sigma(\chi,\xi)$	Reiteration
$T(\chi)$	Upward T-Inference (line 3)
$Der_\Sigma(\chi,\xi) \ \& \ T(\chi)$	& Introduction
$T(\xi)$	$\supset$ Elimination
$\sim Der_\Sigma(\chi,\xi)$	Downward T-Inference
$\sim Der_\Sigma(\chi,\xi)_{\{Der_\Sigma(\chi,\xi)\}}$	$\sim$ Introduction
$\sim Der_\Sigma(\chi,\xi)$	Boundary Rule
$Der_\Sigma(\chi,\xi)$	Der_Σ Introduction

From $\forall x \forall y((Der_\Sigma(x,y) \ \& \ T(x)) \supset T(y))$ one can derive both a sentence and its negation. Let us call the proof above *Proof Sigma*.

At first glance, Proof Sigma looks rather like our original problematic Proof Lambda. But on further investigation, we see that Proof Sigma cannot be disarmed by the same method that defeated Proof Lambda. The fallacy in Proof Lambda turned on using the rule of $\sim$ Introduction for an ungrounded sentence. That fallacy can be avoided by the use of index sets. But even taking into account the index sets, Proof Sigma goes through.

Since the subderivation in Proof Sigma starts on $Der_\Sigma(\chi,\xi)$, which is a boundary sentence, it cannot be blocked by appeal to the index set. Furthermore, such an appeal would be wrongheaded. The rule of $\sim$ Introduction is invalid if the subderivation begins with an hypothesis that is neither true nor false, but a claim like $Der_\Sigma(\chi,\xi)$ is surely either true or false. Since the rules of Σ are purely formal or syntactic, any derivation can be checked algorithmically to determine if the rules have been properly adhered to. Indeed, $Der_\Sigma(\chi,\xi)$ is evidently true, since Proof Sigma itself displays one possible derivation from χ to ξ using only rules from Σ. The problem, of course, is that one can derive $Der_\Sigma(\chi,\xi)$, as well as $\sim Der_\Sigma(\chi,\xi)$, from χ if one has also accepted Der_Σ Introduction. And how can one deny Der_Σ Introduction? It is obviously valid. (One could include Der_Σ Introduction itself in the set Σ, although, as we have seen, this is not necessary to produce the contradiction.)

The solution to Proof Sigma, then, is not to be found in the rules of inference used. The rules of inference are all unassailable. The solution rather must be the recognition that the premise of the proof,

$$\forall x \forall y((Der_\Sigma(x,y) \ \& \ T(x)) \supset T(y)),$$

is not true.

This is a result that is already a consequence of our semantics. Sigma-Validity cannot be true because of cycles in its graph. One cycle becomes evident if we simply graph the sentences that appear in Proof Sigma:

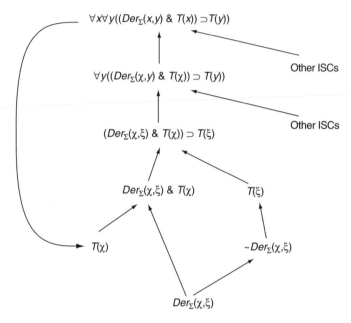

Since $Der_\Sigma(\chi,\xi)$ is true, we can see from this graph that Sigma-Validity cannot be true. It is at best ungrounded, assuming none of its other immediate semantic constituents are false. In order for one of its immediate semantic constituents to be false, there would have to be a *false* sentence that can be derived, using the rules in Σ from a *true* sentence. This, however, cannot happen, so Sigma-Validity is ungrounded.

The problem displayed by Proof Sigma demonstrates that ungroundedness cannot be confined to sentences, such as the Liar and the Truthteller, which are obviously problematic. There are also sentences such as Sigma-Validity, which we would intuitively take to express something true, but which cannot in fact be consistently held to be true. The *cause* of the ungroundedness of Sigma-Validity is not difficult to see, as the graph above illustrates, and the *necessity* of regarding Sigma-Validity as ungrounded is brought home by Proof Sigma. That is, one ought not seek to amend the semantics of the language to make Sigma-Validity true unless one is also prepared to amend the inferential system (how?) to block Proof Sigma. So our best course is simply to accept that it is not true, and for similar reasons even $\forall x(T(x) \supset T(x))$ is not true, although we naively expect it to be. (Proof Sigma also shows that attempts to secure truth for these sentences by using, e.g., restricted quantifiers are bound to run into trouble. If one writes the equivalent of $\forall x \forall y((Der_\Sigma(x,y)\ \&\ T(x)) \supset T(y))$ using restricted quantifiers, the graph for the language becomes unsatisfiable.)

Proof Sigma actually shows something even stronger than the existence of ungrounded sentences that we want to assert and to believe. Since both a sentence and its negation follow by valid inferences from Sigma-Validity, that sentence is not merely ungrounded, it is *self-contradictory* (given the existence of a sentence like $\sim Der_\Sigma(\chi,\xi)$). So sometimes it is appropriate to assert and believe even self-contradictory sentences, sentences which cannot consistently be maintained to be true. This highlights the fact that believing or asserting a sentence, and believing or asserting that the sentence is true, are quite different things. It may be appropriate to believe that one's system of inferences is truth-preserving even when it is provable that the sentence which says the system is truth-preserving cannot be true.

Having shown that Sigma-Validity, the sentence that is the most obvious translation of "The rules in set Σ are all truth-preserving", is not itself true, we are in a position to approach in a new way some important results in metalogic. Let the set Σ^* contain all of the rules of inference that one recognizes as valid. If that set contains the rules used above, then $\forall x \forall y((Der_{\Sigma^*}(x,y)\ \&\ T(x)) \supset T(y))$ will not be true. So if the rules are, in fact, truth-preserving, and if every theorem of the system is true, then $\forall x \forall y((Der_{\Sigma^*}(x,y)\ \&\ T(x)) \supset T(y))$ cannot be a theorem of the system. That is, if a system of rules is truth-preserving, and if it contains the rules listed above, then one cannot prove, using the system, the sentence which says that the system is truth-preserving.

This result misleadingly sounds like a standard result in metalogic: no consistent formal system can prove its own consistency. But this result is quite distinct, and is peculiar to the three-valued semantics. It is not that there is some *truth* stating the validity of the system which is not a theorem, but rather that the relevant sentence is not a truth at all. (If the system is truth-preserving, neither is the relevant sentence a falsehood.) Furthermore, if the rules are truth-preserving, the relevant sentence is *permissible*. For the only way that a sentence of the form $(Der_{\Sigma^*}(m,n)\ \&\ T(m)) \supset T(n)$ could be impermissible is for $\mathscr{F}(m)$ to be true, for $\mathscr{F}(n)$ to be derivable from $\mathscr{F}(m)$ according to the rules of Σ^* and for $\mathscr{F}(n)$ to be either false or ungrounded. But if the rules of Σ^* are truth-preserving, this cannot occur. So $\forall x \forall y((Der_{\Sigma^*}(x,y)\ \&\ T(x)) \supset T(y))$ says just what we want it to: that the rules are truth-preserving. $\forall x \forall y((Der_{\Sigma^*}(x,y)\ \&\ T(x)) \supset T(y))$ can be properly asserted only if the rules are truth-preserving. But still, $\forall x \forall y((Der_{\Sigma^*}(x,y)\ \&\ T(x)) \supset T(y))$ is not true, so no set of truth-preserving rules can be used to prove it.

It might seem at first glance that we have ameliorated the bite of the standard metalogical result. If no consistent formal system can prove its own consistency then, it seems, every such system must be *blind* to a certain important *truth*. But Proof Sigma demonstrates no such thing. We have not shown that Σ is incomplete, in that there are necessary truths, or truths of arithmetic, which it cannot prove, but rather that if the rules of Σ are valid, there is a sentence which *we naively and mistakenly take to be true* which it cannot prove. Nonetheless, even given the three-valued semantics, the standard result is not far behind.

Let's reflect again on what prevents $\forall x \forall y((Der_\Sigma(x,y) \ \& \ T(x)) \supset T(y))$ from being true. The problem is that there are ungrounded sentences that can be validly derived from other ungrounded sentences. For example, the Liar sentence can be validly derived from itself simply by Reiteration, so $Der_\Sigma(\lambda,\lambda)$ is true. $(Der_\Sigma(\lambda,\lambda) \ \& \ T(\lambda)) \supset T(\lambda)$ is a conditional with an ungrounded antecedent and an ungrounded consequent, and so is itself ungrounded. Hence not every instance of $\forall x \forall y((Der_\Sigma(x,y) \ \& \ T(x)) \supset T(y))$ is true.

The problem, once again, is that although we want the generalization to be *about* derivations from true premises, the quantifiers range over all sentences, including ungrounded ones. The conditional can become ungrounded when instantiated on these in the antecedent, even though derivations from *ungrounded* premises are intuitively irrelevant to the generalization.

One way around this problem is to focus not on whether all the derivations are truth-preserving, but rather on whether all the *theorems* of the system are *tautologies*. In standard bivalent systems, these two properties are equivalent to each other, since the inference from A to B is truth preserving in all interpretations just in case $A \supset B$ is true in all interpretations, and in the standard systems of inference B can be derived from A just in case $A \supset B$ is a theorem. Hence, in the standard bivalent semantics it is enough to show that all the theorems are tautologies to show that all inferences are truth-preserving. In our system, however, these equivalences no longer hold. Reiteration, for example, is evidently a valid inference, but not every sentence of the form $A \supset A$ is valid, or a theorem. So it turns out to be a different thing to ask if all the inferences are valid than it is to ask if all the theorems of the system are true.

Given the relation $Der_\Sigma(x,y)$ and given a single theorem, we can define a predicate which is true exactly of the theorems of Σ. For any sentence that can be derived from a theorem is a theorem, and any theorem can be derived from any other. So since $A \supset A$ is a theorem when A is a boundary sentence, we could define theoremhood this way:

$Thm_\Sigma(x) =_{df} Der_\Sigma(\ulcorner A \supset A \urcorner, x)$, where A is any boundary sentence. The claim that all the theorems of Σ are true would then be translated as

$$\forall x(Der_\Sigma(\ulcorner A \supset A \urcorner, x) \supset T(x)).$$

We could proceed in this way at the cost of a bit of tedium: one would show that a sentence is a theorem by deriving it from $A \supset A$ rather than, as we intend, by deriving it from no premises at all. But in order to streamline the proceedings, it will be convenient instead to introduce a theoremhood predicate $Thm_\Sigma(x)$ directly with its own introduction rule:

> Thm_Σ Introduction: If a derivation begins with no premises, and uses only rules from the set Σ, and if the sentence $\mathscr{F}(m)$ is derived (next to the main derivation bar, and with a null index set), one may write $Thm_\Sigma(m)$ on any subsequent line of the proof. Also, if one begins a subderivation with no hypothesis and one is able to derive $\mathscr{F}(m)$ with a null index set *without reiterating into the subderivation any premises or hypotheses from outside it*, then one may dismiss the subderivation and write $Thm_\Sigma(m)$ on any subsequent line.

Thm_Σ Introduction is justified in the same way as Der_Σ Introduction was.[3]

Just as there is a sentence in our language that naturally expresses the claim that the inferences of Σ are truth-preserving, so there is a sentence that expresses the claim that all of the theorems of Σ are true:

$$\forall x(Thm_\Sigma(x) \supset T(x)).$$

It is this sentence that will allow us to argue that if Σ is consistent, then it cannot prove its own consistency, and that this is a failure to prove a *true* sentence.

One way to approach Gödel's theorem informally is to start with a sentence which says of itself that it is not a theorem of a given system, and to show, informally, that if the rules of the system are valid the sentence is true (and hence not a theorem). We now can reproduce this informal reasoning formally. We begin with the *premise* $\forall x(Thm_\Sigma(x) \supset T(x))$ that all theorems provable by means of rules in Σ are true (let Σ be as above). We introduce a sentence, call it τ, which says of itself that it is not a theorem:

$$\tau: \sim Thm_\Sigma(\tau).$$

We can now prove that τ is not a theorem, and hence is true, *from* $\forall x(Thm_\Sigma(x) \supset T(x))$ *as a premise*:

---

[3] $Thm_\Sigma(x)$ is intended to represent the property of being a theorem of the formal system Σ, and to be true of exactly those sentences which can be proven using those rules. So there is a natural sense in which one might call $Thm_\Sigma(x)$ a provability predicate. It should be noted, however, that $Thm_\Sigma(x)$ is not a provability predicate in the sense in which that term is used by logicians (cf., e.g., Boolos and Jeffery 1989: 185). In particular, we make no assumption that every valid sentence in our language is a theorem of Σ. On the other hand, as Boolos and Jeffrey remark, the logician's conditions for being a provability predicate have nothing much to do with proof: "x is a sentence" is, in the logician's lingo, a provability predicate. Our predicate $Thm_\Sigma(x)$ really is tied to proof. If we were being rigorous, we would arithmetize the whole proceeding by assigning Gödel numbers to sentences, and the property of being a theorem of Σ would be translated into a recursive set of numbers.

$$\forall x(Thm_\Sigma(x) \supset T(x)) \qquad \text{Premise}$$
$$Thm_\Sigma(\tau) \qquad \text{Hypothesis}$$

$$\forall x(Thm_\Sigma(x) \supset T(x)) \qquad \text{Reiteration}$$
$$Thm_\Sigma(\tau) \supset T(\tau) \qquad \forall \text{ Elimination}$$
$$Thm_\Sigma(\tau) \qquad \text{Reiteration}$$
$$T(\tau) \qquad \supset \text{Elimination}$$
$$\sim Thm_\Sigma(\tau) \qquad \text{Downward T-Inference}$$
$$\sim Thm_\Sigma(\tau)_{\{Thm_\Sigma(\tau)\}} \qquad \sim \text{Introduction}$$
$$\sim Thm_\Sigma(\tau) \qquad \text{Boundary Rule}$$

Once again, the use of index sets does not interfere with the reasoning, since $Thm_\Sigma(\tau)$ is a boundary sentence. The usual informal argument does indeed demonstrate that τ is not a theorem of Σ, supposing that the rules of Σ are valid. And in this reasoning there is nothing paradoxical.

But suppose that the premise $\forall x(Thm_\Sigma(x) \supset T(x))$ were itself a theorem of Σ, that is, suppose that using the rules of Σ alone one could prove that all of the theorems provable by those rules are true. In that case, there would be no need for *any* premises in the proof above, since $\forall x(Thm_\Sigma(x) \supset T(x))$ could be deduced from no premises. But then $\sim Thm_\Sigma(\tau)$ *would be a theorem* (it is proven on the last line of the proof). Hence the rules of Σ would *not* be truth-preserving, since $\sim Thm_\Sigma(\tau)$ would be a false sentence provable in the system. Furthermore, if we also accept the Thm_Σ Introduction rule, then having proven $\sim Thm_\Sigma(\tau)$ from no premises, we could immediately also write down $Thm_\Sigma(\tau)$ by Thm_Σ Introduction. That is, if $\forall x(Thm_\Sigma(x) \supset T(x))$ is itself a theorem, then the rules in Σ together with Thm_Σ Introduction are inconsistent, since both a sentence and its negation are theorems. So if the rules of Σ are valid, both $\forall x(Thm_\Sigma(x) \supset T(x))$ and $\sim Thm_\Sigma(\tau)$ are truths which are not theorems. If Σ is a finite set of formally specifiable syntactic rules, then by the usual Gödelian procedures one can map the theorems of Σ to a recursive set of integers, so that the translation of $\sim Thm_\Sigma(\tau)$ becomes a mathematical truth which one is unable to establish simply by use of the rules of Σ alone.

Notice that in this case, unlike the case of Proof Sigma, $\forall x(Thm_\Sigma(x) \supset T(x))$ really is a true sentence (supposing the rules of Σ are truth-preserving). For the only way that $\forall x(Thm_\Sigma(x) \supset T(x))$ could fail to be true is for one of its immediate semantic constituents to fail to be true. Such an immediate semantic constituent would have the form $Thm_\Sigma(n) \supset T(n)$. But every sentence of the form $Thm_\Sigma(n)$ is either true or false, since it is a boundary sentence. Further, if the rules of Σ are formally specifiable, then intuitively it is either true or false that a given syntactically specified string can be derived in accordance with them. Every sentence of the form $Thm_\Sigma(n) \supset T(n)$ with a false antecedent is true, so any such sentence which is not true must have a true antecedent and either a false or an ungrounded consequent. But that would mean that some theorem of Σ is either false or ungrounded, so Σ is not truth-preserving. Further, the only way that $Thm_\Sigma(n) \supset T(n)$ can be permissible is for it to be true, so unlike the case of $\forall x \forall y ((Der_\Sigma(x,y) \,\&\, T(x)) \supset T(y))$, we now have identified a Σ-unprovable truth about Σ (assuming Σ to be truth-preserving).

Where does all this leave us? The proof given above explains why we take $\sim Thm_\Sigma(\tau)$ to be a truth about Σ which is not a theorem of Σ. This insight, which plays a central role in most of the hyperbolic claims about Gödel's theorem, is established by a simple ten-line proof using completely syntactically specifiable inference rules. It is the simplicity of this *reductio* argument which has always made it seem ridiculous to assert that our ability to appreciate the truth of a Gödel sentence of a formal system demonstrates something deep about human reasoning, e.g. that human reasoning cannot be explained by any algorithmic procedure. The reasoning to the conclusion that the sentence $\sim Thm_\Sigma(\tau)$ is true and not a theorem is perfectly algorithmic, and proceeds via specifiable rules *from the premise that the theorems of Σ are all true*. The question, then, is really why we accept *that*, i.e. why we accept the truth of $\forall x (Thm_\Sigma(x) \supset T(x))$.

We had better not accept the truth of $\forall x (Thm_\Sigma(x) \supset T(x))$ because it itself is a theorem of Σ, for in that case Σ itself (or Σ fortified with the innocuous Thm_Σ Introduction) is inconsistent. And if we accept $\forall x (Thm_\Sigma(x) \supset T(x))$ because it is a theorem of some other set of rules (call these Σ^*), then the question arises why we take all of the theorems of Σ^* to be true. If we don't, then the fact that $\forall x (Thm_\Sigma(x) \supset T(x))$ is a theorem of Σ^* is insignificant. If we do because $\forall x (Thm_{\Sigma^*}(x) \supset T(x))$ is itself a theorem of Σ^*, then Σ^* is inconsistent. Further, if we do because $\forall x (Thm_{\Sigma^*}(x) \supset T(x))$ is itself a theorem of Σ^*, then we are committing a manifest *petitio principii*: we already have to trust the theorems of Σ^* for the fact that $\forall x (Thm_{\Sigma^*}(x) \supset T(x))$ is a theorem to have any significance. That is, the fact that a valid system cannot prove its own validity is, with respect to a certain epistemological question, insignificant: even if it could, we could not justify our trust in the system on that basis. So why do we trust a system of syntactically specifiable rules to be valid?

John Lucas (1961), and more recently Roger Penrose (1994), have taken the fact that we accept systems of rules as valid to show that *humans have a valid but non-algorithmic ability to recognize the validity of algorithmic procedures*. That is, there is *something* that provides us the insight that a set of rules is valid, but that something cannot itself be reduced to a set of syntactically specifiable rules. In Penrose's case, this conclusion is pushed yet further: the physics which underlies the brain processes that provide this insight cannot even be computable. This is not the place to review those arguments,[4] but at least this much can be said. First, the issue is not the derivation of Gödel sentences like $\sim Thm_\Sigma(\tau)$: as shown above, that is easily done given the premise that the

---

[4] Some observations on Penrose's argument can be found in Maudlin (1996).

theorems of Σ are all true. The issue instead is how one judges that the theorems of Σ are all true. And on this second point, we have seen (I think) that average, and even quite sophisticated, judgments of that sort by humans are wildly unreliable. For example, most people, even most logicians, would not object to the reasoning which leads to the conclusion, in the logic puzzle discussed above, that Sue is telling the truth, even though that conclusion is (as we have seen) not true. Few people would accept the conclusion of Proof Gamma (seeing that such proofs can prove anything), but almost no one can point out any fallacy involved: where is the ability to detect valid (and invalid) inferences in this case? If I am correct, the specific invalidity in Proof Lambda has escaped detection despite millennia of investigation. Also, if I am right, the common acceptance of claims like χ as *true* is a mistake. So the idea that our ability to recognize valid and invalid inferences is highly reliable (much less ideally perfectly reliable) strikes me as plainly false. Indeed, most people would reason to the truth of Gödel sentences like $\sim Thm_\Sigma(\tau)$ by means of an inconsistent system (viz. the predicate calculus with the T-Inferences but without index sets). Occasionally, they notice the invalidity of those inferences (e.g. when confronted with Proof Gamma), and then withdraw assent from the conclusions. But they do not even attempt, much less accomplish, a diagnosis of the problem, and happily accept the conclusions (as in the logic puzzle about Sue) if there are no obvious counter-indications. Actual human reasoning, far from being some mystical but valid process, employs an inconsistent set of rules together with rather vague and unreliable rules of thumb about when to reject a conclusion, even though it seems to be derived by impeccable inferences. (It hardly needs to be said that actual human reasoning is much worse than this: it is rather only in rare circumstances that the results of impeccable reasoning are accepted at all.) The claim that these human capacities cannot be realized in a brain governed by computable physics scarcely demands any refutation.

Even when those most highly trained and scrupulous about inferences are confronted with the problem of detecting invalidity, they get it wrong. Our original Proof Gamma (without index sets) is obviously invalid, otherwise one could deduce anything at all. But the common line among logicians (so I am told) is that the fallacy lies in the use of T-Inferences within subderivations. And there is an obvious *inductive* ground for this judgment: a glance back over this treatise reveals that every problematic inference, including Proof Gamma, Proof Lambda, Proof Sigma, and the reasoning in the logic puzzle, employs some T-Inference within a subderivation. Eliminate the T-Inferences from subderivations and all of one's headaches go away. This conclusion, by a pretty obvious induction, can clearly be arrived at algorithmically.

But does this diagnosis contain any *insight* or understanding? It is hard to see how. As mentioned before, the T-Inferences are *valid*, *truth-preserving* inferences according to every theory of truth in the literature. $T(n)$ is true if and only if $\mathscr{F}(n)$ is true: one would need a counterexample to this to defend the claim that the T-Inferences are not valid. But if they are valid, why *can't* they be used in subderivations? And why can *other* inferences be used? After all, what stronger ground can one have to use an inference than that it be evidently truth-preserving? Further, eliminating all T-Inferences from subderivations disqualifies some obviously valid reasoning. Suppose, for example, that we wish to prove, as a theorem

If "The world is flat" is true then "The world is not flat" is not true.

The reasoning involved in proving this is straightforward and valid (assuming all boundary sentences are either true or false), but it employs T-Inferences in a subderivation. The reasoning *must* employ a subderivation, if it is to prove a theorem, and the use of T-Inferences is unavoidable.

Let us represent "The world is flat" as $F(w)$, and use corner-quotation names to denote sentences. The reasoning proceeds:

$T(\ulcorner F(w)\urcorner)$	Hypothesis
$T(\ulcorner \sim F(w)\urcorner)$	Hypothesis
$T(\ulcorner \sim F(w)\urcorner)$	Reiteration
$\sim F(w)$	Downward T-Inference
$T(\ulcorner F(w)\urcorner)$	Reiteration
$F(w)$	Downward T-Inference
$\sim T(\ulcorner \sim F(w)\urcorner)_{\{T(\ulcorner \sim F(w)\urcorner)\}}$	$\sim$ Introduction
$\sim T(\ulcorner \sim F(w)\urcorner)_{\{\sim F(w)\}}$	Rule of Analysis
$\sim T(\ulcorner \sim F(w)\urcorner)_{\{F(w)\}}$	Rule of Analysis
$\sim T(\ulcorner \sim F(w)\urcorner)$	Boundary Rule
$T(\ulcorner F(w)\urcorner) \supset \sim T(\ulcorner \sim F(w)\urcorner)_{\{T(\ulcorner F(w)\urcorner)\}}$	$\supset$ Introduction
$T(\ulcorner F(w)\urcorner) \supset \sim T(\ulcorner \sim F(w)\urcorner)_{\{F(w)\}}$	Rule of Analysis
$T(\ulcorner F(w)\urcorner) \supset \sim T(\ulcorner \sim F(w)\urcorner)$	Boundary Rule

If one takes the conclusion of this argument to be provable *a priori*, then one had best allow T-Inferences in subderivations. The Draconian solution of forbidding all such inferences is unnecessary, although one does have to keep track of index sets if one is not to fall into contradictions.

To top it all off, if one bans all use of T-Inferences from subderivations *then one cannot accept the proof given above that the sentence τ is true*. Our reasoning to the truth of the Gödel sentence of a formal system *uses a reductio, with T-Inferences in a subderivation*. If we reject all T-Inferences in subderivations, then *we* cannot recognize the truth of the Gödel sentence (even granting that we have accepted that the system in question is valid!), so the idea that humans have some amazing ability to infallibly recognize truths unavailable to computers goes right out the window. Along with it goes the idea that Gödel proved anything of interest, since we have to accept the *informal reductio* (using T-Inferences) to the conclusion that the Gödel sentence is true in order to argue that the system under study is incomplete. Banning the use of T-Inferences in *reductio* arguments eliminates all of the profound results of metalogic.

As soon as a language is rich enough to contain cycles in its graph, the problem of validity of rules of inference becomes non-trivial. Since informal arguments, such as those used to establish the truth of Gödel sentences, use such a rich language, the question of the general validity of the rules used in those arguments is non-trivial. In order to be assured that the Gödel sentence is true, we must trust some reasoning. And typically, I claim, the informal rules we use (with unrestricted T-Inferences and without index sets) are invalid. The fact that we can be convinced of the truth of the Gödel sentences by use of *invalid* rules of inference obviously cannot be used, in conjunction with Gödel's theorem itself, to show that the processes underlying the reasoning are not algorithmic (in *any* sense of algorithmic), much less that the physics of the brain is not computable(!). If we had a capacity to infallibly recognize the validity of any set of inference rules *a priori*, that might cause a problem, but we have no evidence that we have such a capacity, and much evidence to the contrary. Where we do have evidence (e.g. in trying to diagnose the fallacy in Löb's paradox), it appears that we tend to use induction, rather than insight, and that the inductive rule is fallible.

Yet still paradox lurks. Even if in fact humans typically reason by means of an invalid set of inference rules, employing a somewhat vague rule which allows one to reject an argument *ex post facto* if the argument form would apparently allow one to prove anything, still I have been arguing that we can, in fact, do better. We can incorporate the T-Inferences into our usual logical systems by means of appropriate emendations and block all the problematic inferences. The resulting system is, I claim, valid: all the theorems are true, and any sentence that can be derived from a true sentence is true (assuming all the boundary sentences have a classical truth value). Let's leave aside the question of how I have come to *believe* that the rules are valid. The question that we must face directly now is whether that belief—however I have come by it—is itself somehow problematic.

Here's a quick way to approach the puzzle. Suppose that, for whatever reason, I am inclined to accept that some set of inference rules Σ is valid. Then, in the first place, I will be inclined to accept that $\forall x(Thm_\Sigma(x) \supset T(x))$ is true. But more than that: I will also be inclined to accept a certain *inference rule* as valid, viz. the inference from $Thm_\Sigma(n)$ to $\mathscr{F}(n)$. If the rules in Σ are valid, then the theorems of Σ are true, so one ought to be able to infer from the premise that a certain sentence is a theorem to the conclusion that the sentence is true, and hence to the sentence itself. In short, if we accept a set of inference rules as valid, then we are apparently *also* committed to accepting that the rule

Thm$_\Sigma$ Elimination: From *Thm*$_\Sigma(n)$ infer $\mathscr{F}(n)$

is valid.

Thm$_\Sigma$ Elimination obviously resembles the Downward T-Inference. Furthermore, *Thm*$_\Sigma$ Introduction resembles, to a limited extent, the Upward T-Inference. We do not assume, of course, that every true sentence is a theorem: no formal system could have all truths as theorems. But every sentence that can be proven using the rules in Σ from no premises is a theorem. So if we start a proof with no premises, and we confine ourselves to rules in the set Σ, then we can use *Thm*$_\Sigma$ Introduction on any sentence that is derived (with an empty index set) next to the main derivation bar. And even this limited resemblance to the Upward T-Inference is enough to give us pause. For it is resemblance enough to reinvigorate some of our problematic proofs.

Let the set Σ! contain *all the formally specifiable inference rules that we are capable of recognizing as valid.* (Or, if you like, let it contain all the formally specifiable inference rules that we are psychologically constituted to regard as valid after careful consideration.) Then, it seems, we would have to regard (or recognize) the rule *Thm*$_{\Sigma!}$ Elimination as valid, and hence *Thm*$_{\Sigma!}$ Elimination would itself have to be a member of Σ!. And now we appear to be able to reconstruct the Inferential Liar paradox using theoremhood (with respect to Σ!) in the place of truth. All we need to assume is that the set Σ! includes Hypothesis, Reiteration, *Thm*$_{\Sigma!}$ Elimination, $\sim$ Introduction (as emended), the Boundary Rule, and *Thm*$_{\Sigma!}$ Introduction. Let the sentence denoted by ι say of itself that it is not a theorem of Σ!:

$$\mathscr{F}(\iota) = \sim Thm_{\Sigma!}(\iota).$$

We can now recapitulate the Liar argument using $\sim Thm_{\Sigma!}(\iota)$, *which is a boundary sentence*:

$Thm_{\Sigma!}(\iota)$	Hypothesis
$Thm_{\Sigma!}(\iota)$	Reiteration
$\sim Thm_{\Sigma!}(\iota)$	*Thm*$_{\Sigma!}$ Elimination
$\sim Thm_{\Sigma!}(\iota)_{\{Thm_{\Sigma!}(\iota)\}}$	$\sim$ Introduction
$\sim Thm_{\Sigma!}(\iota)$	Boundary Rule
$Thm_{\Sigma!}(\iota)$	*Thm*$_{\Sigma!}$ Introduction

This proof is clearly trouble: it contains both a sentence and its negation as theorems, and it is not blocked by consideration of index sets.

At one level, the feature which leads to this pathology is easy to identify: it arises from the fact that the set Σ! itself contains the rule *Thm*$_{\Sigma!}$ Elimination. From a certain justificatory point of view, this is problematic: we would justify a rule like *Thm*$_{\Sigma!}$ Elimination by arguing for each rule in Σ! that it is valid, but since Σ! contains *Thm*$_{\Sigma!}$ Elimination, we could not complete the justification for it without, in the process, already having convinced ourselves of its validity. In general, no rule of the form Thm_Σ Elimination can allow the set Σ to contain that very rule, lest we fall into the problem illustrated by the proof above.

But this diagnosis does not completely clear up our puzzlement. Begin with any set of rules Σ that we regard as all valid. Then, as already noted, we will also regard the rule Thm_Σ Elimination as valid. But, as we have just seen, Thm_Σ Elimination had better not be part of Σ, else the set of rules is inconsistent (or at least invalid, since it allows one to prove $\sim Thm_\Sigma(\iota)$, which is false). So Thm_Σ Elimination must not be a member of the original set Σ, but it is still a rule whose validity we can apparently recognize. There is therefore a *bigger* set of rules, $\Sigma \cup Thm_\Sigma$ Elimination, all of which we can recognize as valid. Call this set Σ^+. It obviously will not contain the rule Thm_{Σ^+} Elimination, which will in turn be a new rule we can recognize as valid. In short, the process of collecting together formally specifiable rules of inference that we can recognize as valid appears to have no end: no matter how many rules have been collected together into a set, there are yet others that lie outside it.

Notice that the problem is not merely that the set of rules that we can (in principle) recognize as valid is *potentially infinite*: that would hardly be surprising if we idealize the human mind as having unlimited memory, etc. The problem is that the argument appears to work even if the set Σ is infinite: for *any* set of rules, all of which we can recognize as valid, either there is a further rule outside the set we can recognize as valid or the set is inconsistent. It seems to follow that there simply *is* no complete set of rules that we can recognize as valid: our ability to recognize validity outruns even the bounds of set theory. And from that it would seem to follow that our ability to recognize validity must outrun the abilities of any algorithmic system, or any mechanical computer.

Clearly the argument above has run off the rails somewhere. After all, the procedure by which we expanded the set of rules Σ to the larger set Σ^+ did not seem to require any fundamentally new sort of *insight*: it was, rather, itself an algorithmic procedure (otherwise, how could we be assured that our ability to grasp these successive new insights would not give out eventually?). Furthermore, how could it be that the rules whose validity we are able to appreciate do not form a set? How can there fail to be a set like $\Sigma!$ that contains all the rules we could recognize as valid, and how could $Thm_{\Sigma!}$ Elimination fail to be a member of that set?

It is, indeed, the potential infinitude of the rules that we could accept as valid that frees us from the paradox. Just because we could appreciate that *each* member of a set of rules is valid, it does not follow that we could even in principle appreciate that they *all* are valid. Compare: if Goldbach's conjecture is true, then we can, in principle, satisfy ourselves (by direct calculation) that any even number is the sum of two primes, but that does not imply that we can, even in principle, satisfy ourselves that Goldbach's conjecture is true. And again, just because each rule in the set Σ is algorithmic, or syntactically specifiable, it does not follow that the corresponding rule Thm_Σ Elimination is algorithmic, for to check that Thm_Σ Elimination has been followed, one needs to verify that every rule of inference used in a proof is drawn from the set Σ. Without an effective procedure to do that, Thm_Σ Elimination won't itself be an algorithmic rule. Of course if Σ happens to be finite, and to consist in algorithmically applicable rules, then an algorithm can check that a given proof uses only rules from Σ. But if Σ is infinite, then there is no such guarantee. Indeed, all that our "paradox" demonstrates is that, even under ideal and idealized circumstances, we will eventually hit a wall: there will be sets of rules each of which we can recognize as valid even though we cannot convince ourselves of the generalization that every proof constructible using members of the set is valid. For although we can convince ourselves of the validity of any given member, we cannot manage to prove the validity of all the members considered as a group. Our "paradox" shows that there must indeed be such a set of inference rules, and shows as surely that we will never be able to effectively specify the membership of the set. And there is no proof from consideration of Gödel's theorem that these very abilities cannot be instantiated by a formal system.

Given our actual limitations, of course, we will never actually hit this wall: at any time, there will only be finitely many inference rules that we accept as valid, and there will always be more inference rules which we could—given only a bit more time, or patience, or memory, or attention—convince ourselves are valid. It may be instructive to see again how this ever-present potential to expand the set of rules accepted as valid provides the key to diffusing apparent paradoxes.

We saw above how theoremhood validates inferences that are rather similar to those that truth validates—supposing that the inferential rules by which theoremhood is defined are themselves valid. This allowed us to produce a "proof" very similar to the Inferential Liar paradox, using theoremhood in place of truth. That "proof" was diagnosed as follows: if the set Σ itself contains the rule Thm_Σ Elimination, then the set of inference rules is invalid. If the set Σ does not contain Thm_Σ Elimination, then the proof no longer goes through, but if we judge that all of the rules in Σ are valid, then we will also judge that Thm_Σ Elimination is valid—so Σ is not a complete set of the rules we can be brought to regard as valid. In particular, if $\Sigma^+ = \Sigma \cup Thm_\Sigma$ Elimination, then we can come to judge that all of the rules in Σ^+ are valid.

Just as theoremhood can be used to produce a proof similar to Proof Lambda, so can the relation of derivability (by means of a set of rules taken to be valid) be used in place of the horseshoe to produce a "proof" similar to Proof Gamma (Löb's paradox). We proceed as follows.

Suppose that we accept all the rules in Σ as valid. We have already seen that this does not commit us to the truth of the generalization $\forall x \forall y ((Der_\Sigma(x,y) \ \& \ T(x)) \supset T(y))$, since it has immediate semantic constituents that are not true. But even so, accepting the validity of all the rules in Σ would commit us to accepting the *validity* of the rule Der_Σ Elimination: from $Der_\Sigma(n,m)$ and $T(n)$ one may validly infer $T(m)$. For if the premises are both true, then $\mathcal{F}(n)$ is true, and $\mathcal{F}(m)$ can indeed be derived from $\mathcal{F}(n)$ by means of the (supposedly truth-preserving) rules in Σ. Hence $\mathcal{F}(m)$ should be regarded as true. Der_Σ Elimination is obviously rather similar to $\supset$ Elimination, with $Der_\Sigma(n,m)$ playing the role of the sentence of the form $\mathcal{F}(n) \supset \mathcal{F}(m)$. Furthermore, the rule Der_Σ Introduction seems relevantly similar to the rule $\supset$ Introduction, but with this important difference: Der_Σ Introduction does not require the introduction of anything into the index set of the conclusion. Even granting the validity of the rules in Σ, the fact that $\mathcal{F}(m)$ can be derived from $\mathcal{F}(n)$ does not guarantee the truth of $\mathcal{F}(n) \supset \mathcal{F}(m)$ (since $\mathcal{F}(n)$ might be ungrounded) but it does guarantee the truth of $Der_\Sigma(n,m)$.

Mimicking Proof Gamma, then, let us specify the denotation of π as follows: $\mathcal{F}(\pi) = Der_\Sigma(\pi, \ulcorner X \urcorner)$, where $\ulcorner X \urcorner$ is the quotation name of some arbitrary sentence in the language. If we have the rule Der_Σ Elimination where Σ contains the rules Hypothesis, Reiteration, Upward T-Inference, Downward T-Inference, Der_Σ Introduction, and, critically, Der_Σ Elimination itself, then we can prove X as follows:

$Der_\Sigma(\pi, \ulcorner X \urcorner)$	Hypothesis
$Der_\Sigma(\pi, \ulcorner X \urcorner)$	Reiteration
$T(\pi)$	Upward T-Inference
$T(\ulcorner X \urcorner)$	Der_Σ Elimination
X	Downward T-inference
$Der_\Sigma(\pi, \ulcorner X \urcorner)$	Der_Σ Introduction
$T(\pi)$	Upward T-inference
$T(\ulcorner X \urcorner)$	Der_Σ Elimination
X	Downward T-Inference

Once again, we see that Σ had best not contain Der_Σ Elimination, else we are able to prove any sentence whatever. But if Σ does not contain Der_Σ Elimination, there is no bar to accepting Der_Σ Elimination as valid. So accepting all the rules in Σ as valid commits us to accepting all the rules in Σ^+ as valid, where now $\Sigma^+ = \Sigma \cup Der_\Sigma$ Elimination. In this situation, we are able to prove that X can be derived from $Der_\Sigma(\pi, \ulcorner X \urcorner)$, but the proof uses rules from Σ^+, not just from Σ. That is, the proof becomes

$Der_\Sigma(\pi, \ulcorner X \urcorner)$	Hypothesis
$Der_\Sigma(\pi, \ulcorner X \urcorner)$	Reiteration
$T(\pi)$	Upward T-Inference
$T(\ulcorner X \urcorner)$	Der_Σ Elimination
X	Downward T-Inference
$Der_{\Sigma^+}(\pi, \ulcorner X \urcorner)$	Der_Σ Introduction

If we accept all the rules in Σ^+ as valid, then we can be convinced that X can indeed be derived by means of valid inferences from $Der_\Sigma(\pi, \ulcorner X \urcorner)$, just not by means only of the rules that happen to be in Σ.

It is also perhaps worthwhile to note that the use of the T-Inferences in these proofs is gratuitous. For if we believe that all the rules in some set Σ are valid, then we will also accept as valid the following version of Der_Σ Elimination: from $Der_\Sigma(n,m)$ and $\mathscr{F}(n)$ one may validly infer $\mathscr{F}(m)$. Using this version, the problematic proof (if Σ contains Der_Σ Elimination) is pleasingly short and crisp:

$Der_\Sigma(\pi, \ulcorner X \urcorner)$	Hypothesis
$Der_\Sigma(\pi, \ulcorner X \urcorner)$	Reiteration
X	Der_Σ Elimination
$Der_\Sigma(\pi, \ulcorner X \urcorner)$	Der_Σ Introduction
X	Der_Σ Elimination

$Der_\Sigma(\pi, \ulcorner X \urcorner)$ can serve as *both* premises needed for the rule Der_Σ Elimination since $Der_\Sigma(\pi, \ulcorner X \urcorner)$ *is* $\mathscr{F}(\pi)$. For this version of the proof to go through, Σ need only contain Hypothesis, Reiteration, and Der_Σ Elimination (Der_Σ Introduction, while evidently valid, need not be in Σ), which highlights the tight justificatory circle: one could only be convinced that Der_Σ Elimination is valid if one were already convinced that Der_Σ Elimination is valid. This circle is evidently vicious, since those drawn into it would have to countenance a system of inferences capable of proving anything.

We now have corrected classical logic and incorporated the T-Inferences into it in a way that avoids the inferential paradox. We have also seen that there is no bar to introducing predicates that allow us to talk about provability or demonstrability in this system. We have seen that the sentence which says that the system of inferences is truth-preserving is not a theorem, and further is not true (but is permissible), while the sentence which says that all the theorems of the system are true is also not a theorem, but is true. This suffices for a discussion of formally specifiable rules of inference that are *valid*, i.e. that preserve *truth*. But in addition to truth we have introduced another feature that a sentence can have: permissibility. Indeed, many of the most important claims that we have made have turned out to be permissible, but not true. It is therefore incumbent on us also to provide an account of how we reason about what is permissible, i.e. an account of *permissibility-preserving inference*. It is to this task that we turn next.

7 Reasoning about Permissible Sentences

The inferential rules presented in the last chapter are concerned with truth. The rules are designed to be valid: any sentence derivable with an empty index set from a set of true premises will be true. In classical logic, where truth and permissibility coincide, truth-preserving rules are all permissibility-preserving and vice versa; permissible premises are all true premises and conversely. But if, as in our theory, permissibility encompasses a different class of sentences than truth, one must construct two distinct but related inference schemes: one concerned with truth and the other with permissibility. One must also consider cross inferences from one scheme to the other. This is particularly important in our case, since the semantic theory is stated largely by using permissible sentences that are not true, such as "The Liar is not true", "The Truthteller is ungrounded", etc.

Before approaching the detailed structure of a permissibility-preserving set of inferences, we should pause to remark one way in which this project differs from that of specifying the truth-preserving inferences. Permissibility is always a matter of *permissibility according to a specified set of rules*. Just as there is no such thing as theoremhood neat, or derivability neat, but only theoremhood or derivability in accord with an inferential system, so too there is no such thing as permissibility *per se*, but only permissibility according to some normative standard. Properly speaking, then, we ought to subscript any notion of permissibility to indicate the relevant standard being used. If, for example, one adopted the stance that all and only true sentences are permissible, then the permissibility-preserving inferences are just the truth-preserving ones, and the system developed in the last chapter is appropriate. If one adopts a monastic rule of silence (i.e. no sentence can be appropriately asserted), then the search for permissibility-preserving inferences is rendered pointless. In the next chapter, the fact that permissibility is always relative to a normative standard will become crucial to addressing some new paradoxes. As an abstract matter, innumerable possible standards for assertion and denial exist, each supporting a different set of permissibility-preserving inferences. In this chapter, we will be concerned exclusively with an inferential system tailored to the standard of permissible assertion proposed in Chapter 5.

In Chapter 5, we introduced the notion of an *ideal* for standards of assertion: a set of intuitive desiderata for normative rules, all of which could not be simultaneously satisfied once the language contains the truth predicate. In large part, rules of inference that preserve permissibility can be determined simply by reflecting on which of the ideals are satisfied by a given set of normative rules. One ideal is that the rules be *complete*: they should (together with the state of the world) determine for every well-formed sentence that it is either permissible or impermissible to assert. Another ideal is that the rules be *coherent*: no sentence should be categorized as both permissible and impermissible. If a normative standard meets these two ideals, then the language will be *normatively bivalent*: every sentence will either fall into the class of permissible or into the class of impermissible sentences. Another ideal is that the rules should *mimic the logical particles*: for example, if a conjunction is permissible then so should both conjuncts be. We have seen that no rules can mimic all the logical particles, if the truth predicate is included among the logical particles, but there are normatively bivalent rules that can mimic most of them. And insofar as a normatively bivalent set of rules mimics a logical particle, it will render the classical inferences governing that particle permissibility-preserving *without the use of index sets*. That is, in these cases, the permissibility-preserving inferences will be identical to the standard inferences used for language without a truth predicate.

In particular, the rules introduced in Chapter 5 are normatively bivalent and mimic all the logical particles save the truth predicate. Therefore *all of the "classical" logical inferences are permissibility-preserving and all of the "classical" logical theorems are permissible to assert*. One may, for example, properly assert $\forall x(T(x) \supset T(x))$ and $T(\lambda) \supset T(\lambda)$ even though neither of these sentences is true, and one can *prove* each of these sentences as a theorem of the permissibility-preserving system in the usual way, without having to bother about index sets.

Indeed, the *only* logical particles that the rules of Chapter 5 do not mimic are the truth and falsity predicates, so the only truth-preserving inferences that might fail to be permissibility-preserving are the T-Inferences and F-Inferences. Let us therefore focus our attention on these.

The Upward T-Inference does not always preserve permissibility, since a sentence can be permissible even though it is not true (and hence even though the sentence which says it is true is not permissible). But the Downward T-Inference always preserves permissibility. For the only case in which $T(n)$ is permissible is when $\mathscr{F}(n)$ is true, and if $\mathscr{F}(n)$ is true then $\mathscr{F}(n)$ is permissible (because the rules are truth-permissive). So the inference from $T(n)$ to $\mathscr{F}(n)$ always preserves permissibility, and can be admitted to the system. Similarly, if $\Phi(n)$ is permissible, then $\mathscr{F}(n)$ is false, so $\mathscr{N}\mathscr{F}(n)$ is true, so $\mathscr{N}\mathscr{F}(n)$ is permissible. So the Downward F-Inference preserves permissibility, and can be admitted to the system.

Admission of the Downward T- and F-Inferences already provides some notable results. We can, for example, prove that the Liar is permissible:

$T(\lambda)$	Hypothesis
$T(\lambda)$	Reiteration
$\sim T(\lambda)$	Downward T-Inference
$\sim T(\lambda)$	$\sim$ Introduction

This is, of course, just Proof Lambda without the last step, i.e. without the Upward T-Inference which allows one to derive $T(\lambda)$. Once again we see the inaccuracy of the claim that problems are caused by T-Inferences in subderivations: the permissibility-preserving system can allow Downward T-Inferences *everywhere*, and it would be the Upward T-Inference *outside* the subderivation which would fail to preserve permissibility. (A glance back at Proof Gamma shows similarly that the Löb's paradox sentence is provably permissible, but the absence of the Upwards T-Inference blocks the paradox. One can assert $T(\gamma) \supset X$, but one cannot necessarily assert that that sentence is true, and hence cannot detach the consequent by Modus Ponens.)

Use of the Downward F-Inference also allows us to prove that the Liar is not false:

$\Phi(\lambda)$	Hypothesis
$\Phi(\lambda)$	Reiteration
$\sim\sim T(\lambda)$	Downward F-Inference
$T(\lambda)$	$\sim$ Elimination
$\sim T(\lambda)$	Downward T-Inference
$\sim \Phi(\lambda)$	$\sim$ Introduction

Since we can prove both $\sim T(\lambda)$ and $\sim\Phi(\lambda)$, we can obviously prove $\sim T(\lambda)$ & $\sim\Phi(\lambda)$. This in turn allows us to prove that the Liar is ungrounded, with the help of the definitional postulate $\forall x(Y(x) \equiv (\sim T(x)$ & $\sim\Phi(x)))$. This definitional postulate deserves a bit of notice. It is not, of course, *true*, since the instance generated by substituting it with, e.g., the Liar is ungrounded. The definitional postulate is therefore at best ungrounded. If, however, it really is a definitional postulate, then it is guaranteed to be permissible. If $Y(x)$ is everywhere replaceable *salva veritate* and *salva permissibilitate* with $\sim T(x)$ & $\sim\Phi(x)$, then the biconditional is always permissible, even though it is not always true. This comports well with our earlier remarks on "logical truth". Since truth is ultimately rooted in the world, no sentence is made true by its logical form, and no sentence can be known to be true without the use of some presupposition about the world. This holds for "definitional postulates" such as $\forall x(Y(x) \equiv (\sim T(x)$ & $\sim\Phi(x)))$ as well. One is accustomed to saying that certain claims are "true by definition", or "true by stipulation". But one cannot just stipulate the appropriate relation to the world into existence. One can stipulate that a predicate is to have the same meaning as some other predicate, and that guarantees that the relevant biconditional is permissible, but not that it is true.

The definitional postulate $\forall x(Y(x) \equiv (\sim T(x) \And \sim \Phi(x))$ can therefore be used in the permissibility-preserving system but not in the truth-preserving one. This is not upsetting, since no sentence of the form $Y(n)$ is ever true. (It is also notable in this regard that the schema for the T-sentences, $T(n) \equiv \mathscr{F}(n)$ cannot similarly be regarded as "true by definition" or even "permissible by definition", since not only are not all of the instances true, not all of the instances are permissible. For example, the instance for the Liar, which we have called T-Lambda, is not permissible.)

The Downward T- and F-Inferences provide some power to derive semantic claims in the permissibility-preserving system, but the absence of the Upward Inferences is a severe constraint. In essence, one loses information when using the Downward Inferences, and has no means of semantic ascent again. For example, whenever it is permissible to assert that a conjunction is true, it is permissible to assert that each conjunct is true, but the system as we have it does not allow this inference. From the claim that the conjunction is true one can assert the conjunction itself (by the Downward T-Inference), and hence can assert each conjunct (by & Elimination), but since there is no Upward T-Inference one cannot assert that the conjunct is true. Even with the Downward Inferences, the permissibility-preserving system is too anemic to prove things that are obviously permissible.

What we need, then, is something which can provide some of the power of the Upward T- and F-Inferences, but is still weaker than those inferences, The key to enhancing the permissibility-preserving system lies in an observation we have already made: *the semantic theory, when stated in the formal language, is permissible even though it is not true.* We can therefore add the semantic theory as an axiom to the permissibility-preserving system. This addition, along with some truths about ordinals, allows us to derive most of the claims we have made in the course of this chapter.

In its full form, the semantic theory was given as:

$$\forall x(Bound(x) \supset (T(x) \equiv \mathscr{F}(x))) \And \forall x(Bound(x) \supset (\Phi(x) \equiv \mathscr{N}\mathscr{F}(x))) \And$$
$$\exists \Xi((\forall x(Conj(x) \supset (T(x) \equiv \forall y(ISC(y,x) \supset (T(y) \And (\Xi(y) < \Xi(x)))))))) \And$$
$$(\forall x(Univ(x) \supset (T(x) \equiv \forall y(ISC(y,x) \supset (T(y) \And (\Xi(y) < \Xi(x)))))))) \And$$
$$(\forall x(Tau(x) \supset (T(x) \equiv \forall y(ISC(y,x) \supset (T(y) \And (\Xi(y) < \Xi(x)))))))) \And$$
$$(\forall x(Neg(x) \supset (T(x) \equiv \forall y(ISC(y,x) \supset (\Phi(y) \And (\Xi(y) < \Xi(x)))))))) \And$$
$$(\forall x(Phi(x) \supset (T(x) \equiv \forall y(ISC(y,x) \supset (\Phi(y) \And (\Xi(y) < \Xi(x)))))))) \And$$
$$(\forall x(Conj(x) \supset (\Phi(x) \equiv \exists y(ISC(y,x) \And (\Phi(y) \And (\Xi(y) < \Xi(x)))))))) \And$$
$$(\forall x(Univ(x) \supset (\Phi(x) \equiv \exists y(ISC(y,x) \And (\Phi(y) \And (\Xi(y) < \Xi(x)))))))) \And$$
$$(\forall x(Tau(x) \supset (\Phi(x) \equiv \exists y(ISC(y,x) \And (\Phi(y) \And (\Xi(y) < \Xi(x)))))))) \And$$
$$(\forall x(Neg(x) \supset (\Phi(x) \equiv \forall y(ISC(y,x) \supset (T(y) \And (\Xi(y) < \Xi(x)))))))) \And$$
$$(\forall x(Phi(x) \supset (\Phi(x) \equiv \forall y(ISC(y,x) \supset (T(y) \And (\Xi(y) < \Xi(x))))))))).$$

Let's add this as an axiom to the permissibility-preserving system and see what we can prove.

The first two clauses effectively give us both the Upward and Downward T-Inferences and F-Inferences for all Boundary sentences. This reflects our presupposition that Boundary sentences are either true or false: if a Boundary sentence is permissible it is true, so the sentence which says it is true is permissible, and if the negation of a Boundary sentence is permissible, the sentence which says it is false is permissible. If we question this claim about Boundary sentences, the first two clauses must be revised.

The long clause bound by the second-order variable gives the guts of the semantic theory, and we will concentrate on it. Since it is a long existential claim, it is fairly unwieldy, but in practice things are not so complicated. The first move in any derivation, once we have detached the long clause by & Elimination, is to begin a subderivation with an instance of the long clause instantiated on a dummy term for the second-order variable. In essence, we give the function from sentences to the ordinals a dummy name, e.g. Ω, and then use the dummy name in the subderivation. If we can reach any conclusion from which the dummy name has been eliminated, we can write the conclusion outside the subderivation, citing the rule of $\exists$ Elimination. So for all intents and purposes, we can take as our axiom:

$$(\forall x(Conj(x) \supset (T(x) \equiv \forall y(ISC(y,x) \supset (T(y) \,\&\, (\Omega(y) < \Omega(x)))))))\;\&$$
$$(\forall x(Univ(x) \supset (T(x) \equiv \forall y(ISC(y,x) \supset (T(y) \,\&\, (\Omega(y) < \Omega(x)))))))\;\&$$
$$(\forall x(Tau(x) \supset (T(x) \equiv \forall y(ISC(y,x) \supset (T(y) \,\&\, (\Omega(y) < \Omega(x)))))))\;\&$$
$$(\forall x(Neg(x) \supset (T(x) \equiv \forall y(ISC(y,x) \supset (\Phi(y) \,\&\, (\Omega(y) < \Omega(x)))))))\;\&$$
$$(\forall x(Phi(x) \supset (T(x) \equiv \forall y(ISC(y,x) \supset (\Phi(y) \,\&\, (\Omega(y) < \Omega(x)))))))\;\&$$
$$(\forall x(Conj(x) \supset (\Phi(x) \equiv \exists y(ISC(y,x) \,\&\, (\Phi(y) \,\&\, (\Omega(y) < \Omega(x)))))))\;\&$$
$$(\forall x(Univ(x) \supset (\Phi(x) \equiv \exists y(ISC(y,x) \,\&\, (\Phi(y) \,\&\, (\Omega(y) < \Omega(x)))))))\;\&$$
$$(\forall x(Tau(x) \supset (\Phi(x) \equiv \exists y(ISC(y,x) \,\&\, (\Phi(y) \,\&\, (\Omega(y) < \Omega(x)))))))\;\&$$
$$(\forall x(Neg(x) \supset (\Phi(x) \equiv \forall y(ISC(y,x) \supset (T(y) \,\&\, (\Omega(y) < \Omega(x)))))))\;\&$$
$$(\forall x(Phi(x) \supset (\Phi(x) \equiv \forall y(ISC(y,x) \supset (T(y) \,\&\, (\Omega(y) < \Omega(x))))))).$$

Since we can detach each of the conjuncts by & Elimination, we will freely use them as axioms, understanding that the one long sentence is really the only axiom.

Given the semantic theory, there are two main strategies for proving semantic claims. We can show that a sentence has (or fails to have) a certain semantic value in virtue of the semantic value of some of its semantic constituents (whose values have already been established). We can also show that a sentence has a semantic value (or fails to have a semantic value) because of the structure of the graph of the language. We will examine one example of each strategy.

The first strategy can be used to prove that $\forall x(T(x) \supset T(x))$ is ungrounded in a language which contains the Liar. Give the Downward F-Inference and the fact that $\forall x(T(x) \supset T(x))$ is a classical theorem, it is easy to show that $\forall x(T(x) \supset T(x))$ is not false. For convenience, let us introduce the name κ for $\forall x(T(x) \supset T(x))$, so $\mathscr{F}(\kappa) = \forall x(T(x) \supset T(x))$ and $\mathscr{N}\mathscr{F}(\kappa) = \sim\forall x(T(x) \supset T(x))$. The proof runs

$\Phi(\kappa)$	Hypothesis
$\Phi(\kappa)$	Reiteration
$\sim\forall x(T(x) \supset T(x))$	Downward F-Inference
$T(\delta)$	Hypothesis
$T(\delta)$	Reiteration
$T(\delta) \supset T(\delta)$	$\supset$ Introduction
$\forall x(T(x) \supset T(x))$	$\forall$ Introduction
$\sim\Phi(\kappa)$	$\sim$ Introduction

Now all we have to do is prove that $\forall x(T(x) \supset T(x))$ is not true.

In order to follow this first strategy, we need the clause in the semantic theory for material conditionals, a clause we left out for simplicity in our original account. We need three syntactic predicates: $Cond(n)$ which denotes all and only wffs whose main connective is the horseshoe, $Ante(n,m)$ which is true just in case the sentence denoted by n is the antecedent of the sentence denoted by m, and $Conseq(n,m)$ which is true just in case the sentence denoted by n is the consequent of the sentence denoted by m. The more generic notion of an immediate semantic constituent is not sufficient here since the antecedent and consequent contribute asymmetrically to the truth value of the conditional. The semantic clause providing the truth condition for the material conditional is then

$$\forall x(Cond(x) \supset (T(x) \equiv ((\forall y(Ante(y,x) \supset (\Phi(y) \mathbin{\&} (\Omega(y) < \Omega(x)))))$$
$$\lor (\forall y(Conseq(y,x) \supset (T(y) \mathbin{\&} (\Omega(y) < \Omega(x))))))))),$$

or, in other words, a conditional is true just in case either its antecedent is false or its consequent is true, with the relevant antecedent or consequent being assigned a lower ordinal than the conditional. As usual, we write the clause using the dummy name for the function to the ordinals, understanding that any conclusion from which the dummy name is absent can be exported to the main derivation bar (and so is a theorem).

As above, we let κ denote $\forall x(T(x) \supset T(x))$. In addition, we will assign the individual term ζ to $T(\lambda) \supset T(\lambda)$, and the term μ to $T(\lambda)$. (We could use quotation names for these, but this saves space.) Given these assignments for the individual terms, the following sentences are all obviously true: $Univ(\kappa)$, $Cond(\zeta)$, $Tau(\mu)$, $ISC(\zeta,\kappa)$, $Ante(\mu,\zeta)$, $Conseq(\mu,\zeta)$, and $ISC(\lambda,\mu)$. Since they are obviously true, we will use them in the proof with the justification "obviously true". We could, of course, set up some more formal machinery to derive them. We also recall that $\sim T(\lambda)$ and $\sim \Phi(\lambda)$ have been derived above as theorems. Since we have all of the natural deduction rules, we can therefore derive $\sim(T(\lambda) \vee \Phi(\lambda))$ as a theorem.

In order to simplify the proof a bit, we will also use a slightly different falsity clause for the truth predicate:

$$\forall x(Tau(x) \supset (\Phi(x) \equiv \forall y(ISC(y,x) \supset (\Phi(y) \& (\Omega(y) < \Omega(x))))))$$

in place of

$$\forall x(Tau(x) \supset (\Phi(x) \equiv \exists y(ISC(y,x) \& (\Phi(y) \& (\Omega(y) < \Omega(x)))))).$$

This saves a few lines, and makes no material difference.

The proof runs:

$T(\kappa)$	Hypothesis
$T(\kappa)$	Reiteration
$Univ(\kappa)$	Obvious Truth
$\forall x(Univ(x) \supset (T(x) \equiv \forall y(ISC(y,x) \supset (T(y) \& (\Omega(y) < \Omega(x))))))$	Axiom
$Univ(\kappa) \supset (T(\kappa) \equiv \forall y(ISC(y,\kappa) \supset (T(y) \& (\Omega(y) < \Omega(\kappa)))))$	$\forall$ Elimination
$T(\kappa) \equiv \forall y(ISC(y,\kappa) \supset (T(y) \& (\Omega(y) < \Omega(\kappa))))$	$\supset$ Elimination
$\forall y(ISC(y,\kappa) \supset (T(y) \& (\Omega(y) < \Omega(\kappa))))$	$\equiv$ Elimination
$ISC(\zeta,\kappa) \supset (T(\zeta) \& (\Omega(\zeta) < \Omega(\kappa)))$	$\forall$ Elimination
$ISC(\zeta,\kappa)$	Obvious truth
$T(\zeta) \& (\Omega(\zeta) < \Omega(\kappa))$	$\supset$ Elimination
$T(\zeta)$	& Elimination
$Cond(\zeta)$	Obvious truth
$\forall x(Cond(x) \supset (T(x) \equiv ((\forall y(Ante(y,x) \supset (\Phi(y) \& (\Omega(y) < \Omega(x))))) \vee (\forall y(Conseq(y,x) \supset (T(y) \& (\Omega(y) < \Omega(x))))))))$	Axiom
$Cond(\zeta) \supset (T(\zeta) \equiv ((\forall y(Ante(y,\zeta) \supset (\Phi(y) \& (\Omega(y) < \Omega(\zeta))))) \vee (\forall y(Conseq(y,\zeta) \supset (T(y) \& (\Omega(y) < \Omega(\zeta))))))))$	$\forall$ Elimination
$T(\zeta) \equiv ((\forall y(Ante(y,\zeta) \supset (\Phi(y) \& (\Omega(y) < \Omega(\zeta))))) \vee (\forall y(Conseq(y,\zeta) \supset (T(y) \& (\Omega(y) < \Omega(\zeta))))))$	$\supset$ Elimination
$(\forall y(Ante(y,\zeta) \supset (\Phi(y) \& (\Omega(y) < \Omega(\zeta))))) \vee (\forall y(conseq(y,\zeta) \supset (T(y) \& (\Omega(y) < \Omega(\zeta)))))$	$\equiv$ Elimination

(PROOF CONTINUES ON NEXT PAGE)

148 Reasoning about Permissible Sentences

$\forall y(Ante(y,\zeta) \supset (\Phi(y) \ \& \ (\Omega(y) < \Omega(\zeta))))$	Hypothesis
$\forall y(Ante(y,\zeta) \supset (\Phi(y) \ \& \ (\Omega(y) < \Omega(\zeta))))$	Reiteration
$Ante(\mu,\zeta) \supset (\Phi(\mu) \ \& \ (\Omega(\mu) < \Omega(\zeta)))$	$\forall$ Elimination
$Ante(\mu,\zeta)$	Obvious Truth
$\Phi(\mu) \ \& \ (\Omega(\mu) < \Omega(\zeta))$	$\supset$ Elimination
$\Phi(\mu)$	$\&$ Elimination
$\forall x(Tau(x) \supset (\Phi(x) \equiv \exists y(ISC(y,x) \ \& \ (\Phi(y)$ $\& \ (\Omega(y) < \Omega(x))))))$	Axiom
$Tau(\mu) \supset (\Phi(\mu) \equiv \exists y(ISC(y,\mu) \ \& \ (\Phi(y) \ \&$ $(\Omega(y) < \Omega(\mu)))))$	$\forall$ Elimination
$Tau(\mu)$	Obvious Truth
$\Phi(\mu) \equiv \forall y(ISC(y,\mu) \supset (\Phi(y) \ \& \ (\Omega(y)$ $< \Omega(\mu))))$	$\supset$ Elimination
$\forall y(ISC(y,\mu) \supset (\Phi(y) \ \& \ (\Omega(y) < \Omega(\mu))))$	$\equiv$ Elimination
$ISC(\lambda,\mu) \supset (\Phi(\lambda) \ \& \ (\Omega(\lambda) < \Omega(\mu)))$	$\forall$ Elimination
$ISC(\lambda,\mu)$	Obvious Truth
$\Phi(\lambda) \ \& \ (\Omega(\lambda) < \Omega(\mu))$	$\supset$ Elimination
$\Phi(\lambda)$	$\&$ Elimination
$T(\lambda) \vee \Phi(\lambda)$	$\vee$ Introduction
$\forall y(Conseq(y,\zeta) \supset (T(y) \ \& \ (\Omega(y) < \Omega(\zeta))))$	Hypothesis
$\forall y(Conseq(y,\zeta) \supset (T(y) \ \& \ (\Omega(y) < \Omega(\zeta))))$	Reiteration
$Conseq(\mu,\zeta) \supset (T(\mu) \ \& \ (\Omega(\mu) < \Omega(\zeta)))$	$\forall$ Elimination
$Conseq(\mu,\zeta)$	Obvious Truth
$(T(\mu) \ \& \ (\Omega(\mu) < \Omega(\zeta)))$	$\supset$ Elimination
$T(\mu)$	$\&$ Elimination
$\forall x(Tau(x) \supset (T(x) \equiv \forall y(ISC(y,x) \supset$ $(T(y) \ \& \ (\Omega(y) < \Omega(x))))))$	Axiom
$Tau(\mu) \supset (T(\mu) \equiv \forall y(ISC(y,\mu) \supset$ $(T(y) \ \& \ (\Omega(y) < \Omega(\mu)))))$	$\forall$ Elimination
$Tau(\mu)$	Obvious Truth
$T(\mu) \equiv \forall y(ISC(y,\mu) \supset (T(y) \ \& \ (\Omega(y)$ $< \Omega(\mu))))$	$\supset$ Elimination
$\forall y(ISC(y,\mu) \supset (T(y) \ \& \ (\Omega(y) < \Omega(\mu))))$	$\equiv$ Elimination
$ISC(\lambda,\mu) \supset (T(\lambda) \ \& \ (\Omega(\lambda) < \Omega(\mu)))$	$\forall$ Elimination
$ISC(\lambda,\mu)$	Obvious Truth
$T(\lambda) \ \& \ (\Omega(\lambda) < \Omega(\mu))$	$\supset$ Elimination
$T(\lambda)$	$\&$ Elimination
$T(\lambda) \vee \Phi(\lambda)$	$\vee$ Introduction
$T(\lambda) \vee \Phi(\lambda)$	$\vee$ Elimination
$\sim(T(\lambda) \vee \Phi(\lambda))$	Theorem
$\sim T(\kappa)$	$\sim$ Introduction

Note that the ordering constraints involving the function to the ordinals play no role in the derivation. If the Liar is in the language, $\forall x(T(x) \supset T(x))$ can be proven to be ungrounded simply by considering the local truth-functional connections between sentences.

No such proof can show that the Truthteller is ungrounded since assigning it the semantic value true or the semantic value false violates no local constraints. The ungroundedness of the Truthteller is purely a matter of global structure, and so can only be proven by attending to the ordering constraints. The relevant constraint is that no sentence can be assigned an ordinal which is smaller than itself, due to the irreflexivity of the "less than" relation. So to prove that the Truthteller is ungrounded, we need the Irreflexivity Axiom $\sim \exists \Xi \exists y(\Xi(y) < \Xi(y))$: it is not the case that there is a function from the sentences to the ordinals and a sentence such that the ordinal assigned to that sentence is lower than itself. In addition to this axiom, we need the two Obvious Truths $Tau(\beta)$ and $ISC(\beta,\beta)$. We will provide the proof that the Truthteller is not true: the proof that it is not false is similar in the obvious way.

$T(\beta)$	Hypothesis
$\forall x(Tau(x) \supset (T(x) \equiv \forall y(ISC(y,x) \supset$ $(T(y) \,\&\, (\Omega(y) < \Omega(x))))))$	Axiom
$Tau(\beta) \supset (T(\beta) \equiv \forall y(ISC(y,\beta) \supset$ $(T(y) \,\&\, (\Omega(y) < \Omega(\beta)))))$	$\forall$ Elimination
$Tau(\beta)$	Obvious Truth
$T(\beta) \equiv \forall y(ISC(y,\beta) \supset (T(y) \,\&\, (\Omega(y)$ $< \Omega(\beta))))$	$\supset$ Elimination
$T(\beta)$	Reiteration
$\forall y(ISC(y,\beta) \supset (T(y) \,\&\, (\Omega(y) < \Omega(\beta))))$	$\equiv$ Elimination
$ISC(\beta,\beta) \supset (T(\beta) \,\&\, (\Omega(\beta) < \Omega(\beta)))$	$\forall$ Elimination
$ISC(\beta,\beta)$	Obvious Truth
$T(\beta) \,\&\, (\Omega(\beta) < \Omega(\beta))$	$\supset$ Elimination
$\Omega(\beta) < \Omega(\beta))$	$\&$ Elimination
$\exists y(\Omega(y) < \Omega(y))$	$\exists$ Introduction
$\exists \Xi \exists y(\Xi(y) < \Xi(y))$	$\exists$ Introduction
$\sim \exists \Xi \exists y(\Xi(y) < \Xi(y))$	Irreflexivity Axiom
$\sim T(\beta)$	$\sim$ Introduction

One can, by a similar strategy, prove that $\forall x(T(x) \supset T(x))$ is not true (and ultimately ungrounded) even in a language which does not contain the Liar or any other sentence which the local constraints alone require to be ungrounded. Assuming that $\forall x(T(x) \supset T(x))$ is true, one can prove that $T(\ulcorner\forall x(T(x) \supset T(x))\urcorner) \supset T(\ulcorner\forall x(T(x) \supset T(x))\urcorner)$ must be assigned a lower ordinal than $\forall x(T(x) \supset T(x))$, then that $T(\ulcorner\forall x(T(x) \supset T(x))\urcorner)$ must be assigned a lower ordinal than $T(\ulcorner\forall x(T(x) \supset T(x))\urcorner) \supset T(\ulcorner\forall x(T(x) \supset T(x))\urcorner)$, and finally that $\forall x(T(x) \supset T(x))$ must be assigned a lower ordinal than $T(\ulcorner\forall x(T(x) \supset T(x))\urcorner)$. Using a Transitivity Axiom for the "less than" relation, one demonstrates that the ordinal assigned to $\forall x(T(x) \supset T(x))$ must be lower than itself, which contradicts the Irreflexivity Axiom.

Proofs of ungroundedness therefore come in three flavors. The simplest and most intuitive are proofs that use only the natural deduction rules and the Downward T- and F-Inferences. Since all of these inferences are intuitively compelling, the conclusion that the given sentence in neither true nor false seems inescapable, even before doing any theory. The proof that the Liar is neither true nor false is of this first class, which explains why the Liar is so easily recognized as problematic. The second flavor is proofs that employ the semantic theory as an axiom, but do not make use of the clauses about ordering, such as the proof given above that $\forall x(T(x) \supset T(x))$ is not true. Since the local constraints are fairly compelling, proofs of this sort can also be quite convincing, even without having developed an explicit theory. The third flavor are proofs that use the semantic theory as an axiom and which rely on the ordering principles rather than just on the local constraints, such as the proof that the Truthteller is not true. The ordering principle is not so intuitively obvious, and so such proofs are not likely to be accepted without an explicit defense of the theoretical principles involved.

Some anecdotal evidence can be adduced for this ranking of the *prima facie* persuasive power of the three argument forms. Anil Gupta, for example, is happy to accept the paradoxicality of the Liar, but balks at other consequences of Kripke's theory. Among his complaints:

(1) By Kripke's definition various logical laws are sometimes paradoxical. For example, his definition entails that the law $(\forall x) \sim (T(x) \& \sim T(x))$ is paradoxical when there is a liar-type sentence in the language—for now the law does not have a truth value in any of the Kripkean fixed points. ... Intuitively the law does not seem to be paradoxical. In fact even in the presence of paradoxical sentences, far from finding the law paradoxical, we are inclined to believe it.

(2) A related criticism is that according to Kripke's theory the law $(\forall x) \sim (T(x) \& \sim T(x))$ is not grounded but pathological even when there isn't any self-reference of the sort that generates the paradoxes. The sentence $(\forall x) \sim (T(x) \& \sim T(x))$ is never true in the Kripkean minimal fixed point ... [T]he sentence can only become decided when $\sim (T(x) \& \sim T(x))$ is decided for all values of x. This cannot happen until the truth of $(\forall x) \sim (T(x) \& \sim T(x))$ is already decided because it itself is one of the values of x. Result: $(\forall x) \sim (T(x) \& \sim T(x))$ is not grounded in any model—even in models in which there is no vicious self-reference of any sort. It is counterintuitive to say that in such models the logical law should not be asserted to be true. But this is what we would have to say if the minimal fixed point is taken as the model for truth.   (Gupta 1982, in Martin 1984: 209–10)

If by "paradoxical" one means "provably neither true nor false", then the proofs sketched above show how—given the appropriate theory—the two sorts of proofs needed for these results can be regimented. Note that Gupta finds it even more unacceptable that $(\forall x)\sim(T(x)\ \&\ \sim T(x))$ should be paradoxical when the problem stems from the ordering principle than when it stems from the paradoxicality of one of its instances. Note also the critical importance of exactly what one needs to deny, given our account of truth. As Gupta correctly notes, according to our account, we cannot assert that the logical law *is true*. We can, however, correctly assert the logical law itself. If Gupta is "inclined to believe" the logical law he may rightly do so—taking care, however, not to believe it to be true.

Proofs of ungroundedness that use the ordering principles need not rely on circularity (and the Irreflexivity Principle). Infinitely descending chains can also be proven to be ungrounded, albeit with some more powerful machinery. One needs a postulate appropriate for the ordinals: viz. that given any set of sentences (even an infinite set) each of which is assigned an ordinal, there is at least one sentence assigned the lowest ordinal: no member of the set is assigned one lower. This is because every set of ordinals has a least member. One can then prove that any member assigned the lowest ordinal cannot be either true or false, since either would require one of its immediate semantic constituents to have a lower ordinal. In a simple chain, if any member is ungrounded then one can prove that every member above it and below it is ungrounded as well.

This is not to say that every ungrounded sentence is provably ungrounded in this system. If a sentence is unsafe due to an unending non-circular backward path, and if the backward path is never completely unsafe, always having some connections to the boundary, then one might have to verify that none of those connections to the boundary are sufficient to generate a truth value for the sentence. In principle, this could be an infinite task which no finite derivation could accomplish. Of course, *specifying* a sentence with such a semantic structure is a non-trivial task, but the semantics admits the theoretical possibility. Trouble may also come from quantified sentences with an infinite number of immediate semantic constituents, since no finite argument could prove of each constituent individually that it is, for example, ungrounded. Whether we could intuitively recognize the ungroundedness of any such sentence (i.e. a sentence which cannot be proven to be ungrounded in the permissibility-preserving system) is another question.

In the permissibility-preserving system all of the classical inferences are allowable, and the absence of the Upward T- and F-Inferences is largely compensated for if one accepts the semantic theory as an axiom. This makes the system rather cumbersome—one must reason explicitly about semantic structure in order to determine what one can safely say—but the results are quite satisfactory. Given the semantic theory, it is provably acceptable to say the things we have said all along: the Liar and the Truthteller are neither true nor false, as is $\forall x(T(x)\supset T(x))$ and other seemingly undeniable "logical truths". And indeed, all "logical truths", i.e. all *classical* theorems, *are* undeniable. Sometimes, however, one must deny that they are *truths*.

Observations on the Two Inferential Systems

We have now sketched two inferential systems: a truth-preserving system and a permissibility-preserving system. The systems have different rules and preserve different properties. They have different sets of theorems. The truth-preserving system has the Upwards T- and F-Inferences while the permissibility-preserving system does not; the truth-preserving system uses index sets while the permissibility-preserving system does not. The truth-preserving system is a purely inferential system with no axioms, while the permissibility-preserving system has the fundamental semantic theory as an axiom, as well as axioms regarding the structure of the function into the ordinals. Despite these apparent differences there are deep structural connections between the two systems.

In one sense, the truth-preserving system is less comprehensive than the permissibility-preserving system simply because of the asymmetry between truth and permissibility: every true sentence is permissible but not every permissible sentence is true. There are therefore sentences which can be proven in the permissibility-preserving system but not the truth-preserving one, e.g. the Liar and the sentence $Y(\lambda)$ which says that the Liar is ungrounded. Indeed, since no sentence of the form $Y(n)$ is ever true, none can be a theorem of the truth-preserving system. In the other direction, though, the situation is much more benign. Not only is every true sentence permissible, so every theorem of the truth-preserving system can in principle be a theorem of the permissibility-preserving system, but any sentence $\mathscr{F}(n)$ is true *if and only if the sentence* $T(n)$ *is permissible*. So even though the aim of the permissibility-preserving system is to derive permissible sentences, it can nonetheless be used to establish truth: *if it is permissible* (according to our normative rules) *to assert that a sentence is true, then* (according to our semantic theory) *the sentence is true*.

Of course, the lack of the Upwards T-Inferences makes it a non-trivial task to prove, in the permissibility-preserving system, any sentence of the form $T(n)$. In general, one has to use the semantic theory axiom in any such proof. Furthermore, even if one includes the "obvious truths" about the syntactic forms of sentences as axioms, *the permissibility-preserving system has no theorems of the form* $T(n)$ *if one omits the clauses* $\forall x(Bound(x) \supset (T(x) \equiv \mathscr{F}(x))$ *and* $\forall x(Bound(x) \supset (\Phi(x) \equiv \mathscr{N}\mathscr{F}(x)))$ *from the semantic axiom*. This is evident since sentences of the form $T(n)$ are, from the point of view of the classical rules, atomic sentences. The classical rules alone cannot establish either $T(n)$ or $\Phi(n)$, so the classical rules plus the Downward T- and F-Inferences cannot establish any such sentence (since the Downward rules would have nothing to

work on), and the part of the semantic theory that expresses the local constraints cannot be used since one always already has to establish a sentence of
the form $T(n)$ or $\Phi(n)$ in using the local constraints to infer a sentence of
that form. The only way to get semantic output from non-semantic input is
to use the Boundary sentence clauses $\forall x(Bound(x) \supset (T(x) \equiv \mathscr{F}(x))$ and
$\forall x(Bound(x) \supset (\Phi(x) \equiv \mathscr{N}\mathscr{F}(x)))$.

This result is in strict analogy with the results already discussed in the truth-
preserving system. In the truth-preserving system, if one omits the Boundary
Rule then one has no theorems at all. In the permissibility-preserving system if
one omits the Boundary Sentence clauses in the semantic theory, one has no
theorems of the form $T(n)$, and so no theorems that say that a sentence is true.
One can, of course, still demonstrate that some sentences are *ungrounded*
without those clauses; indeed, none of the proofs in the previous section
made use of those clauses. That is because sentences like the Liar are not
made ungrounded by the world: they are guaranteed to be ungrounded no
matter how the world is, in virtue of the graph of the language.

The idea of using a permissibility-preserving system to infer that sentences
are true has been suggested (albeit not in these words) by William Reinhardt.
Reinhardt develops an inferential system, but rejects the usual procedure of
regarding as true all sentences that can be derived in the system. Rather,

[m]y proposal . . . uses KF [formal Kripke-Feferman theory] to state sufficient conditions for the truth of A. The sufficient condition, however, is not that KF $\vdash A$; it is
rather that KF $\vdash T[A]$. The basic proposal then is that
(I)   If A is a sentence for which KF $\vdash T[A]$, then A is true.   (Reinhardt 1986: 232)

Reinhardt does not introduce the notion of permissibility, or explain what
attitude one should take towards sentences which can be derived but for which
$T(n)$ cannot be derived, nor does he employ any ordering principles in the
semantic theory, but one can see from our perspective why his suggestion is
useful. Being a theorem of Reinhardt's system does guarantee having an
interesting property, but that property is not truth. Without the distinction
between permissibility and truth, and without the observation that the inferential system preserves permissibility, Reinhardt's formal technique is a bit
mystifying: after all, if the theorems of the system are not, in general, to be
trusted, why trust those which have the form $T[A]$?[1]

---

[1] Reinhardt is slightly hamstrung in his account by an unfortunate choice of terminology.
Sentences which are neither true nor false, which we call "ungrounded", he calls "non-significant".
Although the content is the same, it seems harder to take a "non-significant" sentence as one
which ought to be asserted or believed than an "ungrounded" sentence. Indeed, Reinhardt is
quite concerned that the axioms of KF are non-significant: he tries to find a method for making
the axioms significant in order to feel justified in using them, even as purely formal devices
(cf. Reinhardt 1986: 236 ff.). He does not try to distinguish non-significant sentences *per se* into
those that can be properly asserted and those that cannot. I am indebted to Vann McGee for
drawing Reinhardt's work to my attention.

It is edifying to compare the relation between the truth-preserving system and the permissibility-preserving system on the one hand, and the relation between the language and the metalanguage in Tarski's scheme on the other. If one adopts Tarski's system, then one cannot do semantics, or explicitly talk about truth, without ascending to the metalanguage. Fundamental semantic principles, such as that a conjunction is true just in case both its conjuncts are true, cannot be stated in the object language at all. In Tarski's system, no claims about truth can be made in the object language so all theories of truth must be framed in a more powerful language.

In our system there is no distinction between language and metalanguage: there is but a single language which contains its own truth predicate. Using that language one can frame many true sentences, including sentences which contain the truth predicate. If $\mathcal{F}(n)$ is true, then so is $T(n)$. And in that language one can *frame* the complete semantic theory: one can say, for example, that a conjunction is true if and only if its conjuncts are. But since the semantic theory itself does not come out true, one cannot *assert* the semantic theory *if one is restricted to asserting only true sentences*. To talk about semantics, one does not need to *enlarge the language*, one rather needs to *relax one's standards*. One must be content to assert claims that are not true (although they are permissible). By casting the relevant distinction as that between truth and permissibility rather than that between language and metalanguage we can see why certain claims involving truth are completely unproblematic (viz. those which are true) while others involve us in particular difficulties (viz. those which are merely permissible but not true).

One might well be tempted to reject the truth-preserving system altogether in favor of the permissibility-preserving system: if one happens to be interested in whether a sentence $\mathcal{F}(n)$ is true one simply sees if the sentence $T(n)$ can be derived. Such an approach may be workable, but it is perhaps not advisable.

First, one might wonder why the truth-preserving system should be rejected even if it is in some sense redundant: after all, it still is a perfectly good system for its purpose. Further, there are some derivations that will be much easier in the truth-preserving system. Suppose, for example, one wants to prove that $\forall x(M(x) \supset M(x))$ is *true*. We have already seen how to derive this sentence in the truth-preserving system using the Expanded Boundary Rule. One can then also derive $T(\ulcorner \forall x(M(x) \supset M(x)) \urcorner)$ by the Upward T-Inference. Deriving $T(\ulcorner \forall x(M(x) \supset M(x)) \urcorner)$ in the permissibility-preserving system, by using the semantic theory axiom, would require some new machinery. The problem derives from the fact that any universal claim has an infinitude of immediate semantic constituents. There is no problem showing, in the permissibility-preserving system, that any given constituent of $\forall x(M(x) \supset M(x))$, for example $M(\lambda) \supset M(\lambda)$, is true. Since $M(\lambda)$ is a boundary sentence, the Boundary Sentence clauses can be used to prove that it is either true or false, and from this it can be shown that $M(\lambda) \supset M(\lambda)$ is true. But since there are an infinite number of such constituents of $\forall x(M(x) \supset M(x))$ one cannot show directly that they all are true. Some generalizing techniques may be able to do the job, but there is no pressing reason to replace a more elegant system with a more cumbersome one. Further, when we come to study the formal properties of the two systems, we find that the truth-preserving system has some rather intriguing characteristics.

Each system allows us to define a notion of a consequence of a sentence, but we will focus first on the truth-preserving system. We will say that Y is a *logical consequence* of X just in case Y can be derived with any empty index set in the truth-preserving system using only X (with an empty index set) as a premise. Similarly, a logical consequence of a set of sentences is a sentence that can be derived from premises drawn from that set. A theorem is a sentence that can be derived from no premises. As usual, we use the symbol $\vdash$ to represent logical consequence. $\vdash X$ indicates that X is a theorem.

The notions of logical consequence and theoremhood are evidently dependent on the specification of a particular inferential system, and so ought properly to be subscripted to indicate the system of rules under consideration. In classical contexts where complete systems are available, the relativity of these notions to an inferential system can be safely ignored: all of the sets of inference rules likely to be employed will generate the same relations of logical consequence. We cannot be so cavalier: no complete set of rules (complete in that every logically necessary truth is a theorem) may exist, and different systems of inference may generate different relations of logical consequence. These particular differences will not concern us, so in the sequel we will act as if there is one unique set of truth-preserving inference rules and so one unique relation of logical entailment.

Given the graph of a language, we can also define a notion of semantic entailment. Every graph has a boundary, and every language has a set of primary truth values (as usual, we consider a language whose primary values are truth and falsity). Consider the set of all possible assignments of primary truth values to the boundary sentences. Each such assignment generates a unique assignment of truth values to all of the sentences in the language, i.e. each such assignment of primary values to the boundary sentences generates a unique interpretation of the language. When defining semantic entailment, we consider this set of interpretations as the complete set of admissible interpretations of the language. Given two sentences X and Y, we say that X *entails* Y iff every admissible interpretation which assigns X the value true also assigns Y the value true. As usual, we represent the relation of semantic entailment as $X \models Y$. $\models X$ indicates that X is a logically necessary truth, a sentence true in all interpretations.

The relations between logical consequence and semantic entailment in our system are rather different from their relations in classical logic, and so repay some scrutiny.

Since the Upward and Downward T-Inferences are both part of the truth-preserving system, we always have every instance of the schema

$$\mathscr{F}(n) \vdash T(n)$$

and

$$T(n) \vdash \mathscr{F}(n).$$

Representing this in an obvious way, we have

$$T(n) \dashv\vdash \mathscr{F}(n),$$

which looks suspiciously like the schema for the T-sentences.

Since every interpretation which makes $\mathscr{F}(n)$ true makes $T(n)$ true, and vice versa, we also have $T(n) \models\!\!\!\dashv \mathscr{F}(n)$, which again looks suspiciously like the schema for the T-sentences. But neither $\vdash$ nor $\models$ is a truth-functional connective, so the problems which arose from accepting all of the T-sentences as true do not recur. The key is that the inferential structure does not guarantee $X \supset Y$ to be a theorem whenever Y is a logical consequence of X, and the semantics does not guarantee $X \supset Y$ to be a necessary truth when Y is entailed by X. That is, we can have

$$X \vdash Y$$

but not

$$\vdash X \supset Y,$$

and

$$X \dashv\vdash Y$$

but not

$$\vdash X \equiv Y.$$

Similarly for entailment, we can have:

$$X \models Y$$

but not

$$\models X \supset Y,$$

and

$$X \models\!\!\!\dashv Y$$

but not

$$\models X \equiv Y.$$

So the fact that $T(n)$ always both logically implies and entails $\mathscr{F}(n)$, and vice versa, does not mean that all of the T-sentences are theorems nor that they are necessary truths.

Logical implication and entailment do not have exactly the same properties in the truth-preserving system; a few examples suffice to drive this point home. Consider first the Truthteller sentence β: $T(\beta)$. Since it is completely unsafe, no interpretation makes it true. It therefore entails every sentence. But not every sentence is a logical consequence of it. Indeed, from the point of view of the inferential system, $T(\beta)$ is just like an atomic *non*-semantic sentence, since applying the Upward and Downward T-Inferences to it just yields the same sentence. No safe sentence that is not a theorem is a logical consequence of the Truthteller.

The Liar sentence $\sim T(\lambda)$, since it is completely unsafe, also entails every sentence. Furthermore, the Liar sentence is *self-contradictory*: it logically implies two sentences that contradict each other (i.e. one of which is the negation of the other), namely itself and $T(\lambda)$ (among other pairs). But even so, the Liar does not logically imply every sentence. It does not, for example, imply the Truthteller. In classical systems, every self-contradictory sentence logically implies every other sentence by use of *reductio ad absurdum*, but the use of index sets blocks these inferences in our system, at least in some cases. The schema for the proof of an arbitrary sentence X from the Liar runs as follows:

$\sim T(\lambda)$	Premise
$\sim X$	Hypothesis
$\sim T(\lambda)$	Reiteration
$T(\lambda)$	Upward T-Inference
$\sim\sim X_{\{\sim X\}}$	$\sim$ Introduction
$X_{\{\sim X\}}$	$\sim$ Elimination
$X_{\{X\}}$	Analysis

This is not yet a proof of X since the index set is not empty. If X happens to be a non-semantic sentence, then the index set can be emptied by use of the Expanded Boundary Rule, and if X is completely safe then it can be eliminated by use of the Expanded Boundary Rule and the Rule of Analysis. But to prove the Truthteller by this means, one would have to be able to empty out an index set which contains $T(\beta)$, which cannot be done. $T(\beta)$ cannot be removed by the Boundary Rule, and it cannot be removed by the Discharge Rule without already having derived $T(\beta)$ or $\sim T(\beta)$, which is just what we are trying to do. So not every sentence is a logical consequence of a self-contradictory sentence.

Semantic entailment, then, does not coincide with logical implication. We have, for example, $T(\beta) \models T(\lambda)$ but not $T(\beta) \vdash T(\lambda)$. But it still may be that every logically necessary truth is a theorem and every theorem a logically necessary truth. That is, it may be that $\models X$ just in case $\vdash X$. In standard classical systems, if all and only the theorems are logically necessary, then the relation of semantic entailment must coincide with the relation of logical implication, for in standard logical systems, $X \models Y$ obtains just in case $\models X \supset Y$ does, and $X \vdash Y$ obtains just in case $\vdash X \supset Y$ does. Since all of the inference rules are truth-preserving, every theorem is a logically necessary truth, but I do not know whether, for the system here described, all logically necessary truths are theorems. Given the possibility of infinite graphs whose structure could not be captured in any finite derivation, this seems very unlikely.

Once we have the notion of logical implication, we are able to define a self-contradictory sentence: a self-contradictory sentence logically implies both some sentence and its negation. And this in turn provides us with one definition of a *paradoxical* sentence: a sentence is paradoxical iff both it and its negation are self-contradictory. This definition does not capture all of the various uses of "paradoxical", but does indicate in precise terms one way in which the Liar is paradoxical and the Truthteller is not. Paradox arises when one cannot consistently maintain either a sentence or its negation. Paradox is naturally defined in terms of inferential structure, since it arises in the context of providing arguments for and against theses.

What can one infer from the fact that a sentence is paradoxical? If a sentence is self-contradictory, then it cannot be true, and so is either false or ungrounded. If both a sentence and its negation are self-contradictory, then both the sentence and its negation must be ungrounded. So one can always properly assert that a paradoxical sentence is ungrounded, and deny that it is either true or false. A self-contradictory (or paradoxical) sentence itself may be either permissible or impermissible. It may sound odd to say that one can appropriately assert a self-contradictory sentence, but recall that the sentence $\forall x \forall y ((Der_\Sigma(x,y) \,\&\, T(x)) \supset T(y))$, which says that a system of rules Σ is truth-preserving, is self-contradictory if the language is sufficiently rich. If we want to be able to say that our system of inference rules is truth-preserving we must sometimes be able assert self-contradictory claims. Our system allows this, although it obviously also forbids our ever appropriately saying that a self-contradictory sentence is true. The Liar is an example of a paradoxical sentence that we intuitively think it appropriate to assert.

If we define "self-contradictory sentence" and "paradoxical sentence" as above, then the question of whether "logical laws" are themselves paradoxical becomes rather subtle. We will focus on two examples: the sentences $\forall x (T(x) \vee \sim T(x))$ and $\forall x (T(x) \supset T(x))$, i.e. "All sentences are either true or not true" and "All true sentences are true". Both of these sentences are ungrounded, and both are necessarily permissible: they are permissible no matter what truth values are put at the boundary. Indeed, one would expect that these sentences ought to be *synonymous*, since the three-valued truth table for $A \supset B$ is identical to the truth table for $\sim A \vee B$. Initially, we did not even treat the horseshoe explicitly in the semantics—we merely stipulated that the other connectives can be defined from negation and conjunction in the usual way. But once one defines paradoxicality or self-contradictoriness in terms of the *inferential* structure rather than the *semantics*, semantic identity is not enough to guarantee identity in all respects.

There are two distinct cases: one when the language contains the Liar or an appropriately similar sentence, and the other when it does not. Let us assume, first, that the language contains the Liar. Then the first thing to note is that $\forall x(T(x) \vee \sim T(x))$ is a self-contradictory sentence: from it, one can validly infer both $T(\lambda)$ and $\sim T(\lambda)$. The derivation of $T(\lambda)$ is as follows, and that of $\sim T(\lambda)$ is similar in the obvious way (using a Downward T-Inference):

$\forall x(T(x) \vee \sim T(x))$	Premise
$\forall x(T(x) \vee \sim T(x))$	Reiteration
$T(\lambda) \vee \sim T(\lambda)$	$\forall$ Elimination
$T(\lambda)$	Hypothesis
$T(\lambda)$	Reiteration
$\sim T(\lambda)$	Hypothesis
$\sim T(\lambda)$	Reiteration
$T(\lambda)$	Upward T-Inference
$T(\lambda)$	$\vee$ Elimination

Since one can validly derive both $T(\lambda)$ and its negation from $\forall x(\sim T(x) \vee T(x))$ (assuming the language contains the Liar or some such paradoxical sentence), $\forall x(\sim T(x) \vee T(x))$ is self-contradictory. If the inferential structure is rich enough (e.g. if it contains de Morgan's laws), then one can also derive a contradiction from the negation of $\forall x(\sim T(x) \vee T(x))$, so "Every sentence is either not true or true" would be paradoxical. Of course, all that follows from this result is that the sentence must be ungrounded, which is a result confirmed by the semantics. The sentence is still permissible: every sentence *is* either true or not true.

The interesting thing is that $\forall x(T(x) \supset T(x))$ may still not be self-contradictory (and *a fortiori* not paradoxical) even though $A \supset B$ is semantically identical to $\sim A \vee B$! It all depends on the set of *inference rules* that one accepts for the horseshoe. If the only $\supset$ Elimination rules one has are Modus Ponens and Modus Tollens, then it is clear that no contradiction can be derived from $\forall x(T(x) \supset T(x))$. $\forall$ Elimination can yield $T(\lambda) \supset T(\lambda)$, but Modus Ponens and Modus Tollens cannot get anything further out of that: in each case, the second premise one needs to derive the conclusion is the conclusion itself. If one could derive $\sim T(\lambda) \vee T(\lambda)$ from $T(\lambda) \supset T(\lambda)$, then one could get a contradiction by means of the derivation given above, but there is no guarantee that these sentences can be derived from one another even though their semantic structure is identical. If they *can't* be derived from one another, then one can argue that they are not *synonymous* even though they are semantically identical. This would be a somewhat pleasing result since "Either the Liar is true or it is not true" does not intuitively seem to be synonymous with "If the Liar is true then it is true".

On the other hand, one could *insist* that $\sim T(\lambda) \vee T(\lambda)$ and $T(\lambda) \supset T(\lambda)$ be interderivable by adding the requisite inference rule to the inferential scheme. That is, if one intends to *define* the horseshoe by means of the tilde and the wedge, by *stipulating* that the semantics of $A \supset B$ be identical to that of $\sim A \vee B$, one might also insist that the direct inferences from $\sim A \vee B$ to $A \supset B$ and back again be added to the inferential structure. Those inferences must obviously be valid. If one does this, then $T(\lambda) \supset T(\lambda)$ is self-contradictory, and so is $\forall x (T(x) \supset T(x))$, in a language which contains the Liar.

In the standard natural deduction systems one can make do with a single rule for, e.g., $\supset$ Elimination since the free use of subderivations allows other inferences to be built up from a small set. In a normal natural deduction system, $\sim A \vee B$ can be derived from $A \supset B$ as follows:

$A \supset B$	Premise
$\sim (\sim A \vee B)$	Hypothesis
A	Hypothesis
A	Reiteration
$A \supset B$	Reiteration
B	$\supset$ Elimination
$\sim A \vee B$	$\vee$ Introduction
$\sim (\sim A \vee B)$	Reiteration
$\sim A$	$\sim$ Introduction
$\sim A \vee B$	$\vee$ Introduction
$\sim (\sim A \vee B)$	Reiteration
$\sim\sim (\sim A \vee B)$	$\sim$ Introduction
$\sim A \vee B$	$\sim$ Elimination

In the standard predicate calculus, then, there is no need to posit a specific rule for inferring $\sim A \vee B$ from $A \supset B$: the natural deduction rules allow it. Once we add index sets, though, the situation changes. The conclusion of the derivation given above would not have an empty index set, since A would be introduced at the first use of $\sim$ Introduction and $\sim (\sim A \vee B)$ at the second. By successive uses of the rule of analysis, the final index set could be reduced to $\{A,B\}$. But unless A and B are safe sentences, or can be proven to have a classical truth value, $\sim A \vee B$ cannot be derived with an empty index set, and cannot be shown, by this proof, to be a logical consequence of $A \supset B$. Without adding some special inference rules, $\sim T(\lambda) \vee T(\lambda)$ is not a logical consequence of $T(\lambda) \supset T(\lambda)$.

The relevant rule, allowing one to infer $\sim A \vee B$ directly from $A \supset B$, is obviously valid, since the two sentences are semantically identical. So one *could*, without harm, add the rule. On the other hand, since in the case of safe sentences the derivation already goes through, one might wonder whether it is really worthwhile to add the rule. Of course, there is an extended sense of "self-contradictory" according to which $T(\lambda) \supset T(\lambda)$ is self-contradictory no matter what one decides to do because a contradiction can be derived from it by use of valid rules of inference, whether one has accepted those rules or not. In this extended sense $\forall x(T(x) \supset T(x))$ is self-contradictory in any language which contains the Liar. Thank goodness, then, that our semantics has already determined that it is not true.

Suppose we accept enough inference rules so that every inference which can be determined to be valid by inspection of truth tables can be made without adding to the index set, i.e. without use of $\sim$ Introduction or $\supset$ Introduction.[2] In particular, suppose the inference from $A \supset B$ to $\sim A \vee B$, the de Morgan inferences, the inference from $\sim T(n)$ to $\mathscr{N}\mathscr{F}(n)$ and the inference from $\Phi(n)$ to $\mathscr{N}\mathscr{F}(n)$ can all be made without adding to the index set (as well as the inferences we have already accepted). Then paradoxicality will be fairly contagious in the language. If some sentence $S(= \mathscr{F}(\sigma))$ is paradoxical, so are $S \vee \sim S$, $T(\sigma) \vee \sim T(\sigma)$, $T(\sigma) \vee \Phi(\sigma)$, $S \supset S$, and $T(\sigma) \supset T(\sigma)$. The generalizations $\forall x(\sim T(x) \vee T(x))$, $\forall x(\Phi(x) \vee T(x))$, and $\forall x(T(x) \supset T(x))$ will also obviously be paradoxical, and so can be recognized as ungrounded by reflection on what can be inferred from them. Once again, we see that these inferences do not comport with a supervaluational semantics in which all classical theorems come out true.

The situation for $\forall x(T(x) \supset T(x))$ and $\forall x(\sim T(x) \vee T(x))$ in a language *without* the Liar (or an equivalent paradoxical sentence) is somewhat different. Each sentence will, of course, still be ungrounded, but there may be no way (using a given inferential scheme) to validly derive a contradiction from either. This confirms Gupta's intuition that in such a language these sentences are not *paradoxical* (or self-contradictory). It does not follow, of course, that in such a language either sentence is *true*.

It is notable that as the relation of semantic entailment and of logical consequence come apart, we are left with conflicting ways of talking about what is *entailed by* or *follows from* the truth of a sentence. What would be the case if $\forall x(\sim T(x) \vee T(x))$, or if the Liar itself, were true? A semantic approach

---

[2] Examples of rules which are valid but which cannot be determined to be so simply by inspection of truth tables are the $Cons_\Sigma$ Rule, the Thm_Σ Rule, and the rule which allows one to infer anything from the Truthteller (since the Truthteller is necessarily ungrounded).

directs your attention to models of the language in which they are true, and asks what else is true in all those models. Since neither sentence is true in any model, we have a degenerate case: we can't make a distinction between what would and would not be the case if these sentences were true. But we can still ask what *validly follows from* each of these sentences. Here we can make discriminations: the Truthteller, for example, validly follows from neither, at least not by any rule whose validity is provable merely from the semantics of the logical particles.[3] So the semantics and the inferential structure give us different tools to approach the question "What if this sentence were true?".

I have, up to this point, been dancing around a subtle question which should be forthrightly addressed. We know that not every instance of the Tarski schema

$$T(n) \equiv \mathscr{F}(n)$$

is true: if $\mathscr{F}(n)$ happens to be ungrounded, the biconditional will also be ungrounded. We have also said that the corresponding semantic and inferential "biconditionals", viz.

$$T(n) \dashv\vDash \mathscr{F}(n)$$

and

$$T(n) \dashv\vdash \mathscr{F}(n)$$

always do "obtain" or "hold". But does that means that the instances of these schemata are always *true*, or merely that they are always *permissible*?

We should first note that since $\vdash$ and $\vDash$ are not truth-functional connectives, the instances of these schemata are, *prima facie* at least, atomic sentences (or perhaps conjunctions of two atomic sentences, one asserting that the relation hold left-to-right, the other right-to-left). There is therefore no reason to insist that the instances must be ungrounded when $\mathscr{F}(n)$ is ungrounded. But the deep logical structure of the relations appears to be quantificational: $X \vdash Y$ obtains just in case *there exists* some sequence of sentences starting with X (with an empty index set) and ending with Y (with an empty index set) such that each sentence is written down in accordance with some one of a set of syntactically specified rules. The concept of logical implication invokes an implicit existential quantification over sequences of sentences. And $X \vDash Y$ obtains just in case *every* interpretation which assigns X the value true also assigns Y

---

[3] There is a degenerate sense in which the inference rule:

From $\forall x (\sim T(x) \lor T(x))$ infer anything at all

is truth-preserving: since the premise cannot be true, the inference cannot lead from a true premise to a conclusion which is not true. But the validity of the rule does not follow from consideration of just the truth-functional connectives and semantic predicates: global structural properties of the graph must be invoked as well.

the value true. Here there is an implicit *universal* quantification over the set of admissible interpretations. These quantificational claims have as their immediate semantic constituents assertions about particular sequences of sentences and particular interpretations (e.g. "such-and-such a sequence of sentences starts with the sentence X", or "such-and-such interpretation assigns the sentence Y the value true"). And these in turn, if not boundary sentences themselves, ultimately resolve into boundary sentences. If, then, all boundary sentences are either true or false, then claims about logical implication and about semantic entailment will all turn out to be true or false. When we say that $X \models Y$ or $X \vdash Y$ obtains, we commit ourselves to $X \models Y$ or $X \vdash Y$ being *true*.

There may yet be a puzzle, though, about just what makes such claims true. We have said that all truth is ultimately rooted in the non-semantic world, i.e. all true sentences are either boundary sentences or have boundary sentences as semantic constituents, and their truth value can be ultimately traced back to the truth value of boundary sentences. But claims like $T(\beta) \models T(\lambda)$ and $\sim(T(\beta) \vdash T(\lambda))$ are, if true, *necessary* truths, and similarly the boundary sentences which are their semantic constituents are necessarily true or necessarily false. The "world" which makes them true or false must be a Platonic world of eternal, non-contingent facts.

This is, of course, just the usual problem about the nature of mathematical truth. Indeed, questions about semantic entailment can be translated, in an obvious way, into questions about possible assignments of numbers to nodes of directed graphs in accordance with certain rules, and these latter would be regarded as purely mathematical issues. So statements about entailment and about logical implication have the same status as mathematical statements. If, as I do, one regards such mathematical claims as either true or false, then so will these others be. If, on the other hand, one has some other account of the semantic status of mathematical claims, then that account can presumably be adopted to claims about entailment and logical implication.

One general strategy, though, ought to be avoided. That strategy seeks to somehow ground or legitimize mathematics by reducing it to logic. The general metaphysical impetus behind this strategy is this: mathematical claims, taken at face value, seem to assert that mathematical *objects* (such as numbers, or lines, of manifolds, or directed graphs) have certain *properties* or bear certain *relations*. But these objects do not appear to be *physical* objects at all: they do not inhabit, or depend on, the world of space and time. Such putative objects are therefore weird or peculiar, and so ought to be avoided in one's ontology. If mathematical claims could somehow be translated into the language of pure logic, and mathematical truth reduced to theoremhood in some formal system, these odd Platonic objects can be purged from one's ontology in favor of a non-problematic notion of *logical truth*.

What is wrong with this strategy is the last step. Even if the proposed reduction of mathematics to pure logic could be carried out, the idea that logical truth or theoremhood is itself ontologically unproblematic does not stand up to scrutiny. To say that a sentence is a theorem of some logical system is to say that there is a sequence of sentences starting with no premises and ending with the given sentence, where each member of the sequence bears an appropriate syntactic relation to some of the sentences which precede it (or to some axioms or axiom schemata), or is otherwise justified by the rules. But the theorems of any logical system far outrun the set of *actually produced* sequences of sentences that satisfy the given conditions. The envisioned sequences of sentences are no more physical entities than numbers or geometrical objects, and "facts" about them are just as ghostly and weird (or just as little ghostly and weird) as facts about numbers and Euclidean triangles. "Logic" cannot magically produce truth out of nothing: there are truths about which sentences are theorems only if there are truths about sequences of sentences conforming to specified rules, and these further truths cannot be grounded in yet further rules and so on *ad infinitum*. The truths of logic may ultimately be grounded in a Platonic world of logical facts and logical objects, but such a world seems no great improvement over a Platonic world of mathematical facts and objects, if improvement was sought for.

Further, we have seen that without the presupposition that boundary sentences have classical truth values, a logical system has no theorems at all. So even the set of "purely logical truths" rests on the presupposition that something makes the boundary sentences either true or false. If the boundary sentences are about numbers or sets, then there must be numbers and sets to make those sentences true or false.

Given the graph of a language and the rules for generating interpretations from assignments of primary values to boundary sentences, the relation of semantic entailment is fixed once and for all. The same is not true of logical implication. As we have remarked, the Truthteller entails the Liar (since it entails every sentence) but does not have the Liar as a logical consequence. This mismatch could be remedied by additions to the inferential system. One could, for example, simply stipulate that any sentence be derivable directly from the Truthteller. Or, more helpfully, one could link the truth-preserving inferential system back to the permissibility-preserving system in this way: if $Y(n)$ is a theorem of the permissibility-preserving system, then any sentence can be written as a logical consequence of $\mathscr{F}(n)$ in the truth-preserving system. It is not clear, though, just what interest such enhancements of the inferential system hold: they are clearly not instances of intuitively acceptable inference forms.

So much, then, for the formal features of the truth-preserving system. The features of the permissibility-preserving system that we have outlined are much more prosaic. Since there are no permissibility gaps, and since all of the standard inference rules hold without modification, the results are what one expects from standard systems. If we denote the derivability in the permissibility-preserving system by $\vdash_p$, then we have

$$X \vdash_p Y \text{ if and only if } \vdash_p X \supset Y$$

and similarly

$$X \models_p Y \text{ if and only if } \models_p X \supset Y.$$

Since the Downward T-Inference is part of the system we also have

$$T(n) \vdash_p \mathscr{F}(n),$$

but lacking the Upward T-Inference we do not always have

$$\mathscr{F}(n) \vdash_p T(n).$$

Correspondingly, we have:

$$T(n) \models_p \mathscr{F}(n)$$

but not always

$$\mathscr{F}(n) \models_p T(n).$$

We have subscripted the notions of logical consequence and entailment to distinguish those notions concerned with *truth* and *truth-preserving inference rules* from the notions concerned with *permissibility* and *permissibility-preserving rules*. We have also noted that if we were being careful we would subscript each sort of logical consequence to indicate the exact system of inferences under consideration. But when it comes to the notion of permissibility, we must also bear in mind that the notions defined are *relative to a specified normative standard of what is permissible to assert*. Since we have up until now had only one such standard under consideration, the existence of other standards is likely to escape notice, but it is nonetheless there. Other standards of permissibility will obviously underwrite different accounts of which inferences preserve permissibility, or when the permissibility of one sentence guarantees the permissibility of another.

Consider, as an extreme example, the *Monastic Rule of Silence*: it is never permissible to assert any sentence. The "logic" of this notion of permissibility is evidently quite distinct from the logic appropriate to our rules. Or even more intriguing, the *Relaxed Monastic Rule*: one may only speak truths that can be formulated in sentences of less than five words. There are evidently non-trivial permissibility-preserving inference rules for these monks, but those rules would have a rather baroque form. The point (which will become of crucial importance in the next chapter) is that permissibility itself is a notion that adverts—directly or indirectly—to a normative standard, and the various derivative notions such as permissibility-preserving inferences inherit that dependence. In the remarks made above, $\vdash_p$ and $\models_p$ refer to permissibility *as defined by the rules outlined in Chapter 5, for the language discussed there.* Different standards of permissibility, or standards defined for different languages, may not display these features.

Having outlined a truth-preserving system of inferences and a permissibility-preserving system, there is one last inference rule that recommends itself to our attention. We have seen that even if a sentence is self-contradictory, it does not follow that the negation of the sentence is a theorem in the truth-preserving system: the rule of $\sim$ Introduction requires the introduction of an index set, and if the self-contradictory sentence is ungrounded it may not be possible to empty the index set. Still, it is evident (in some sense) that a self-contradictory sentence cannot be *true*, for if it were true, and the relevant inferences really were truth-preserving, then both of the two contradictory sentences which logically follow from it would have to be true, which is impossible. The key to understanding this reasoning lies in observing that the claim that the self-contradictory sentence is not true is (a) not the same as the denial of the self-contradictory sentence and (b) itself a claim that, while always *permissible*, is sometimes not *true*.

What follows from this is the acceptability of the following inference rule in the *permissibility*-preserving system. Suppose one starts a subderivation with a premise $\mathscr{F}(n)$. And suppose one can reason from $\mathscr{F}(n)$ to both a sentence and its negation *using rules from the truth-preserving system.* Then one can dismiss the subderivation and write $\sim T(n)$. This rule is obviously akin to $\sim$ Introduction (both in the form in which it appears in the truth-preserving and the permissibility-preserving system), but is a distinct rule, since the conclusion is not the negation of the hypothesis but the negation of the claim that the hypothesis is true. It is obviously also a curious rule since it allows inferences within the subderivation that are not allowed outside it (such as the Upward T-Inference) because they are not permissibility-preserving. I don't think that there are any conclusions that can be reached by means of this rule that cannot be reached by a more drawn out derivation without the rule (using the truth theory as an axiom), but this rule seems to capture some of our intuitive reasoning more directly.

One final consequence of our system is worthy of note, if only for its curiosity. We remarked above that according to our account, many logic puzzles are ill-posed: the inferences used to arrive at the "correct" conclusion are not valid. Objections to common logic puzzles actually run much deeper than this. Consider puzzles of the "knights and knaves" genre, in which knights are supposed to be capable of only telling the truth, knaves only of lying (i.e. uttering falsehoods). It is commonplace in such puzzles for an individual to assert "I am a knight". This is not typically *useful* information (since, intuitively, a knight can truly say it and a knave falsely), but is still supposed to be *consistent* for a knight to say. But if "I am a knight" is equivalent to "Every sentence I utter is true", then no knight can say it. For if every *other* sentence the person says is unproblematically true, then the relevant portion of the graph for the language reduces to a Truthteller cycle. That is, in the most favorable case, every immediate semantic constituent of "Every sentence I utter is true" will be true save one, the one which links back to that sentence itself. The sentence is at best *ungrounded*, not true, and so cannot be uttered by someone who utters only truths. (It is easy to see this if "I am a knight" is the *only* sentence the person utters: then it is obviously a form of the Truthteller.)

It may seem odd that there can be knights (i.e. people who only state truths) but they cannot truly say they are knights. But this is really no more odd than that there can be monks who never say anything at all, and who cannot truly *say* that they never speak. The act of producing the sentence changes the facts in a relevant way. One can, if one has been scrupulously honest, truly say "Everything I've said before this sentence is true", and can further truly assert "And the sentence I just uttered is true" *ad infinitum*, but one cannot truly say of *all* of one's assertions at once that they are true.

It is amusing to imagine a land with lesser knights and knaves, the former of which are confined to uttering *permissible* sentences and the latter to *impermissible* ones. On safe topics, such as the weather or the right road to the castle, these would be as trustworthy (or untrustworthy) as the original sort: lesser knights always state the truth when using safe sentences, lesser knaves always state falsehoods. If a lesser knight has only spoken on safe topics, and so only spoken truths, he still cannot say "I only speak the truth" or even "I am a lesser knight" (i.e. "I only assert permissible sentences"[4]): the Truthteller is not only not true, it is not permissible. But a lesser knight can appropriately (but not truly) say "I never utter a falsehood". The version of the Truthteller that runs "This sentence is not false" is ungrounded but permissible. Presumably this is why the eminent logician George Washington phrased his self-description as "I cannot tell a lie": although what he said could not be true, it could be permissible. "I always tell the truth" cannot be.

---

[4] This sentence is problematic for other reasons as well, which will be discussed below.

8 The Permissibility Paradox

Every proposed solution to the Liar paradox gives rise to a new difficulty. This has sometimes been called the revenge problem, the basic idea being that concepts that are adequate to solve a given Liar paradox must themselves permit the formulation of a new, unresolved paradox. Let us look at the general phenomenon first, and then consider the form it takes for us.

A Liar paradox can typically be solved for an object language with a certain stock of semantic predicates by employing more semantic characterizations in the metalanguage than are available in the object language. Thus, the Liar which is formulated as "This sentence is false" can be solved by claiming that the sentence falls into a truth-value gap, or the Liar formulated as "This sentence is not true" solved by saying that the sentence at issue is not *determinately* true. But as soon as the object language is enriched to include predicates like "falls in a truth-value gap" or "is not determinately true", then a new Liar sentence can be formulated, yielding a new paradox which seems not to be soluble except by again expanding the metalanguage. Tyler Burge remarks:

> Even apart from these problems, the response merely encourages the paradox to assume a different terminology. This can be seen by considering versions of the Strengthened Liar adapted to fit the very words of the response:
>   (i) (i) is either false or undefined
>   (ii) (ii) is not determinately true.
> After claiming that (β) [i.e. (β) (β) is not true] is neither true nor false (or "bad" in some other sense), the gap–theorist must still face a precisely analogous Strengthened Liar tailored to his favorite description of the gaps.   (Burge 1979, in Martin 1984: 89)

At one level, our theory avoids the revenge problem. The original Liar is ungrounded, and the relevant version of the Strengthened Liar (in Burge's sense), viz. $\Phi(\varepsilon) \vee Y(\varepsilon)$, where $\mathscr{F}(\varepsilon)$ is that very sentence, is already formulable in the language. The semantic predicate $\Phi(n) \vee Y(n)$ is both truth-functionally identical to the original Liar predicate $\sim T(n)$ and identical with respect to its permissibility. Indeed, our language is expressively complete with respect to semantic predicates: every possible semantic predicate can be formulated, so long as the language has both the truth and falsity predicates.

The claim that every possible semantic predicate can be formulated demands a bit of clarification. For two semantic predicates to be identical in meaning, they must be both truth-functionally identical (i.e. guaranteed to have the same truth value when predicated of the same sentence) and permissibility-identical (guaranteed to have the same permissibility value when predicated of the same sentence). Since according to our rules all true sentences are permissible and all false sentences impermissible, two predicates that agree in their truth-functional structure can disagree in their permissibility only when the sentence is ungrounded. Since a monadic semantic predicate must yield an ungrounded sentence when predicated of an ungrounded sentence, and a sentence with a classical truth value when predicated of a sentence with a classical truth value, there are exactly four possible truth functions for monadic semantic predicates. These can be identified by their truth functions thus: $<T,T,U>$, $<T,F,U>$, $<F,T,U>$, $<F,F,U>$, where the first slot gives the truth value when predicated of a true sentence, the second the truth value when predicated of a false sentence, and the third the truth value when predicated of an ungrounded sentence. But each semantic predicate comes in two permissibility flavors: one which yields a permissible sentence when applied to an ungrounded sentence, and the other which yields an impermissible sentence. The eight possibilities can be represented in an obvious way: $<T,T,U/A>$, $<T,T,U/D>$, $<T,F,U/A>$, $<T,F,U/D>$, $<F,T,U/A>$, $<F,T,U/D>$, $<F,F,U/A>$, $<F,F,U/D>$.

If the language's only semantic predicate is the truth predicate, only four of these possible predicates can be expressed: $<T,T,U/A>$, $<T,F,U/D>$, $<F,T,U/A>$, and $<F,F,U/D>$, expressed by $T(n) \vee \sim T(n)$, $T(n)$, $\sim T(n)$, and $T(n) \& \sim T(n)$ respectively. Every truth function can be constructed, but not every truth function *cum* permissibility value. If we add the falsity predicate, then the other four possible predicates can be constructed: $<T,T,U/D>$, $<T,F,U/A>$, $<F,T,U/D>$, and $<F,F,U/A>$ are expressed by $T(n) \vee \Phi(n)$, $\sim \Phi(n)$, $\Phi(n)$, and $\sim T(n) \& \sim \Phi(n)$ respectively. The ungroundedness predicate $Y(n)$ is equivalent both truth-functionally and with respect to permissibility to $\sim T(n) \& \sim \Phi(n)$: ungrounded sentences are not true and not false (equivalently, neither true nor false). We started with a language that contains only a truth predicate, and which is therefore not complete with respect to expressive power. But once we add a falsity predicate, the language is expressively complete: every possible semantic predicate can be expressed. And the apparatus that we used to solve the original Liar is adequate to every sentence constructible in this language.

But there is another doubt. Even though truth, falsity, and ungroundedness are the only truth values in this language, and even though there are no truth-value gaps, what about the predicates "permissible" and "impermissible"? These have made an appearance in the account, but are not represented in the formal language. Perhaps a permissibility paradox lies in wait. Indeed there does, but we must approach it with extreme care.

In describing our language, we have used, in the metalanguage, the predicates "is permissible" and "is impermissible". We have not, however, introduced these predicates into the formal language itself. Does this not show that there is still an important language/metalanguage distinction?

It is certainly correct that the language we have been discussing up to now is importantly *incomplete*: it does not contain "permissibility predicates", and must be expanded to include them if it is to become as expressively rich as English. And it is also correct that expanding the language to include these predicates will cause us some headaches. But, as we will see, it is not so obvious that much is gained by characterizing the expanded language as a *metalanguage*, at least not if that tacitly suggests that there ought to be an even more expansive meta-metalanguage. Furthermore, as we will see, the permissibility predicate is not in any obvious way "above" the truth predicate in some hierarchy: just as one can have a language with a truth predicate but no permissibility predicates, so one could have a language with permissibility predicates but no truth predicate. The sort of iterated problematic characteristic of the revenge problem, iteration that ultimately gives rise to an infinite hierarchy of truth predicates or semantic values, simply will not arise for us. Once we admit the permissibility predicates, we will have some problems, but we will be done. But in the first instance we must be very precise about the structure of the permissibility predicates we admit. In particular, we must be careful to distinguish the nature of permissibility from the nature of truth.

As has already been mentioned, this work offers an *analysis* of truth, a single, comprehensive account of the nature of the truth predicate and the conditions under which a sentence is true. We have therefore only introduced a single truth predicate (there are no distinct "levels" or "types" of truth that need to be differentiated). In contrast, we have offered only an *ideal* for rules of permissible assertion, a set of desirable conditions that we wish such rules to meet, all of which cannot be simultaneously satisfied. So there is no unique sort of permissibility, rather there are infinitely many different possible rules for permissible assertion and denial of sentences, each of which will satisfy, and fail to satisfy, the ideal in its own way. And there is no unique fact, concerning a particular sentence, whether it is permissible or impermissible to assert. Rather, any sentence will be permissible according to some rules, impermissible according to others. Indeed, the sentence will be neither permissible nor impermissible according to some (incomplete) rules, both permissible and impermissible according to some (pragmatically incoherent) rules. It may even be indeterminate whether the sentence is permissible or not if the rules are sufficiently vague. The obvious point is that permissibility and impermissibility are always *relative to a set of rules*. There is simply no content to the question of whether a sentence *per se* is permissible or not.

The critical implication of the foregoing is that there is not a single permissibility predicate: there ought to be at least as many predicates as there are articulable rules. So there is an infinitude of permissibility predicates, just as there is an infinitude of possible rules, although most of these rules fail to satisfy the ideal in such radical and unjustifiable ways that we would never seriously consider them as rules *to adopt*. Nonetheless, in order to keep things clear we always need to subscript any permissibility predicate to indicate the rules it is associated with. For example, in association with the Monastic Rule of Silence we could introduce the predicate $P_{MRS}(x)$. Since the rule forbids all assertion, every atomic sentence of the form $P_{MRS}(n)$ would be false.

Instead of expanding the language to include a single permissibility (and impermissibility) predicate, we have expanded the language to include an infinitude of such predicates, all at one fell swoop. And this collection of predicates does not, in any obvious way, *have a structure* or *form a hierarchy*. There are not different "levels" of predicates. We may, of course, introduce or define some structure on them, if need be, but the need may well not arise. In any case, the immediate proliferation of such predicates is not a symptom or a consequence of any revenge problem or iteration: as an abstract matter, all the rules are there all along.

But now the "form" of the revenge problem that does occur can be easily stated. Let $P_{\Sigma_i}(x)$ be any of the permissibility predicates, with Σ_i some set of rules. Form the sentence:

$$\omega: \sim P_{\Sigma_i}(\omega),$$

i.e., a sentence which says of itself that it is not permissible according to the rules Σ_i. According to the rules in Σ_i is ω permissible to assert or not?

Since we have not specified what the rules Σ_i are, we obviously cannot directly answer this question. But we can say that no matter how the rules are written, *the ideals of permissibility are bound to be violated in a serious way*.

Let's review the ideals of permissibility. If all our fondest wishes could be granted, we would have rules of permissibility to

1. *Be truth-permissive*: they should allow the assertion of any true sentence.
2. *Be falsity-forbidding*: they should prohibit the assertion of any false sentence.
3. *Be complete*: they should render a decision about every sentence, either permitting or forbidding that it be asserted.
4. *Be pragmatically coherent*: they should not have as a consequence that the assertion of any sentence is both permitted and forbidden.
5. *Mimic the logical particles*: if a sentence is permitted, then its negation ought to be forbidden, if a conjunction is permitted, then both conjuncts should be, and so on. Considering (as we do) the truth predicate as a logical particle, we would similarly like it to be the case that if $\mathscr{F}(n)$ be permitted, so should $T(n)$.
6. *Be simple*.

7. *Harmonize with the statement of the semantic theory*: they should permit the assertion of those sentences which we use to convey the theory of truth.

Before the introduction of the truth predicate into the language, there was a unique rule that would satisfy all but the last desideratum: the rule that says one is permitted to assert all and only truths. Of course, before the introduction of the truth predicate, no rule can satisfy the last desideratum, since one cannot formulate any theory of truth without using a truth predicate.

Once a truth predicate has been added, the last desideratum can be met, but not all of the rest. We settled on a set of rules that satisfy all but the fifth, and violates it only with respect to the truth (and falsity) predicate. This is a bit of a price to pay, but is tolerable and fairly easily accepted.

But once the permissibility predicates are added to the language, we see that for each permissibility predicate *one of the first four desiderata must be violated*. For if desiderata 3 and 4 are met, then the rules will render a unique judgment for each sentence: either it will be permitted (and not forbidden) or forbidden (and not permitted). But if the sentence $\sim P_{\Sigma_i}(\omega)$ is permitted, then one is permitted to assert a falsehood, and desideratum 2 is violated. And if $\sim P_{\Sigma_i}(\omega)$ is forbidden, then one is forbidden to assert a truth and desideratum 1 is violated. So you're damned if you do and damned if you don't (and damned if you both do and don't, and damned if you refuse to make any decision).

No doubt, the first four desiderata are more important to us, more dear to our heart, than the last four. It hurts more to give up any of the first four than to give up the others. The resulting rules are, in a certain sense, more *defective*, more seriously in conflict with our ideal. But for all that, we cannot rightfully refuse to admit the permissibility predicates into our language: after all, sentences are permitted and forbidden according to the various rules. There are many truths that can only be formulated with the help of those predicates. If admitting them to the language also necessarily forces us in a certain way farther from our ideal, *c'est la vie*.

Given the parameters of the problem, there is simply no way to avoid unpleasantness here. For any set of rules, the corresponding ω: $\sim P_{\Sigma_i}(\omega)$ can be formulated in the language, and if the rules for permissibility yield a judgment in every case, then the rules either permit asserting a falsehood or forbid asserting a truth. One would prefer to have rules that do not have this feature, but one cannot always have what one prefers. It is as if, to make an obvious analogy, one is playing a game which uses a deck of cards, in which some of the cards have strings connecting them to other cards. The object of the game is to sort the cards into two piles, in a way that satisfies certain constraints. One of the constraints is that a card always goes into the opposite pile as the card it is attached to. All goes well, until one finds that the deck includes a card with a string attached to itself. One can put the card on either of the piles, but no matter where it goes, one cannot satisfy the constraint.

Sentence ω is such a card: the rules of permissibility can be so formulated to make it true or so formulated to make it false, but if true it is not permissible and if false it is. There is no use trying to avoid the problem: it cannot be avoided. One simply cannot sort such cards into piles that satisfy all the constraints.

The only real question left to us is which of these defective rules of permissibility we ought to accept. And the "ought" in the last sentence is evidently a *purely normative* matter: there is no "fact" about which system of rules is best, just a fact about which ideal or ideals each system of rules violates. Is it "better" to allow the assertion of a falsehood, or to forbid the assertion of a truth, or to fail to provide a judgment in a particular case? My own taste tends toward the second option, towards rules that produce not-properly-permissible truths, but *de gustibus non est disputandum*. If others prefer a different set of rules, I will not gainsay them.

There is, however, a seductive observation that must be resisted. Every set of rules will have its own problematic sentences. And for every problematic sentence, *some other set of rules will solve that problem*. Suppose, for example that for some set of rules Σ_0, the sentence

$$\omega_0: \sim P_{\Sigma_0}(\omega_0)$$

is forbidden. Then Σ_0 will forbid the assertion of at least one truth. And there is obviously nothing to prevent some *other* system of rules, call it Σ_1, to *permit* the assertion of that truth. That is, $\sim P_{\Sigma_0}(\omega_0)$ may be permissible according to Σ_1 while it is forbidden according to Σ_0, and *to that extent* Σ_1 may better accord with our ideals than Σ_0. But it would obviously be a mistake to conclude that Σ_1 is *better overall* than Σ_0, or that one ought to abandon Σ_0 for Σ_1, or that there is a hierarchy of rules in which Σ_1 is superior to Σ_0. For Σ_1 will obviously have its own problematic sentence $\omega_1: \sim P_{\Sigma_1}(\omega_1)$, and however that sentence turns out to be problematic (whether an impermissible truth or a permissible falsehood), there is no need for that sentence to be problematic *for Σ_0*.

So every set of rules for permissibility will have some serious local problems, some sentences for which the rules fail to be either truth-permissive or falsity-forbidding or complete or pragmatically coherent. If we were to settle on a set of rules of permissibility once and for all, we would have to resign ourselves to these anomalies. But every such local problem can be locally solved by some other set of rules. And this creates a very strong incentive or temptation for us to be *fickle*: to abandon one set of rules for another that happens to be better suited to the particular sentences under consideration at the moment. Insofar as we are focused on just those problematic sentences, the switch will appear to be an improvement, and the new rules to be better (which, for those sentences they are). But is it evident that all this switching is really just pushing around the same bump in the rug. The local improvement does not imply that there is any global advantage to be had by switching rules or that the new rules come closer overall to the ideal than the ones that are being abandoned.

Of course, the idea that we ever commit to a particular set of rules is an unrealistic idealization. There is no exact criterion for permissibility that any of us actually uses, and the overwhelmingly vast majority of our everyday discourse satisfies all of the myriad sets of rules that we might be inclined to adopt. There is no specific set of rules of permissibility endorsed by typical English speakers, or by any individual English speaker, and so no determinate content to a sentence like

> This sentence cannot be permissibly asserted according to the standard normative rules governing discourse in English.

What the standard normative rules are is indeterminate or vague since we have neither collectively nor individually endorsed a particular set of rules. No doubt, certain *gratuitous* departures from the ideals would be universally rejected (such as not being permitted to assert "Snow is white" even though it is true), but as we have seen, not every departure from the ideals is gratuitous.

One task we might pursue at this juncture is the formulation of some complete, explicit sets of rules of permissibility. But since we would in all likelihood not stick to any such set in all circumstances, it hardly seems worth the effort to make all the detailed decisions needed to formulate the rules. As a simple example, let's suppose that for our set of rules (call it Σ_0) we decide to allow the sentence $\sim P_{\Sigma_0}(\omega_0)$ to be impermissible and hence true. We still have many other decisions to make. What about $T(\omega_0)$? It is true: ought we allow it to be asserted or not? It meets the ideal of truth-permissiveness to allow it, but of course would demand a further violation of the fifth ideal, viz. mimicking the logical particles. That is, if $T(\omega_0)$ is permissible but $\sim P_{\Sigma_0}(\omega_0)$ is not, then the *Downward* T-Inference will not preserve permissibility, unlike in our original scheme. This does not seem so bad, since the Upward T-Inference has already been rejected, but there are even more annoying cases.

Having decided that $\sim P_{\Sigma_0}(\omega_0)$ shall not be permissible, we naturally want to say (because it is true) that there are some sentences that are both true and not permissible according to the rules of Σ_0, i.e. we want to assert

$$\exists x(T(x) \ \& \ \sim P_{\Sigma_0}(x)).$$

Nothing stands in our way in allowing this to be permitted. What if someone asks after an instance of the existential generalization? We are inclined to provide $\sim P_{\Sigma_0}(\omega_0)$ itself as an instance, that is, we are inclined to assert

$$T(\omega_0) \ \& \ \sim P_{\Sigma_0}(\omega_0).$$

Our rules could permit this (true) sentence to be asserted.

But of course our rules *forbid* asserting $\sim P_{\Sigma_0}(\omega_0)$. So we now have rules that permit a conjunction but forbid one conjunct. Yuck.

At this point one might be tempted to claim that such a set of rules is Pragmatically Incoherent, since to assert a conjunction is *ipso facto* to assert each conjunct and therefore to permit the assertion of a conjunction is *ipso facto* to permit the assertion of each conjunct. And one might further assert that a violation of Ideal 4 (Pragmatic Coherence) is so severe as to render the rules unacceptable, or, worse, not even rules at all. It is not clear to me how to evaluate this claim. As an abstract matter, it is clearly possible to have rules which sort sentences into two classes, and to have a conjunction in one class and one of its conjuncts in the other. And it is possible to denominate the two classes respectively "Sentences Permissible to Assert" and "Sentences Impermissible to Assert". And there is a straightforward sense in which such rules can permit a conjunction while forbidding one conjunct. And I suppose an official Rule Enforcer could slap the wrist of anyone who asserted the latter and praise anyone who asserted the former. Beyond that, the metaphysical status of assertion is not clear enough to me to know how to evaluate this situation.

What all this does point up, though, is that the hope for any simple, universal, syntactic rules of *permissibility-preserving inference* are likely to be dashed. Under the scheme just proposed, the rule of & Elimination would no longer always preserve permissibility, which is a distressing result. Clearly, which inference rules preserve permissibility is dependent on which rules of permissibility one is discussing: the inference rules all have to be subscripted to indicate the sort of permissibility under consideration. And equally clearly, the divergence of the permissibility-preserving rules from the truth-preserving ones will be much more extreme than we considered back in Chapter 7. And no doubt, if one ever were to wander into a discussion of the sorts of sentences that violate & Elimination, the temptation would be overwhelming to switch (during the course of the conversation) to *using* a different set of rules for permissible assertion. No matter how much we clean up a given notion of permissibility, it will never command our unwavering allegiance in all contexts of conversation. So the task of exactly specifying any set of rules for permissibility will not repay the effort put into completing it.

(Note that the truth-preserving inferences are quite unaffected by any of this—they continue to be *valid* irrespective of the standards of assertion one might adopt. Of course, if one feels compelled to assert the conclusion of a valid argument whenever one feels compelled to assert the premises, one is likely to get into some trouble with any given rules for permissibility.)

Indeed, the practical advice one is likely to offer with respect to rules of permissibility is this: simply try to *avoid* conversational contexts which lead into problematic areas (e.g. discussion of sentences like $\sim P_{\Sigma_0}(\omega_0)$). There are many rules of permissibility (like the rules of Chapter 5) that can nearly meet the ideals outside of these contexts, or at least need not violate any of the first four ideals outside of these contexts. And there is no need to even consider the problematic sentences unless one is engaged in some useless pursuit like philosophy.

At this point, there may well be a great gnashing of teeth and rending of garments. For if, at the end of the day, the best practical advice concerning the Permissibility Paradox is simply to avoid discussing it, why, at the beginning of the day, was not the best advice concerning the Liar paradox to simply avoid discussing it? Put another way, if we can't meet all the ideals of permissible assertion, what has been gained in the investigation up to this point? Haven't we striven mightily to provide an account of truth merely to be done in at the end by the problems surrounding permissibility? I don't think that these charges are accurate, but they deserve our careful consideration.

What has been Accomplished?

The revenge problem as it arises in the context of the semantic paradoxes carries with it a certain threat. Schematically, the revenge problem begins when one introduces a new concept in the course of solving a semantic paradox, as one might introduce the notion of determinate truth when discussing the Liar framed in terms of (regular) truth, or as we have introduced the notion of permissibility when dealing with fallout from our trivalent semantics. The revenge occurs if the new concept can then be used to construct a sentence which is, generically, as problematic as the original Liar. As we would seem to need to introduce a new concept to solve this problem, the familiar hierarchy of problems and solutions arises. Once the iteration of problems has begun, there appear to be only two options. Either the problems never stop, but always recur, in which case it is unclear that any real progress has been made. Or else the problems somehow stop at some level, in which case one wonders why the multiplication of concepts had to be started in the first place. If one reaches a point where there are resources to resolve all problems, why did one have to ever go beyond the concept of truth in the first place?

In our solution, the regress is stopped, in a sense, after the first step. In discussing the resolution of the Liar, we introduced the (generic) normative notion of permissibility. That general normative notion has an infinitude of specific instances, all possible rules of permissibility, but those specific instances do not form a hierarchy and are not generated by any iterative procedure. The notion of permissibility, as we have seen, begets its own problems, but those problems are not to be solved by the introduction of any further concept. Indeed, those problems, severe failure to meet the ideals, are not to be solved at all. So one question that remains is: why introduce the notion if it will leave unresolved problems? Are we really better off than we were with our original problems?

I hope that it is clear that the nature of the problems associated with the permissibility paradox is, in fact, completely different from the problem we started with. Our original problem was to understand the nature of *truth*. The Liar paradox demands our attention in part just because of its peculiarity, but much more importantly because it seems to stand in the way of a natural account of the nature of truth. At least, it stood in the way of Tarski's attempt to provide what he considered to be an adequate account of truth in a natural language. But we have been able to circumvent Tarski's problem altogether: what is on offer is a complete analysis of truth in a natural language, an analysis both of the truth predicate and of truth itself, insofar as it admits a general analysis. We have had to abandon Tarski's demand that all the T-sentences be regarded as true, but Tarski never adequately motivated that requirement as a *sine qua non* for a theory of truth.

The generic *nature* of permissibility is also perfectly clear, or at least as clear as is any fundamentally normative notion. Abstractly, there are rules that specify what is and is not permitted. There are then the further questions of what it is for an agent to endorse a specific set of rules, and on what grounds one might decide to endorse a specific set of rules for permissibility. The general problem of the nature of endorsement of normative rules is not peculiar to semantics, and need not detain us here. As for possible grounds for endorsement, we have spelled those out with some precision in the Ideal.

It is the Ideal of permissibility that explains why we need two notions (truth and permissibility) rather than one. For we need the notion of truth to *specify* the Ideals of being truth-permissive and falsity-forbidding. We do not need the notion of truth to explicate the generic notion of permissibility, but we do need it to explain the features that we would like rules for permissible assertion to have.

The remaining problem, the Permissibility Paradox, is therefore not a problem that obstructs any understanding of the notion of truth or the notion or permissibility. It is rather a material problem: it shows that, no matter what we do, truth and permissibility (and falsity and impermissibility) cannot possibly *match up* in quite the way we would like them to. This is not a conceptual problem, but a practical one. It is a problem we must learn to live with.

9   The Metaphysics of Truth

Our account of the Liar paradox and related paradoxes is now complete. It is time to take stock, review the results, and confront some very tempting objections to the whole enterprise.

One rather obvious objection goes like this:

> "According to your own theory of truth, your theory of truth is not true. So why should anyone take it seriously?"

This deserves some comment.

There are two quite distinct ways to understand this objection. In one form, it is supposed to point out an *internal* problem with the theory: the theory is supposed to be somehow self-contradictory or self-undermining or self-stultifying in a way that makes it simply impossible to take seriously. It is as if part of the theory itself were the injunction not to take the theory seriously: in such a case, it is impossible to take the theory seriously no matter how hard one tries. In the second form, the objection is rather that the theory is materially inadequate, since any *correct* or *acceptable* theory of truth must itself be true. This is presumably because of the nature of truth. Let's take these objections in turn.

The first form of the objection is just incorrect: the theory of truth explicated in Chapter 3 together with the standard of permissibility developed in Chapter 5 is not self-defeating.[1] If one accepts the theory and the standard of permissibility, then one is permitted to assert the theory and also to assert that the theory is not true. This would only be self-contradictory if one also claimed that only true sentences should be asserted, but this is something we deny. The whole theory may be lunacy, but at least it is coherent lunacy.

The second form of the objection is much more interesting and subtle. It relies on an intuition that truth is the sort of topic for which there ought to be a (presumably unique) complete true theory. Just as there are facts about physics, and it is the job of the physicist to get those facts right and produce a true theory, so the job of the philosopher is to discover the facts about truth

---

[1]   As we have seen, the standards of permissibility would need to be amplified and complicated once the permissibility predicates are added to the language, but the objection, if it works at all, would work even for the language that only has the truth predicate added. So it is enough to show that the objection does not work there.

and produce a true account of truth itself. If this is correct then the theory I have proposed, since it judges itself not to be true, could not be acceptable.

The question before us, then, is to what extent (if any) there are *facts* about truth which any correct theory of truth is obliged to get right, and whether those facts are sufficient to render the theory of truth itself true.

Putting the issue in terms of facts may be a bit problematic, but it allows us to make contact with some other philosophical problems. Consider, for example, the problem of vagueness. If John is a borderline case of baldness, then we are inclined to say both that there is no fact about whether John is bald or not and that the sentence "John is bald" fails to have a classical truth value. One is inclined to say that if "John is bald" is true, then it is a fact that John is bald, and if "John is bald" is false, then it is a fact that John is not bald. So in some way or other, the failure of a classical truth value corresponds to a failure of factuality. And the failure of a theory of truth to have a classical truth value would indicate a failure for the facts to settle or determine the truth values of all sentences.

In order to get a grip on the connection between factuality and truth we need to clarify both the nature of facts and the way that facts render (interpreted) sentences true. The example of baldness can be of some service here. Grant for the sake of argument that Moe is not bald, Curly is bald and John is an indeterminate borderline case. Grant also that there is a determinate set of hair-distribution facts for each individual: these include the exact number, position, length and thickness of each hair on the head of each man. (Each of these facts might itself be subject to vagueness worries, but that is of no moment for the example, and can be safely ignored.) The basic intuition about baldness, an intuition that is typically phrased in terms of supervenience, is that whether or not an individual is bald is completely determined by the set of hair-distribution facts for that person. Two individuals cannot agree on their hair-distribution and differ with respect to baldness. Therefore, whether someone is bald or not is not a metaphysically *additional* fact over and above the hair-distribution facts. It is at best something like a *generic feature* of the totality of hair-distribution facts. Otherwise, it is hard to see why two individuals could not match with respect to hair distribution yet differ with respect to baldness.

Whether or not someone is bald is determined, then, by the totality of hair-distribution facts together with some *function* from hair distributions onto the predicates "bald" and "not bald", or perhaps better together with some function from hair distributions and the predicate "bald" to the values true and false. Borderline cases can occur when the function is only a partial function, so that some distributions do not get associated with either truth value. It is exactly because one holds the view that the only "real" or first-order facts relevant to this case are hair-distribution facts that the failure of John to be either bald or not bald does not reflect any objective vagueness or fuzziness in the world: John's hair distribution is just as determinate as anyone else's, the only vagueness is in whether that distribution should count as being bald or not.

Suppose one accepts this rather prosaic account of the way "John is bald" can fail to have a classical truth value. (Further remarks on the problem of vagueness can be found in Appendix C.) Then one will also want to be careful about exactly how the term "fact" is used in the description of this case. Whether one is bald, or not bald, or indeterminate with respect to baldness is determined by the facts about one's hair. But then being bald, or not being bald, had best not themselves be facts, or at least not facts of the same ontological order as the hair-distribution facts. Otherwise, it is hard to see how the hair distribution comes into the story at all: the truth value of "John is bald" would then be determined *directly* by the fact that he is (or is not) bald. And then it would be a mystery (1) why the supervenience thesis connecting hair distribution to baldness holds and (2) how the sentence could fail to have a classical truth value without there being some corresponding "objective vagueness" in John.

The right way to talk about this case, then, seems to be the following. The hair-distribution facts exhaust the relevant set of facts in this case. The hair-distribution facts are the ultimate grounds for the truth values of sentences concerning John's hair. There are some sentences, such as "John has more than 89 hairs", whose truth values are determined by the hair-distribution facts in such a straightforward way that any question or doubt about the truth value of the sentence would have to derive from some question or doubt about what the hair-distribution facts are. But other sentences, such as "John is bald", can be such that their truth value is not settled even though no hair-distribution fact is in question. In these cases, is seems appropriate to say that the facts about John's hair are not indeterminate. It is only indeterminate whether those facts are sufficient to render him bald.

Note that on this way of speaking, we should resist saying even in the case of Curly that it is a fact that he is bald. We should better say that it is (unproblematically) *true* that Curly is bald, and bald in virtue of facts about the distribution of his hair. If we speak this way about this case, then we can maintain that all the truths about Curly's and Moe's and John's hair (including the truth that Curly is bald and that Moe is not) are *grounded* in facts about their hair, but we can deny that there is a simple correspondence between the truths and the facts. Otherwise, the failure of "John is bald" to have a classical truth value would have to imply some failure of factuality about John's head (relative, at least, to Curly and Moe), and that seems incorrect. On this analysis, the colloquial "There is no fact about whether John is bald" is misleading, since there are *never* facts about baldness. One would better say "The facts about John do not fix a truth value for the sentence 'John is bald'".

The same remarks could be made, *mutatis mutandis*, about properties. At a fundamental ontological level, there is no property of baldness: baldness is not an ontological constituent of any object. Presumably, the fundamental onto-logical properties of an object are its physical properties, like mass and charge. Physicalism can then be stated either as the supervenience of all other proper-ties on the physical properties or, more accurately, as the denial that there are any properties beside physical properties. Of course, if all one wants are sets of objects, then one can get them: if the physical properties ultimately determine the truth values of all sentences of the form "*x* is bald", then one can collect together all the objects that satisfy "is bald", and one can say that these objects all have a property in common (or even that the set *is* a property). This corresponds to what David Lewis calls an *abundant* property: to every set of objects there corresponds at least one such property, viz. the property of being a member of that set (Lewis 1986: 59). Abundant properties evidently cut no metaphysical ice: sharing an abundant property does not imply that two objects have anything at all in common.

Rather, a fundamental metaphysical project is the delineation of what Lewis calls *sparse* properties:

The sparse properties are another story. Sharing of them makes for qualitative similar-ity, they carve at the joints, they are intrinsic, they are highly specific, the sets of their instances are *ipse facto* not entirely miscellaneous, there are only just enough of them to characterize things completely and without redundancy.   (ibid. 60)

Note in particular the last clause: since the sparse properties characterize things without redundancy, there are no supervenience relations among them. The search for sparse properties is part of Lewis's quest for metaphysical atoms that can be promiscuously recombined, so as to generate the set of possibilities through a sort of combinatorial algorithm. Lewis's own choice for the meta-physical atoms (at least for the actual world) is encapsulated in his thesis of Humean supervenience: the atoms are point-sized bits of space-time that instantiate sparse properties and are externally related only by spatio-temporal relations. I have criticized almost every aspect of Lewis's proposal elsewhere (Maudlin forthcoming), but here I want to emphasize the attractiveness of one foundational aspect of the project: there ought to be some set of atomic facts about the world such that (1) every truth about the world is determined by those facts and (2) none of the facts supervene on any others. The fundamental facts may take the form of small objects instantiating prop-erties, or they may not: so long as they serve to make *sentences* of subject/predicate form true, one might be lulled into the mistaken notion that the facts themselves have the metaphysical form of individuals instantiating (sparse) properties. That is, *all* properties might be merely abundant properties or supervenient properties like baldness, to which no fundamental metaphysical item corresponds.

Let us assume, then, that there is some set of fundamental atomic facts. And let us say that a sentence is *factual* just in case it is true. Then the sentence "Curly is bald" can be factual without Curly's being bald being a (fundamental) fact, or indeed, without it being a fact at all.

Note that we now have two distinct indications that in a certain realm of discourse there are more truths than there are corresponding facts. One indication is failure of bivalence: if some sentences fail to have classical truth values, then not all the predicates used in those sentences can correspond to (sparse) properties, since there can be no "objective vagueness" about the instantiation of those properties. Bivalence fails when the truth values of some sorts of sentences are *indirectly* determined by the facts, and when the *means of determination* fails: even though the set of facts is complete, the connection between the facts and the truth values for the sentences fails to determine a truth value. The second indication of having more truths than there are corresponding facts is *supervenience*: if the truth of certain sentences guarantees the truth of some other, then the facts that make the former sentences true cannot be completely distinct from the facts that make the latter sentence true. If the facts are to be both complete and non-redundant, then the truth values of sentences that *directly* correspond to the facts must be metaphysically independent of each other: the truth values of any set of such sentences cannot guarantee the truth value of any sentence outside the set.

Let's now apply this general scheme to logic. What immediately comes to our attention is that logic *is exactly the study of the supervenience of truth values of sentences*. An inference is deductively valid exactly when the truth of the premises is sufficient to guarantee the truth of the conclusion. So the considerations above immediately suggest that for the sentences studied by logic *the true sentences are not in direct one-to-one correspondence with the facts that make them true*.

Just as a sentence like "Curly is bald" can be true even though Curly's being bald is not a fact, so a disjunction such as "Curly is bald or Curly is left-handed" can be true (and hence factual) even though there is no corresponding "disjunctive fact" of Curly being either bald or left-handed. Indeed, there had better not be any such "disjunctive fact" if the (atomic) facts are to play the role that Lewis prescribes: to characterize things "completely and without redundancy". For if it is a fact that Curly is bald (or if there are facts which suffice to make "Curly is bald" true), then it is clearly redundant to add that he is either bald or left-handed. And similarly if there are facts that suffice to make "Curly is left-handed" true. But "Curly is bald or Curly is left-handed" is factual if and only if either there are facts that make "Curly is bald" true or facts that make "Curly is left-handed" true, and in either case adding any *further* disjunctive fact would be redundant. So even though disjunctions can be true, and hence factual, there are no disjunctive facts to which they correspond. This is, of course, a good thing: it explains how the truth of either disjunct can suffice to guarantee the truth of the disjunction. If there had to be "disjunctive facts" to make disjunctions true, then one might worry why the world might not contain enough facts (or states of affairs, or whatever one wants to call them) to make one disjunct true but fail to contain the disjunctive fact that makes the disjunction true.

I take it that the foregoing account of disjunction is both attractive and plausible: anyone would find disjunctive facts hard metaphysical fare. All we need to do now is apply the very same morals to the truth predicate, and hence to truth.

There are facts which suffice to make "Curly is bald" true, and these very facts also suffice to make "Curly is bald or Curly is left-handed" true. Similarly, the facts which make "Curly is bald" true suffice to make " 'Curly is bald' is true" true. Just as one does not need to appeal to disjunctive facts to make disjunctions true, and one does not have to appeal to facts about baldness to make claims about baldness true, so one does not need to appeal to *facts* about truth in order to make claims about truth true (and hence factual). Indeed, one had best not make there be facts about truth, since the truth value of " 'Curly is bald' is true" supervenes on the truth value of "Curly is bald".[2] So in order for the facts not to be redundant, there cannot both be facts about the truth of sentences *and* facts about, say, the distribution of hairs on Curly's head which are sufficient to make "Curly is bald" true. To avoid redundancy, we must make a choice between having hair-distribution facts and having truth facts, but the choice here is obvious. Claims about sentences being true can be factual, but there are no facts about truth.

It bears repeating that the supervenience criterion indicates situations where there cannot be a direct one-to-one correspondence between truths and facts, but it does not tells us which (if any) of the truths do correspond directly to the facts, which predicates correspond to sparse properties, etc. The truth value of " 'Curly is bald' is true" supervenes on the truth value of "Curly is bald", but equally the truth value of "Curly is bald" supervenes on that of " 'Curly is bald' is true". The term "supervenience" etymologically conjures up images of a *hierarchy*, with one set of truths "above" another, but the formal condition for supervenience evidently allows for the truth value of each of a pair of sentences to supervene on the truth value of the other. Supervenience tells us that there are more truths than facts, but does not by itself indicate which, if any, of the truths directly corresponds to a fact. In the case of " 'Curly is bald' is true" and "Curly is bald", we have already argued that *neither* of these

---

[2] One might object: the truth of "Curly is bald" does not supervene on the facts about Curly's hair distribution since he could have the same hair distribution but "Curly is bald" could be false if "Curly is bald" meant something other than what it does. Fair enough. Let the truth of "Curly is bald" supervene on the facts about Curly's hair distribution and the facts which make "Curly is bald" mean what it does (in English, in a given context). Still, the supervenience base does not contain facts about truth, only about hair and about meaning.

sentences directly corresponds to a fact. All that the supervenience tells us is that they don't *both* directly correspond to facts.

Logical particles allow us to construct sentences whose truth values are determined by the truth values of other sentences, and the semantic graph of a language indicates the asymmetric dependency relation among these truth values. According to our theory of truth, the *graph* can have cycles in it, but the dependency of classical truth values of sentences on one another never displays any such cycle: we can trace any classical truth value in the graph back to its ultimate source at the boundary of the graph without ever going around in a circle. The boundary of the graph contains *logically* atomic sentences, and, as far as logic is concerned, the logically atomic sentences could correspond directly to the metaphysically atomic facts. Of course, logical structure is only a small part of metaphysical structure: the truth value of "Curly is bald" is *logically* independent of the truth values of all the sentences that describe Curly's hair distribution, but it is not metaphysically independent of them. The task of the metaphysician is to *extend* the graph of the language to show ontological dependency relations in addition to narrowly logical ones. In a perfected metaphysical graph, the boundary nodes would be ontologically independent of each other: every distribution of primary truth values at the boundary would correspond to a metaphysically possible state of the world, and each distinct distribution would correspond to a metaphysically distinct state. Our theory of truth therefore forms a fragment of a more general ontological account of the world.

When I introduced the notion of the graph of a language back in Chapter 2, I remarked that the arrows on the graph represent relations of direct metaphysical dependence. We have now been arguing that the dependence is such that no sentence in the interior of the graph can directly correspond to a fact; facts are directly represented only at the boundary, where the language meets the world. (Or at least, where the language meets the world *as far as logic is concerned*. As we have seen, the boundary sentence "John is bald" does not directly represent a fact.) It is therefore important to regard the graph of the language as more than just an instrument for calculating truth values from other truth values, or for displaying covariation among truth values. For distinct graphs, with distinct metaphysical implications, can be instrumentally equivalent for this purpose.

For example, take the graph of a language and make the following global substitution: wherever a boundary sentence $\mathscr{F}(n)$ occurs, replace it with the sentence $T(n)$, and vice versa. Since $\mathscr{F}(n)$ and $T(n)$ have identical truth values, this will make no difference at all to the overall distribution of truth values given some assignment of truth primary truth values at the boundary. But still the metaphysical picture would be quite different: the truth value of $\mathscr{F}(n)$ would be *derived from* and hence *metaphysically dependent on* the truth value of $T(n)$. And of course, the truth values of $T(n)$ and $\mathscr{F}(n)$ would still supervene on each other. So if we follow the general recipe we have been discussing, we would now assert that all the basic ontological facts are facts about the truth values of sentences, rather than, say, facts about the physical properties of physical objects. It is not a fact, we would say, that the electron has negative charge, even though the sentence "The electron has positive charge" is true, and hence factual. Rather, it is a fact that the sentence "The electron has positive charge" is true. It is this fact in the world that makes the (now boundary) sentence " 'The electron has positive charge' is true" true, and it is the truth value of this sentence that makes "The electron has positive charge" true.

The metaphysical picture just described is evidently quite bizarre, even though the resulting theory of possible distributions of truth values to sentences is unchanged. Although I doubt that anyone would seriously try to defend this ontological picture, it is still worthwhile to point out some of its defects. The ontology suggests that truth is a basic, irreducible, fundamental logical property of sentences, that there is no deeper logical account of how sentences get the truth values they have (just as, in the original picture, there is no deeper account of how the electron gets its negative charge). But then, one might legitimately wonder why only, e.g., the Truthteller sentence cannot have this basic property. Why are there not distinct possible worlds that differ *only* in the following respect: in one the Truthteller is true while in the other the Truthteller is false? We do not regard this as a real metaphysical possibility, but the question is: why not?

It will not do to say that the Truthteller cannot get a primary truth value because it is neither on the boundary of the graph nor connected to the boundary. Under the exchange of sentences outlined that will be correct, but if sentences of the form $T(n)$ are allowed to be on the boundary at all, then it is hard to see why the graph ought not to be modified to make the Truthteller a boundary sentence. After all, the Truthteller simply ascribes truth to a particular sentence, so why should it be treated differently from other such sentences? In our scheme, all such sentences are treated the same: none are boundary sentences. If one wishes to make some such sentences boundary sentences, then it is unclear why one would not make them all. (Or, to put it another way, although the swap of sentences in the graph described above yields a perfectly determinate graph, it is unclear what sort of *metaphysical* account of truth could generate that graph directly.)

How exactly could the world make a sentence like "This electron has negative charge" (as an example of a plausible metaphysical boundary sentence) true? No doubt because the world contains electrons and negative charge as irreducible ontological components. And the world cannot make a sentence like "The Truthteller is true" true because, although it contains the sentence, it does not in the same way contain truth. (No doubt there are *more* facts involved in making "This electron has negative charge" true than just facts about the electron and its charge: there are also facts about what gives the sentence, and its components, the meanings and referents they have. These are facts about English usage, and the position of the person using the demonstrative "this", and so on. But for our purposes we may hold these facts as given: even granted that it is determined what "this electron" and "negative charge" and "The Truthteller" and "truth" mean or refer to, it remains that the state of the world can make the one sentence, but not the other, true.)

The world, then, does not contain truth or facts about truth. And hence we have no right, *ab initio*, to expect any theory of truth to be factual (i.e. true). If the world contained truth as it does electric charge, then we could rightly expect any particular claim about the truth of a sentence to be either true or false, and hence any generalization about truth to be either true or false. Failure of a theory of electric charge to be true implies that the theory is false: it is untrue to the facts. It (directly or implicitly) implies that the facts are other than they are. But a theory of truth can meet a different fate. Since there are no facts about truth, claims about truth can be true or false or ungrounded. True claims about truth, such as " 'Snow is white' is true" ultimately derive their truth from the facts (in this case facts about snow), and do not imply that the facts are other than they are. False claims about truth do imply that the facts are other than they are. But ungrounded claims about truth do not imply anything at all about the facts: they fail to be connected to the boundary of the graph in a way that achieves this.

Given the standards of permissibility we have adopted, a theory of truth may be permissible to assert even though it is not true. Further, there is a relevant distinction to be made among ungrounded permissible sentences. Some permissible sentences are only contingently permissible. For example, "Snow is white and the Liar is not true", $W(s)$ & $\sim T(\lambda)$, is ungrounded, and permissible just in case snow is white. The permissibility of that sentence therefore has straightforward factual implications: it's being permissible implies something about the facts. On the other hand, there are necessarily permissible ungrounded sentences. These have no factual implications at all: they will be permissible no matter how the world happens to be. Our theory of truth is both ungrounded and necessarily permissible. But this is as it should be. After all, the theory of truth should only be about the generic characteristics of truth, not about any other feature of the world. But since truth is not itself an element of the world, the theory of truth *per se* is completely non-factual. It ought to be necessarily permissible: otherwise, there would be constraints on how the world must be for the theory of truth to be acceptable. But that would imply that the truth is a constituent feature of the world itself.

It might help to bring these assertions about the non-factuality of truth down to earth with an example. Consider one case in which the theory offered here disagrees with other popular theories. According to our account, the sentence $T(\lambda) \supset T(\lambda)$ is not true. According to any account that uses supervaluational techniques, or that uses the maximal intrinsic fixed point, it is. Exactly what kind of a dispute is this? How could it possibly be resolved? We generally think that we can resolve theoretical disputes about electric charge by experimentation, i.e. by consulting the world. Even where this fails, we think that we can describe how the world according to one theory differs from the world according to the other. But what is there *in the nature of the world* that would settle a dispute about the truth value of $T(\lambda) \supset T(\lambda)$? There seems to be nothing at all—and hence the question itself seems not to be one of a factual nature.

Do not now go on to add: but then *it is a fact* that there is no fact which settles the truth value of $T(\lambda) \supset T(\lambda)$. If the truth value is not settled by the facts, then it is not settled by the facts. *Expanding* the set of facts to include its non-settlement just invites confusion: it would now be that the status of the sentence *is* settled by the facts: it is settled by the fact that it is not settled by the facts. We have not come all this way to be sucked back into that quagmire.

With this sketch of facts and factuality on the table we can now directly address several perennial lines of attack against any proposed solution to the Liar. I have left them to the end because they could not be properly answered until the complete metaphysical picture of truth and permissibility had been presented. Answering these objections allows us the chance to show the theory again in a slightly different light, and to resolve some lingering doubts.

One objection stems from the old Aristotelian saw: "To say of what is that it is not, or of what is not that it is, is false; while to say of what is that it is, or of what is not that it is not, is true" (*Met.* 1011^{b}26–28). Now suppose, says the objector, that the Liar sentence *really is not true*. Then when you say, as you do, that the Liar sentence is not true, you speak the truth. And if you speak the truth by uttering the Liar sentence itself, then the sentence really is true. The only way to deny this is to deny that the Liar sentence *really is not true*. But if you do so, why do you persist in *saying* that the Liar sentence is not true?

There is a popular tactic to respond to this objection, namely by saying that when *I*, in the course of presenting my semantics, say "The Liar is not true", my sentence does not *mean the same thing*, or *express the same proposition* as the Liar sentence itself. To be more vivid, suppose both Sam and I say, at the same moment, "What Sue is now saying is not true". And suppose that, at that very moment, Sue happens to be saying "What Sam is now saying is true". According to the strategy under consideration, the sentences Sam and I produce do not have the same meaning, or express the same proposition, or have the same truth value. Indeed, what Sam says expresses no proposition at all, while what I say, by using the very same words at the same time and in what is, to all obvious respects, the same circumstances, is true. Such a strategy is followed in Skyrms (1984).

It should first be obvious that I am rejecting this approach root and branch. Both Sam's sentence and my sentence say the same thing, and have exactly the same truth value. Both of our sentences are ungrounded, as is Sue's, and both of our sentences are permissible, exactly because Sue's is ungrounded. Sam is right to say what he does, and Sue is wrong, even though neither speaks truly or falsely. And I am right to say what I do for exactly the same reason that Sam is right. I remain right in saying what I do, even if I am engaged in developing a semantic theory.

A variant of this objection harks not to Aristotle but to Tarski. It begins with the claims that it is obvious—an undeniable truism—that all of the T-sentences are necessarily true. And if the T-sentences are necessarily true, then the sentences on either side of the biconditional are logically equivalent. And if they are logically equivalent, then if someone asserts one, she must assert the other. But the T-sentence for the Liar is "The Liar is true iff the Liar is not true". So if one is willing to assert that the Liar is not true, one must be willing to assert that it is true, and so willing to contradict oneself.

Again, we have rejected this argument in its entirety. It is not so that the T-sentences are undeniable. Lo, I deny some of them. The T-sentence for the Liar is not true: it is ungrounded. Furthermore, it is not even *permissible*: one side is permissible and the other impermissible, so the biconditional is impermissible. Since I refuse to even assert the T-sentence, much less assert that the T-sentence is true, I am hardly bound by it to assert one side if and only if I assert the other. Indeed, I assert one side, viz. "The Liar is not true" and deny the other, viz. "The Liar is true".

Tarski himself does not put his argument this way. He rather regards the T-sentences as a useful starting-point for a general definition of truth, a starting-point which leads to difficulties when faced with sentences like the Liar. Tarski nowhere claims that these difficulties cannot be overcome, just that the prospects for a "semantical definition" of truth are dim. He would certainly recognize that a theory which *denies* the truth of some T-sentences can evade his antinomy (since it is a premise of his antinomy that the T-sentences all be regarded as true), and might even admit that an equally good *alternative* starting-point for a theory is the claim that the semantics of the truth predicate be characterized by the identity map from the truth value of $\mathscr{F}(n)$ to the truth value of $T(n)$. If the semantics is bivalent and there are no truth-value gaps, it follows from this starting-point that all T-sentences will be true. But if the semantics is not bivalent, the truth predicate can be characterized by the identity map without the T-sentences all being true.

Other authors have raised the status of the T-sentences to inviolability. Crispin Wright, for example, defines the Disquotational Schema (DS) as the schema

"P" is T if and only if P.

He assesses the status of the schema as follows:

Why does it seem that any competitive account of truth must respect the DS? Relatedly, why just that starting point for the deflationary conception? The answer, I suggest, is that standing just behind the DS is the basic, platitudinous connection of assertion and truth: asserting a proposition—a Fregean thought—is claiming that it is true. The connection is partially constitutive of the concepts of assertion and truth, and it entails the validity of the analogue of the DS for propositional contents (sometimes called the Equivalence Schema):

It is true that P if and only if P.

The DS proper—the schema for sentences—is then an immediate consequence, provided we have determined that a sentence is to count as true just in case the proposition it expresses is true, and are so reading the quotation marks that each relevant instance of

"P" says that P

holds good.   (Wright 1992: 23–4)

It is hard to know how to deny something characterized as a "basic, platitudinous connection" except baldly: there is no such connection between asserting a proposition (or asserting a sentence) and claiming that it is true. I assert that the Liar is not true. I deny that it is true that the Liar is not true. I assert that the system of inferential rules developed in this book is truth-preserving, even though I can prove that the sentence that says they are truth-preserving is self-contradictory, and hence not true. I have something to back up these claims: namely a complete, explicit, coherent account of both truth and permissibility, an account which allows truth and permissibility to come apart. Opposed to this account stand only, as far as I can see, the words "basic" and "platitudinous". So much the worse for platitudes.

One might worry, though, that if asserting a sentence is not just claiming it to be true, our expressive powers have been grievously diluted. Suppose that I really do wish to claim that a sentence is true, to do more than indicate that the sentence can be properly asserted. How can I do this if assertion no longer carries with it the implicit commitment to the truth of what is asserted?

The answer is perfectly straightforward: to convey one's belief that a sentence is true, one need merely assert *that it is true*. For the only circumstance in which $T(n)$ is permissible is when $\mathscr{F}(n)$ is true, so by asserting $T(n)$ one commits oneself to the truth of $\mathscr{F}(n)$. Asserting $\mathscr{F}(n)$ itself can sometimes be proper even when $\mathscr{F}(n)$ is not true, asserting $T(n)$ never is. So there are no such inexpressible beliefs or contents: if one believes a sentence to be true one can convey that by saying so.

In offering a semantics and an account of permissibility, I have provided two quite different theories. One is a theory of how the truth values of sentences are fixed by the logical structure of the language and by the world. The other is a set of recommendations about which sentences one ought to assert. There has been a mutual adjustment between these two theories: in explaining the semantics, I have often used sentences, such as "The Liar is not true", which, according to the semantics, are not true. Fortunately, according to the rules of permissibility, it is nonetheless appropriate to assert these sentences. One could, as we have seen, accept the semantic theory and conjoin it with a different set of rules of appropriate assertion, such as the rule that it is only appropriate to assert true sentences. But one would then be reduced to silence when asked to *explain* the semantic theory one has accepted. One might adopt a set of rules according to which it is always appropriate to assert false sentences, although what the supposed advantages of such rules might be I can't imagine.

There is no issue, then, about whether a set of rules for permissibility are true or not: such normative rules aren't even candidates for truth. Nor is there an interesting question about whether such a theory is permissible: it is easy enough to make it so by its own lights. There is, of course, the question of coherence: whether the rules can always be followed. And if there is a *sui generis* notion of appropriateness according to which it is always appropriate to assert truths and deny falsehoods, we have tried to provide at least one account of permissibility and impermissibility that yields this result, insofar as possible. But if some simple declarative sentences are neither true nor false, then provision must be made for them, and coherence alone does not decide the issue. Various coherent rules for dealing with such sentences can be formulated. One can only be induced to accept or reject a set of rules by seeing them in action. The rules offered above allow one to appropriately assert the very sentences one needs to explain the semantics, and they allow one to assert many sentences one is pre-analytically disposed to assert (e.g. "All true sentences are true"). Perhaps more appealing rules can be found, but the only way to establish this is to find them.

What of a theory of truth? Must it, by its own lights, be a *true* theory? Not if that means that, by its own lights, all of the claims it makes are true. Our theory of truth claims that a conjunction is true just in case both its conjuncts are true, and also that that very sentence, while permissible, is not true. In order for the project of constructing a semantics *cum* rules for permissibility to succeed, the theory of truth and rules of permissibility ought to be permissible (by their own lights), but neither need be true. But if a theory of truth cannot be defended by claiming that it is true (and that all rival theories are therefore false), what can be said in defense of a theory of truth? Perhaps no more than that it is coherent, complete, and *hangs together*.

This account of truth, and of permissibility, and of factuality, and of the Liar hangs together.

Achievements and Prospects

The theory of truth and permissibility here presented is not the final word. There may be alternative, equally coherent, expansive, simple ways of dealing with these issues. They should, by all means, be developed. But the accomplishments of this theory can still be *touted*: they are its sole recommendation.

Tarski despaired of developing any theory of truth for a language which contained its own truth predicate: thus began the tradition of distinguishing the object language and metalanguage and restricting the domain of the truth predicate to the object language. Our theory demands no such distinction. Further, Tarski's antinomy seemed to apply to any language that had merely a *truth* predicate. We have developed a theory for a language with truth, falsity, and ungroundedness predicates, i.e. with enough semantic predicates to express the whole of the semantics. We have developed a theory of truth for a language that can serve as its own metalanguage.

The semantic theory is unique: every sentence has a determinate truth value. The theory is in a certain way *principled*: the truth values of sentences like the Liar are traced not to their apparent inconsistency, but to straightforward global properties of the graph of the language. The Truthteller is seen to be equally ungrounded even though it is not, in the usual sense, paradoxical.

We have solved the Inferential version of the Liar paradox in a principled way: given the semantics, the weakness of standard logic can be diagnosed and corrected. The diagnosis also explains why the weakness, though inherent in rules like $\supset$ Introduction and $\sim$ Introduction, does not become apparent until the truth predicate and the T-Inferences are added to the language. We have shown that the weakness does not lie in the T-Inferences themselves, whether used within subderivations or not. This is a welcome result since on any decent theory of truth the T-Inferences are truth-preserving.

We have produced an explicit set of inferential rules appropriate to the three-valued semantics, which recovers all the results of classical predicate calculus for the fragment of the language without semantic predicates. We have also produced a complete theory of permissibility and impermissibility for this fragment of the language, and at least some algorithmic inferential rules for determining whether a sentence is permissible. We have indicated why a complete set of such algorithmic rules (i.e. a set of rules such that every necessarily permissible sentence is a theorem) is likely not to exist.

We have explained why the demand that all the T-sentences come out true is ill-advised, although appropriate to a two-valued semantics. We have explicated the essence of the truth predicate instead in its being the identity map from the truth value $\mathcal{F}(n)$ to that of $T(n)$.

We have shown why Tarski's and Kripke's approaches are different approaches designed to solve the same problem: that of cycles in the graph of the language which are unsatisfiable if the only truth values available are truth and falsity.

We have explained how the theory of truth for boundary sentences differs from that for true or false non-boundary sentences, which differs again from that for completely unsafe sentences. We have sketched a picture of how all truth and falsity is ultimately grounded in the world. Part of that picture is a radical critique of the claim that a sentence can be true or false in virtue of its logical form. We have traced the foundations of classical logic, and shown its dependence on the assumption that all boundary sentences are either true or false. We have shown that once that assumption is eliminated, the appropriate logical system has no theorems at all. We have raised the hyper-Kantian question, viz. "How is *a priori* analytic knowledge possible?", and answered it: it isn't.

We have displayed a new "paradox" which lies at the heart of metalogic: in any plausible inferential system for a language with a truth predicate and unlimited means of referring to sentences, the sentence which says that the inferential system is truth-preserving is self-contradictory, and hence not true. We have recommended simply accepting this result: the sentence in question is not true, even though it is permissible to assert it. This paradox drives home the necessity of distinguishing truth from permissibility, and of rejecting the claim that asserting or believing a sentence is *ispo facto* asserting or believing that the sentence is true.

We have discussed the permissibility paradox and the unavoidability, once the language has been expanded to include claims about the permissibility of sentences according to various normative rules, of severe violations of the ideal by which those rules are evaluated. It is at this point that the cycle of problems spawned by the Liar finally comes to an end. The end is a *defeat*: we cannot have rules of permissibility that always satisfy even our most dearly held desires. But defeat is not dishonor when it is logically unavoidable. At least we now *understand* what the defeat is, and why it cannot be avoided. And we see why this defeat does not, in itself, indicate any shortcoming of our account of the *nature* of truth or of permissibility.

It is equally important to stress what we have not done. We have not given a complete account of any natural language. The language we have dealt with is an artificial one, with limited expressive resources. The theory of truth applies only to a language with two sorts of predicates: predicates such that atomic sentences containing them are always made true or false by the world, and semantic predicates. We have given some attention to the particular predicates "permissible" and "impermissible", and the problems associated with them. But there is no reason to believe that the predicates of any natural language fall into only these groups. We have not attempted any account of modal discourse, or temporal discourse, or any of the other locutions susceptible to formalization.

So the theory presented in this book can be expanded in various ways. One can try to produce formal languages capable of modeling more of a natural language. One can obviously also produce theories of other functions of language than making assertions or stating truths: e.g. making commands or asking questions.

Expanding in another direction, one can try to develop (rather as the logical positivists envisioned) a *metaphysically perfect* language. The picture of truth we have so far traces truth and falsity ultimately to the boundary sentences: these, in turn, are made true or false by the world. The world provides the *boundary conditions* for the language. It would be pleasant and useful to have a language in which *all combinatorically possible boundary conditions represent metaphysically possible worlds*. If one could achieve this, then talk of possible worlds could be reduced to talk of the possible boundary conditions for the metaphysically perfect language.

Natural language is not, in this sense, metaphysically perfect. English contains the terms "gorse", "furze", and "whin", which allows for the construction of three distinct boundary sentences: "That is gorse", "That is furze", and "That is whin" (referring to the same plant). But since gorse *is* furze and whin, no metaphysically possible world can give those three boundary sentences different truth values. Nor can a metaphysically possible world make "That is a glass of water" true and (when pointing at the same glass) "That liquid is predominately H_2O" false, even though these are distinct boundary sentences. So trying to model the features of natural language is a very different project than trying to construct a metaphysically perfect language.

The positivists thought that the project of constructing a metaphysically perfect language could be conducted *a priori*, by reflecting on the meanings of terms (where those meanings were accessible to introspection). As the work of Putnam and Kripke has shown, this is not so. Construction of a metaphysically perfect language will depend on substantive empirical knowledge, knowledge of the nature of things like water. What a physicalist would like, ultimately, is a language in which every possible distribution of boundary values corresponds to a unique and distinct possible physical state of the world, and the truth value of every other sentence which has a truth value is then determined by the boundary conditions.

Yet another interesting project is the examination of languages in which the boundary sentences can have more than two truth values. The problem of vagueness falls here.[3] It seems as though the world together with the totality of linguistic practices do not jointly make a sentence such as "John is bald" either true or false, but in an entirely different way than happens for ungrounded sentences. Natural language contains such predicates, so the project of modeling natural language must confront them. Arguably, a metaphysically perfect language would not contain such predicates, again showing how the two projects diverge. At any rate, if classical logic depends, in the way we have argued, on the presupposition that every boundary sentence is either true or

---

[3] We have addressed the problem of vagueness briefly above. It is taken up slightly less briefly in Appendix C.

false, then the existence of boundary sentences that are neither will demand a revision of logic itself, even of our logic which can tolerate ungrounded sentences. For although we have explained why, e.g., "The Liar is true or the Liar is not true" must be ungrounded, since its immediate semantic constituents are, it does not seem equally obvious that "John is bald or John is not bald" must be construed as *vague* (or given a truth value other than true) even if its immediate semantic constituents are neither true nor false.

Yet another project would examine discourse for which the very existence of a world to make boundary sentences true or false is in doubt. For the non-Platonist, the language of mathematics, and perhaps of set theory, seems to be of this kind. Perhaps we can come to understand the inferences in such a language as dependent on the *inappropriate* presupposition that the boundary sentences are true or false, so that mathematical claims will cease to have classical truth values. Or perhaps there is some other way of understanding what makes the boundary sentences true or false.

There is, then, much to be done. But the paradox of the Liar, and the other semantic paradoxes, need not stand in our way.

Appendix C: Vagueness

It has been one of the contentions of this chapter that the logical puzzles surrounding the Liar and related paradoxes have nothing at all to do with vagueness. It is natural enough to suspect some connection between the Liar sentences and sentences like "John is bald", where the appropriately semi-hirsute John seems to be a borderline case of baldness. In each case, one is inclined to claim that the sentence lacks a classical truth value: it is neither true nor false. I agree with this assessment. But the reason for the lack of a classical truth value, and the implications of the lack, are quite different in the two cases. There is nothing vague about the Liar because there is nothing vague about its components: the Liar sentence is a grammatical composition of the negation operator, the truth predicate, and a singular term whose referent is not in dispute. The semantics of the negation operator and the truth predicate are not vague: each is a specifiable truth-function of the truth values of its argument (or the denotation of its argument). The lack of classical truth value in this case derives from the global structure of the graph of the language, and neither the graph, nor the relevant graph-theoretic facts, are vague. Furthermore, as we have seen, the very nature of the new semantic value (ungroundedness) puts constraints on the sorts of truth-functional operators that can exist in the language.

Vagueness has none of these features. It does not arise on account of the structure of the graph of the language. Attributions of vague predicates to borderline cases (e.g. "John is bald") are typically logically atomic, and so appear at the boundary of the graph of the language. And if the existence of borderline cases of vague predicates requires the introduction of a new truth value, it is not obvious that the nature of this new truth value constrains the available truth-functional operators in the way that the nature of ungroundedness does. Indeed, I will argue, it does not. This observation is critical for diagnosing the flaw in an argument by Timothy Williamson to the conclusion that vagueness is merely epistemic.

From the point of view of logic, problems with vagueness appear at the boundary of the language, and so reflect a problem having to do with the relation between the language and the world. But of course the world itself is not vague: there is no fundamental ontological vagueness. Vagueness is a defect of language, not an inadequacy of the non-linguistic. Our project now is to sketch how that problem arises and what implications it has for logic.

The basic outline of the problem has already been given in this chapter. Logic only exhausts a small portion of the metaphysical relations among sentences. From the point of view of logic alone, the sentence "John is bald" has no relation to the myriad sentences that describe in precise detail the distribution of hair on John's head, but the truth values of the latter suffice to fix the truth value of the former. In an ideal complete metaphysical analysis, the graph of language would therefore be extended in such a way that "John is bald" is no longer a boundary sentence: it would have as "metaphysical constituents" the detailed claims about John's hair distribution. Associated with the predicate "bald" would be a function from the truth values of the latter to the truth value of the former. Sufficient conditions for baldness correspond to a partial function from the truth or falsehood of some detailed claims to the value true for "John is bald", necessary conditions for baldness correspond to a partial function from the truth or falsehood of some detailed claims to the falsehood of "John is bald". Borderline cases arise exactly when the necessary and the sufficient conditions do not jointly partition the space of detailed hair distributions, so that some distributions map neither to true for "John is bald" nor to false.

This picture explains how in the completed "metaphysical graph" of the language there could be only classical truth values at the boundary (hence no "ontological vagueness"), but still fail to have those classical values percolate up to sentences like "John is bald", and why fault lies, as it should, with the imprecision of the predicate "bald". Let us assume, for the moment, that this picture is correct. Then beside true and false, we need a new truth value for sentences like "John is bald" when John's hair distribution facts fall outside the partial functions that map distributions to true and to false. Let us call this new truth value *borderline* and represent it with a *B*. Sentences can get the truth value B even though every backward path through the metaphysical graph from the sentence reaches the boundary, so the source of borderline cases has nothing to do with the source of ungroundedness.

Logical operators are again to be understood as truth functions from the truth values of a set of immediate semantic constituents to the truth value of a sentence with the operator, but the available truth values now include true, false, ungrounded, and borderline. Since the existence of ungrounded sentences has no direct bearing on vagueness, we will leave it out of account in this discussion: it could be added back in the obvious way if needed. In the case of ungroundedness, we saw that the nature of the truth value put constraints on the possible logical operations: for example, any monadic operator applied to an ungrounded sentence must yield an ungrounded sentence. It follows that there only exists a single extension of classical negation: negation must map truth to falsehood, falsehood to truth, and ungroundedness to ungroundedness. But no similar argument exists for borderline sentences. There is nothing in the nature of the truth value that forbids a monadic logical operator that maps borderline sentences to non-borderline sentences. In particular, nothing rules out the existence of two *distinct* extensions of the classical negation operator to cover the new truth value. Let's call them Kleene negation and Vagueness-Strong (or V-Strong) negation:

A	$\sim$A
T	F
F	T
B	B

Kleene Negation

A	$\neg$A
T	F
F	T
B	T

V-Strong Negation

(The third possible extension is not distinct: it is equivalent to $\sim\neg\sim$A or $\neg\neg\sim$A.) Similarly, there is nothing in the nature of the truth value that forbids a semantic predicate that allows one to *truly* say that a sentence is borderline. The natural way to define a *borderline predicate* is unobjectionable:

$\mathscr{F}(\alpha)$	B (α)
T	F
F	F
B	T
Borderline	Predicate

Again, none of the problems that haunted ungroundedness appear. We do not need to invoke a special account of permissible assertion to explain why one can appropriately say " 'John is bald' is borderline": that sentence can just be true.

Although there is no objection to having logical operators that map borderline sentences to sentences with classical truth values, there is something uneasy about the converse: a logical operator that takes classical truth values as input and yields a borderline sentence as output. Why is that?

As we have been, the truth value *borderline* enters into a language only because of imprecision in the language itself: places in the metaphysical graph where there is only a partially defined function from the input to the output. But one mark of a *logical* notion seems to be precision: each logical particle is defined by a definite truth function from the immediate semantic constituents to the truth value of the sentence with the operator. To say that a logical operator maps some classical truth values to B is to say that it is an only partially defined function which fails to be defined for this input, but also that it is defined by the mapping to B in this case. That is a contradiction. So we have the following constraint: no logical operator maps classical truth values to B, but there is no objection to logical operators that map B to classical values. Again, this stands in clear contrast to the nature of ungroundedness.

The existence of the two distinct forms of negation provides the key to responding to one of Timothy Williamson's arguments for bivalence. Williamson attempts to prove the incoherence of the denial of bivalence by a *reductio ad absurdum*. As it is brief, it will be worthwhile to quote Williamson's argument in full.[4]

To generalize the argument, consider a language L with negation ($\sim$), disjunction ($\vee$), conjunction (&), and a biconditional ($\leftrightarrow$). Extend L to a metalanguage for L by adding a truth predicate (T) for sentences of L and quotation marks ("...") for naming them. The falsity of a sentence of L is identified with the truth of its negation. Thus the supposition at issue, the denial of bivalence for a sentence of L, is equivalent to the denial that either it or its negation is true:

   (1) $\sim [T(``P") \vee T(``\sim P")]$

Two instances of Tarski's disquotational schema for truth are:

   (2a) $T(``P") \leftrightarrow P$
   (2b) $T(``\sim P") \leftrightarrow \sim P$

The argument uses (2a) and (2b) to substitute their right-hand sides for their left-hand sides in (1):

   (3) $\sim [P \vee \sim P]$

It then applies one of DeMorgan's laws to (3) giving

   (4) $\sim P \;\&\; \sim\sim P$

This is a contradiction, whether or not the double negation is eliminated. Thus (1) reduces to absurdity. In effect, one uses Tarski's schema to equate bivalence ($T(``P") \vee T(``\sim P")$) with the law of excluded middle ($P \vee \sim P$), and then argues from the incoherence of denying the latter to the incoherence of denying the former.   (Williamson 1992: 145–6)

On general principles, we should be extremely suspicious of this argument. Intuitively, borderline cases arise due to imprecision in language. How could any purely *logical* argument demonstrate that language cannot be imprecise? Furthermore, we have already seen that inference is the handmaiden of semantics: valid inferences preserve truth, but we have to settle what truth values there are (e.g. that there is ungroundedness as well as truth and falsity) before we can determine which inferences do preserve truth. The inferences of a standard natural deduction system will preserve truth if one is concerned only about sentences with classical truth values, but fail to preserve truth once ungrounded sentences are admitted into consideration. We have to *settle the semantics* before we can *validate the inferences*, so we cannot blindly accept the validity of the inferences in order to prove that the semantics must be bivalent.

Enough of generalities. Williamson has provided an argument: let's see where it goes wrong.

As we have already seen, if we admit the truth value *borderline* into the language, then there will be two distinct extensions of negation, and there will similarly be distinct extensions of the other logical particles. For the moment, let's focus on negation. Williamson's argument acknowledges only one form of negation—he obviously does not tell us which of the two distinct forms considered above he has in mind. Since the form of Williamson's argument is to reduce the opponent of bivalence to absurdity, let's

---

[4] Essentially the same argument appears in Williamson (1994: 187 ff.). The argument there is a bit more extensive, using a falsity biconditional rather than simply identifying the falsity of a sentence with the truth of its negation, but for our purposes the arguments are identical, and are subject to the same sort of response.

consider the most charitable reading of what the opponent has to say. As Williamson states, the opponent claims that there is at least one sentence that is neither true nor false. Call the relevant sentence P. Then the opponent wants to say something true (or at least permissible!—but truth will do here) when he says "P is neither true nor false". Since we do not yet know the charitable way to translate this sentence into the formal language (we are trying to figure out, for example, what sort of negation the opponent of bivalence is using), let's begin by representing the claim as

$$\text{Not}(T(\text{``}P\text{''}) \vee \Phi(\text{``}P\text{''})).$$

The word "Not" is used as long as we have not yet determined the form of negation that the opponent means to use. Williamson next identifies falsehood with truth of the negation, but again does not seem to be aware that (if the opponent is right) there are several forms of negation, so for the moment we will use the translation

$$\text{Not}(T(\text{``}P\text{''}) \vee T(\text{``Not } P\text{''})).$$

Keeping to the two distinct forms of negation mentioned above, there are four possible readings of this claim. Which does the opponent have in mind?

The four readings are:

(1) $\sim(T(\text{``}P\text{''}) \vee T(\text{`` }\sim P\text{''}))$
(2) $\sim(T(\text{``}P\text{''}) \vee T(\text{``}\neg P\text{''}))$
(3) $\neg(T(\text{``}P\text{''}) \vee T(\text{`` }\sim P\text{''}))$
(4) $\neg(T(\text{``}P\text{''}) \vee T(\text{``}\neg P\text{''}))$

Assuming our usual interpretation of the truth predicate as defined by the identity map from the truth value of $\mathscr{F}(n)$ to the truth value of $T(n)$, and taking the only natural truth-functional form of disjunction, for which the disjunction of two borderline sentences is a borderline sentence, it is easy to derive the truth values of each of these sentences when P is borderline. Sentence 1 is borderline, sentence 2 is false, sentence 3 is true and sentence 4 is false. So by the principle of charity, we must interpret the opponent of bivalence as asserting sentence 3: at least by his own lights, he is thereby asserting something true.

Indeed, it is obvious at least that the second negation must be the Kleene negation. We want to represent the falsity of a sentence as the truth of its negation: $\Phi(\text{``}P\text{''})$ is supposed to be equivalent to $T(\text{``Not P''})$. So $T(\text{``Not P''})$ should be true just in case P is false. If the truth predicate is the identity map, the negation *must* be Kleene negation; if V-Strong negation is used, $T(\text{``Not P''})$ will be true when P is borderline.

We grant Williamson's use of the disquotational schema: if the truth predicate is the identity map, then disquoting preserves truth value (again permissibility will not come into the game here). The result of disquoting within sentence 3 is

(5) $\neg(P \vee \sim P)$.

By the opponents lights, this is also true—the disquotation has changed nothing.

Now comes the application of deMorgan's law. Under the natural extension of disjunction and conjunction, deMorgan's laws hold for both Kleene negation and for V-Strong negation. So we are indeed allowed, as Williamson says, to convert 5 into

(6) $\neg P$ & $\neg \sim P$.

But so what? *Contra* Williamson, sentence 6 is not a contradiction, i.e. it is not the conjunction of a sentence with its negation. It is rather the conjunction of a sentence with the (V-Strong) negation of a *different* sentence. And not surprisingly, according to the semantics of the opponent sentence 6 is true if P is borderline. (Indeed, sentence 6 is true if and only if P is borderline: just what we want.) Williamson only derives a "contradiction" because his language has only one form of negation. But according to the foe of bivalence, there are two forms of negation, and one needs both of them to truly state the opponent's thesis. And of course, the only argument that Williamson might have that there is only one form of negation is going to be a *petitio*.

Nor can the conclusion be turned into a contradiction by the rule of double negation. As the truth tables show, eliminating a double negation is a valid inference if both negations are of the same type, but validity fails exactly for the "mixed" double negation $\neg \sim$:

A	$\sim\sim A$	$\neg\neg A$	$\neg\sim A$
T	T	T	T
F	F	F	F
B	B	F	T

Logic cannot possibly prove the truth of bivalence because one will have to assume bivalence (or else not assume it) when it comes to justifying the adequacy of the logical apparatus.

If one wants to represent higher-order vagueness, the formal apparatus needed is similarly easy to construct. John presents a borderline case of baldness. James's situation is not so clear—having less hair than John, he is a borderline borderline case. How do we deal with him?

Nothing simpler. We need yet another semantic value—call it *BB*—to take care of borderline borderline cases. We need to extend the semantics of the borderline predicate in the obvious way:

$\mathscr{F}(\alpha)$	$B(\alpha)$
T	F
F	F
B	T
BB	B

Now when we say that "James is bald" is borderline, the assertion we have made is itself borderline. And so on.

So nothing in the formal apparatus of logic stands in the way of the recognition of vagueness, higher-order vagueness, and so on. And since Williamson's argument turns out to be bankrupt, one is tempted to rest the case of the sheer incredibility of the idea that our linguistic practices determine to the hair when Socrates became bald, or to the penny when Bill Gates became rich, or to the nanosecond when Muhammad Ali became famous. But perhaps something more enlightening may be ventured.

There are, after all, arguments that establish conclusions that seem to be frankly incredible, and some of them appear to be relevant to problems of vagueness. Here is a nice example.

Consider a train car with a board affixed to the floor on a frictionless hinge, as shown in figure C.1.

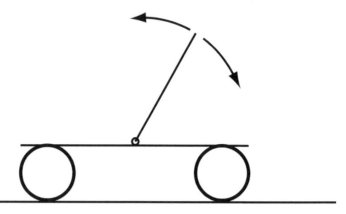

FIG. C.1. Hinged Board

Now imagine the train takes a trip from one city to another, along a fixed route and schedule. The train can accelerate, slow down, back up, wait overnight in a train yard, whatever one likes. If the board ever falls to the floor on the right or on the left it will remain there for the rest of the trip. A simple continuity argument demonstrates the astonishing conclusion that, for a fixed trip, there is some initial position of the hinged board such that, at the end of the trip, the board will be standing upright!

The board can start out in any position from lying on the right to lying on the left. If it starts out lying on the right it will end up lying on the right; if it starts lying on the left it will end up there. Now if the dynamics is continuous, any continuous set of possible initial conditions will be mapped onto a continuous set of final positions. So the continuous set of possible initial conditions, which stretch from lying on the right to lying on the left, must map to a continuous set of final states that also stretch from lying on the right to lying on the left. Hence there must be at least one initial state that leads to a final state in which the board is upright.

No doubt, for any real board and any real train trip, the critical position will always be beyond our ken, much less beyond our practical ability to set. Still, the argument demonstrates that some such (unknowable) critical initial state does exist. Is the critical penny that separates the rich from the non–rich like that?

Here is an even closer case. One is shopping for a new car. One enters a car dealership with a certain car in mind, but not having decided whether or not to buy it. It seems incredible to assert that in such a case one must be disposed with respect to the maximum amount one is willing to pay for the car, down to the penny—that is, it is incredible that there is a precise amount such that one will pay that much for the car but not one penny more. In any case, such a critical amount is certainly not available to introspection.

Yet a similar "continuity" argument appears to secure this surprising result. Grant that the relevant physical dynamics is deterministic, so every possible initial state of the world will evolve into a unique final state. The relevant initial conditions clearly include how much the dealer is willing to sell the car for. Surely, if the dealer is willing to sell the car for a penny, you will buy it, and if the dealer will not accept less than a million dollars you will not. Now consider all of the initial conditions that differ only with respect to the price the dealer will accept. There must be a greatest amount such that you would buy the car for that much—and the amount must be precise down to the penny. That much, and not a penny more, you would be willing to pay, even though you cannot tell by introspection where the critical penny lies. If you have such absolutely precise, but epistemically inaccessible, dispositions to purchase items, is it much more surprising that there might be an absolutely precise, but unknowable, line that your linguistic dispositions draw between the rich and the non-rich?

There is, however, something quite misleading about the description just given of one's dispositions with respect to automobile purchases. Let's approach the problems in stages.

First, the description above suggests—but does not state—that there is a "critical penny" dividing amounts one is willing to pay for the car from amounts one is not willing to pay, just as there is to be a penny dividing the rich from the non-rich. But the argument demonstrates no such thing. If, for example, seven happens to be someone's lucky number, then that person might be disposed to pay $21,777 for the car but balk at paying $21,666. This seems to be irrational—to be willing to pay more and unwilling to pay less—but recall that these dispositions are not available to introspection. It is likely that somewhere in the borderline area between amounts one knows one is willing to pay and the amounts one knows one is not willing to pay, the dynamics of reflection becomes chaotic. Seemingly irrelevant factors—like the presence of a seven in the price—could tip the end result one way or another.

Of course, when we say that someone might be willing to pay $21,777 but unwilling to pay $21,666, we mean that they might be disposed to accept an *initial* offer to sell at $21,777 and disposed to reject an *initial* offer at $21,666. Having accepted the initial offer for $21,777, one would then certainly also accept a *subsequent* offer to reduce the price to $21,666. And similarly, having rejected an initial offer to sell at $21,666, one would reject a *subsequent* offer at $21,777. It is because one has the (introspectable) firm disposition not to *change* one's response from rejection to acceptance if the price is raised, or from acceptance to rejection if the price is lowered, that one is inclined to accept the truth of "If I am willing to pay $21,777, then I am willing to pay $21,666". But the latter might be *false*, when the "if . . . then" is interpreted in the usual truth-functional way.[5]

---

[5] Some work on vagueness has been directed at the problem of making certain conditional sentences *true* even in the "penumbral" region of borderline cases. For example, if John has less hair than Joe, one wants "If Joe is bald then John is bald" to be *true* even if both Joe and John are borderline cases. This "if . . . then" cannot be truth-functional. But one could allow the truth

Once we remark that the final accepted sales price can depend on the order in which offers are made, it becomes obvious that in the "chaotic" regime one's final decision could equally depend on factors other than the asking price for the car. Perhaps, subconsciously or not, one dislikes mustaches. One might be willing to pay more for a car if the salesman doesn't have a mustache than if he does. Evidently, the end result also depends on factors like the exact sales pitch, the length of negotiations, the quality of the coffee offered, the presence or absence of flies in the showroom, how much one had for breakfast, and so on. Fix all of the other factors, allowing only the price to vary, and there will be a maximum price one is willing to pay. But equally, fix the price somewhere in the border area, and the decision to purchase or not may be changed by varying the room temperature, etc. So there simply is no such thing as "the maximum price one is willing to pay—to the penny": there is at best the maximum price one is willing to pay *in such-and-such precisely defined circumstances*, to the penny. And finally—this is the crucial observation—when the outcome depends on non-financial matters such as the presence or otherwise of mustaches, there simply is no such *psychological item* as "the amount one is willing to pay". In the chaotic zone, it is neither correct nor incorrect to say that one is willing to pay the stated amount.

Similarly, if I am asked to categorize people into the categories "rich" and "not rich", there are certain values for net worth such that my decision is completely determined by the net worth. If you have only a penny to your name, you are not rich; if you are a billionaire, you are. Other considerations are irrelevant. But in the middle ground between rich and poor, my categorizations will depend on the order in which questions are asked, on how wealthy I happen to feel that day, on how tired I am, and so on. In these cases, we may say that the decision I make is made on *non-semantic* grounds: the outcome may better be attributed to my having a headache at the moment than to the "meaning" of "rich". So these dispositions of mine no longer provide *semantic foundations* for interpreting the word "rich". Given all the facts there are (facts that determine how I would behave in any specific circumstance), still the extension of "rich" is not settled down to the penny.

Nor is even the edge of the "borderline" region settled exactly. In the example of the car, we might admit everything said so far but still ask after the maximum amount one is willing to pay *considering all possible circumstances*. This, surely, must be determined down to the penny. And it is at that very penny, it seems, that the borderline region begins.

But this is too quick. There are some circumstances in which I would be willing to pay a great deal for the car—for example if the salesman took out a gun and threatened to kill me if I didn't pay. But we would not normally take this sort of scenario into consideration when asked how much one would be willing to pay for the car. Rather, there is supposed to be some tacit restriction to normal circumstances, usual methods of negotiation, and so on. But the exact boundaries of what counts as "normal" are obviously going to be a matter of dispute. So we cannot get rid of vagueness by "quantifying over" the variations in circumstances: the exact domain of the quantification will also be vague.

---

value of the conditional to be *borderline*, and explain the intuition as stemming instead from a normative *commitment*: if we should come to regard Joe as bald, then we are thereby committed to coming to regard John as bald, just as accepting to buy the car at any price would thereby dispose us with certainty to buy it at any lower price.

So, contrary to first appearances, there is no precise maximum amount I am willing to pay for the car, even if all the (precisely specified) counterfactuals about my car-buying behavior have unproblematic truth values. Those counterfactuals do not suffice, taken as a whole, to draw the desired boundary. And surely there is nothing more than those counterfactuals that could be relevant to the question. Similarly for the exact extension of "rich" vis-a-vis our linguistic behavior. There is no precise extension, even if precisely enough specified counterfactuals about what we would say have perfectly determinate truth values. Once the way the counterfactuals would come out begins to depend on paradigmatically non-semantic parameters (such as how tired one is), the determinacy of the counterfactuals cannot be parlayed into determinacy of extension. And surely there would be nothing beyond the counterfactuals that could determine the extension.

There is nothing in either logic or semantics that can rule out the existence of vague terms, and hence the existence of sentences that lack a classical truth value. I see no reason to question the usual view that such vague terms exists, and that for this reason some sentences in natural language lack classical truth values. But in the end, none of this has any bearing whatever on the status of the Liar.

References

BOOLOS, G. and JEFFREY, R. (1989), *Computability and Logic*, 3rd edn. (Cambridge: Cambridge University Press).

BURGE, T. (1979), "Semantical Paradox", *Journal of Philosophy* 76: 169–98. Reprinted in Martin (1984: 83–117).

CARNAP, R. (1959), "The Elimination of Metaphysics through Logical Analysis of Language", in A. J. Ayer *Logical Positivism* (ed.), (New York: The Free Press), ch. 3.

FRIEDMAN, H. and SHEARD, M. (1987), "An Axiomatic Approach to Self-referential Truth", *Annals of Pure and Applied Logic* 33: 1–21.

GUPTA, A. (1982), "Truth and Paradox", *Journal of Philosophical Logic* 11: 1–60. Reprinted in Martin (1984: 175–235).

KETLAND, J. (1999), "Deflationism and Tarski's Paradise", *Mind* 108: 69–94.

KRIPKE, S. (1975), "Outline of a Theory of Truth", *Journal of Philosophy* 72: 690–716. Reprinted in Martin (1984: 53–81).

LEWIS, D. (1986), *On the Plurality of Worlds* (Oxford: Basil Blackwell).

LUCAS, J. (1961), "Minds, Machines and Gödel", *Philosophy* 36: 112–27.

LEBLANC, H. and WISDOM, W. (1976), *Deductive Logic*, 2nd edn. (Boston: Allyn and Bacon).

MCGEE, V. (1990), *Truth, Vagueness and Paradox* (Indianapolis: Hackett).

MARTIN, R. (ed.) (1970), *The Paradox of the Liar* (New Haven: Yale University Press).

—— (ed.) (1984), *Recent Essays on Truth and the Liar Paradox* (Oxford: Oxford University Press).

MAUDLIN, T. (1996), "Between the Motion and the Act . . . ", *Psyche* 2: 40–51.

—— (forthcoming), *The Metaphysics within Physics* (Oxford: Oxford University Press).

PENROSE, R. (1994) *Shadows of the Mind: A Search for the Missing Science of Consciousness* (Oxford: Oxford University Press).

REINHARDT, W. (1986), "Some Remarks on Extending and Interpreting Theories with a Partial Predicate for Truth", *Journal of Philosophical Logic* 15: 219–51.

SKYRMS, B. (1984), "Intensional Aspects of Semantical Self-reference", in Martin (1984: 119–31).

SOAMES, S. (1999), *Understanding Truth* (Oxford: Oxford University Press).

TARSKI, A. (1956), "The Concept of Truth in Formalized Languages", in Tarski, *Logic, Semantics, Metamathematics*, trans. and ed. J. H. Woodger (Oxford: Oxford University Press), 152–278.

TENNANT, N. (2002), "Deflationism and the Gödel Phenomena", *Mind* 111: 551–82.

VAN FRAASSEN, B. (1968), "Presupposition, Implication, and Self-reference", *Journal of Philosophy* 65: 136–52.

—— (1970), "Truth and Paradoxical Consequences", in Martin (1970: 13–23).

WILLIAMSON, T. (1992), "Vagueness and Ignorance", *Proceedings of the Aristotlian Society, Supp. Vol.* 66: 145–62.

—— (1994), *Vagueness* (London: Routledge).

WRIGHT, C. (1992), *Truth and Objectivity* (Cambridge, Mass.: Harvard University Press).

YABLO, S. (1993), "Paradox without Self-reference", *Analysis* 53: 251–2.

Index

a posteriori 74
a priori 74, 116
abundant property 181
acyclic graph 36–40, 54–5
Analysis, Rule of 114–5
Ante(*x*, *y*) 146
Aristotle 187

β, defintion of 40
baldness 179–82
Boolos, G. 66–7, 129
borderline, truth value 195–9
borderline cases 72
Bound(*x*) 79
Boundary Rule 114–17
boundary sentence 70, 80, 86, 109
  definition of 30–1
boundary value problem 31
Broakes, J. xi
Burge, T. 168

Carnap, R. 73–5
Classical logical systems 10–13
Clio xi, 39, 59–63, 77, 97, 100
closing off the truth predicate 27, 46,
  51–2, 98–9, 103
Common Sense 90
completely unsafe sentence 49–50, 76,
  81
  definition of 42
compositional semantics 29
Cond(*x*) 146
conditional proof 109
Conj(*x*) 79
conjunction
  Medium Kleene 54
  Strong Kleene 54, 80, 110
  Weak Kleene 54, 80, 110
connective
  Kleenesque 44

non-Kleenesque 64
Conseq(*x*, *y*) 146
Continued Fractions 88–94
Contrarian, the 90
corner quotes 24, 26
cycles 40

deflationary concept of truth 9
Der$_\Sigma$ Introduction 123–4
Der$_\Sigma$(*x*, *y*), definition of 122
determined by the assignment,
  definition of 55
Diagonalization Lemma 66
directed graph 29, 40
Discharge Rule 115, 121, 157
Downward F-Inference 112, 142, 152
Downward T-Inference 112, 142, 152
  definition of 8

entailment 65
Expanded Rule of Analysis 115, 118

$\mathcal{F}(x)$ 79
  definition of 4
F-sentences 71
facts about truth 178–9, 182–7
falsity predicate 54
Field, H. xi
fixed point 9, 27, 44–9, 52, 56, 76,
  120
  minimal 57, 120
France, hexagonality of 31, 70–1
Friedman, H. 23

Gödel, K. 133
Gödel sentence 133–4
Gödel's theorem vii–ix, 129–31
graph of a language 35, 184
  definition of 29
Gupta, A. 4, 6, 69–70, 150–1, 161

Hall, N. xi
Humean supervenience 181

ideal of permissible assertion 96, 141, 170
impermissible sentence, definition of 97
index set 107
infinitely continued fractions 83
interpretation of a language 65
Intuitionist Logic 15
$ISC(x,y)$ 79

Jeffrey, R. 66–7, 129

Kant, I. 76, 116, 192
Ketland, J. 23
Kleene connectives 27, 37, 44–5, 57,
    112–4
Kleene negation *see* negation, Kleene
Kleenesque connective
    definition of 44
Kripke, S. 5–6, 14, 17, 48–9, 56, 64,
    98–9, 103, 120, 191–3
    theory of truth 4, 8–10, 26–8, 42–54,
    76, 150

λ, definition of 5
Language L 4
LeBlanc, H. 21
Lewis, D. 39, 181
Liar paradox
    in language L 5–10
    inferential version 6, 13–21, 105–21
    informal version 1–4
    semantic version 5
Liar sentence 41, 65
Löb's Paradox 15–6, 40–1, 105, 134,
    137–8, 143
local constraints 41
    definition of 45
logic puzzles 16, 119–20
logical consequence 155
logical equivalence 65
Lucas, J. vii, 131

Martin, R. 3–4, 17
Maudlin, V. xi
Maxwell 39, 59–3, 77, 97, 100, 118

McGee, V. xi, 101–2, 106, 120, 153
Medium Kleene conjunction 54
metalanguage 46–9, 52, 103, 154, 170
metaphysical graph of a language 184,
    195
metaphysically perfect language 193
minimal fixed point 57, 64
Modus Ponens 109
Modus Tollens 109
Monastic Rule of Silence 165

Natural Deduction system 13
    rules of 21–3
$Neg(x)$ 79
negation
    Kleene 36–8, 41, 196
    Strong 36–8, 41
    Vagueness-Strong 196
$\mathcal{NF}(x)$ 79
    definition of 71
non-classical truth value 38
non-Kleenesque connectives 52, 64
Noonan, J. xi
normal connective, definition of 44

ordinal 84–6

Paraconsistent Logic 15
paradoxical sentence 158, 161
Penrose, R. vii, 131
permissibility 141
permissibility paradox 103
permissible sentence, definition of 98
$Phi(x)$ 79
physics 31–35
pragmatic coherence 96, 171, 175
primary truth value 72
    definition of 44
Proof Gamma 15, 18–20, 105–7, 116,
    132, 137–8, 143
Proof Lambda 8–9, 14–5, 18, 25, 105–6,
    125, 132
Proof Sigma 125–7
provability predicate 129
Pryor, J. xi, 90
Putnam, H. 193
puzzles, logic *see* logic puzzles

quantification 59–64
quantifiers
  restricted 62–4, 126
  unrestricted 62

rank of a sentence 36
redundancy theory of truth 68–71
Reinhardt, W. 153
Relevance Logic 15
revenge problem 168, 176
revision theory 4
Robinson arithmetic 66
Rule of Analysis 114–15
rules for eliminating sentences from
    index sets 113–15

safe sentence, definition of 42
Salmon, N. 17–18
self-contradictory sentence 127, 157–8
semantic entailment 155
Sheard, M. 23
Sigma-Validity 124–7
  definition of 122
Skyrms, B. 102–3, 187
Soames, S. 17–18
sparse property 181
Strong Kleene conjunction 54, 80,
    110
Strong negation *see* negation, Strong
Strong truth predicate 52
supervaluation 27–8, 58, 111, 161, 186
supervenience 182–4

T-Lambda 144
  definition of 5
Tarski, A. 2–6, 17–19, 58, 68–70, 73,
    154, 177, 188, 191
Tarski biconditional 67–9
Tarski schema 162
Tau(x) 79
tautology 65
Tennant, N. 23
theorem 155

Thm_Σ Elimination 135–6
Thm_Σ Introduction 129–30
Thm_Σ(x) 129
time machine 33
truth predicate 68
  semantics of 29–30
truth-functional connectives 53–4
truth-predicate 67
Truthteller 41, 50, 65, 71, 76, 86,
    149, 185
  definition of 40
T-Elim 23
T-In 23
T-Inference
  definition of 8
T-Inferences 116, 132, 139, 191
T-Intro 23
T-Out 23
T-sentences 4, 58, 68–70, 156, 177,
    188, 191

ungrounded sentences 50, 57, 75–7
  definition of 49
ungrounded on an assignment, definition
    of 56
Univ(x) 79
unsafe sentence 115
  definition of 42
Upward F-Inference 112
Upward T-Inference 112, 142–3
  definition of 8

vagueness 31, 72, 179, 193–203
valid inference 12
valid sentence 65
van Fraassen, B. 4, 6, 27

Weak Kleene conjunction 54, 80, 110
Williamson, T. 195–9
Wisdom, W. 21
Wright, C. 188–9

Yablo, S. 57